APR 1 5 2014

TWO WEEKS

D1289296

30 YEARS AT
Ballymaloe

30 YEARS AT Ballymaloe

DARINA ALLEN

A celebration of the world-renowned cooking school with over 100 new recipes

Photography by Laura Edwards

Kyle Books

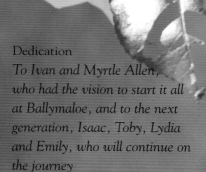

Dedication
To Ivan and Myrtle Allen,
who had the vision to start it all
at Ballymaloe, and to the next
generation, Isaac, Toby, Lydia
and Emily, who will continue on
the journey

Published in 2014 by Kyle Books
www.kylebooks.com
general.enquiries@kylebooks.com

Distributed by National Book Network
4501 Forbes Blvd., Suite 200
Lanham, MD 20706
Phone: (800) 462-6420
Fax: (800) 338-4550
customercare@nbnbooks.com

First published in Great Britain in 2013 by
Kyle Books, an imprint of Kyle Cathie Limited

10 9 8 7 6 5 4 3 2 1

ISBN: 978-1-909487-13-0

Library of Congress Control Number: 2013954350

Darina Allen is hereby identified as the author
of this work in accordance with Section 77
of the Copyright, Designs and Patents Act 1988.

All rights reserved. No reproduction, copy or transmission
of this publication may be made without written permission.
No paragraph of this publication may be reproduced, copied
or transmitted save with written permission or in accordance
with the provisions of the Copyright Act 1956 (as amended).
Any person who does any unauthorized act in relation to this
publication may be liable to criminal prosecution and civil
claims for damages.

Text © Darina Allen 2013
Photographs © Laura Edwards 2013,
except for those listed on page 319
Design © Kyle Books 2013

"Other Worlds" from *Amarcord* by Marcella Hazan and Victor
Hazan, copyright © 2008 by Marcella Hazan and Victor Hazan.
Used by permission of Gotham Books, an imprint of Penguin
Group (USA) LLC appears on pages 110–111.

Editor: Vicky Orchard
Design: Louise Leffler
Food Photography: Laura Edwards
Food Styling: Linda Tubby
Props Styling: Polly Webb-Wilson
Production: Nic Jones and David Hearn

Color reproduction by ALTA London
Printed and bound in China by 1010 printing Ltd.

Contents

Foreword by Alice Waters   6

Introduction   8

1983   The First 12-week Course; Equipping the School   20

1984   Local Artisan Producers; The Farm Shop   32

1985   Claudia Roden   42

1986   The Herb Garden   48

1987   Game; Deh-Ta Hsiung   60

1988   Irish Food   68

1989   The Fruit Garden; The Beginning of Television   76

1990   Keeping Cows; Rose Gray and Ruth Rogers   88

1991   Foraging; The Library; Barbecue Course   100

1992   Marcella Hazan   110

1993   Myrtle Allen   116

1994   Versatile Vegetables   124

1995   Keeping Pigs; Cooking with the Clergy; The Shell House   138

1996   Slow Food   148

1997   The Maze; The Memory Arboretum   158

1998   The Wood-burning Oven   164

1999   Going Organic; Patrick Holden   174

2000   Farmers' Markets   188

2001   Madhur Jaffrey   198

2002   Food Allergies   204

2003   Rory O'Connell   214

2004   Cooking with Spices   222

2005   Keeping Chickens   230

2006   Butchery; Dawn Chorus   244

2007   Self-sufficiency; Beekeeping   252

2008   Sustainable Fishing   262

2009   Thomasina Miers   272

2010   The Soft Fruit Garden; Mike Butt Award   278

2011   Rachel Allen; Long-table Dinners   286

2012   The New Nordic Movement; Thanksgiving   296

The Students   304

Index   316

Acknowledgments   320

Foreword by Alice Waters

Darina invited me for my first visit to Ballymaloe in her characteristic expansive fashion: "Come any time!" she told me. "Celebrate your birthday here!" I had, of course, heard of the Cookery School and knew about the groundbreaking work that Darina was doing with Irish food—but even so, I was not prepared for the full attraction of the place. The first time I came, I stayed in the hotel that Myrtle Allen, Darina's mother-in-law, had created, and it was magical: windows that opened right onto the garden, freshly picked flowers brought into your room every day. They always had a big buffet on Sundays and invited all their family and friends, with Myrtle and her husband Ivan there at the end of the table. I was so touched by those dinners, and the fact that I was so effortlessly included in them. The message was always "come as you are, bring your friends, and join us on Sunday night." It was such a loving, lively scene every Sunday: the kids in the family would come in still dripping from the sea and have this beautiful meal around the table with their parents, aunts and uncles, cousins, and grandparents. Sometimes one daughter would sing, or another would play music for the hotel guests. This is how Ballymaloe is: you are instantly made to feel completely at home—you are included, no matter what.

Darina took me out to see the Cookery School, and we did everything: we went out to the lobster boats in Ballycotton and saw the daily catch, visited the fat, happy pigs that rooted through the fields, gathered herbs from the garden and eggs from the henhouse. The School at that time was already a bustling, well-established institution but was ever-evolving: they were developing their greenhouse, making cheese from the milk of their Jersey cows, inviting renowned chefs from all over the world to teach classes, and, of course, teaching all the fine forgotten traditions of Irish cooking. I remember Darina's brother Rory, a chef and teacher himself, cooked a soup for me with wild garlic, which remains one of the best things I've ever had. I learned about the sweet, milky pudding they make that's so delicious, thickened with foraged carrageen moss, that my daughter Fanny now loves; and Darina's husband Tim taught me to make the Irish soda bread I now make every Christmas. Almost every year since that first visit I have found myself back there, celebrating my birthday with friends it seems I have known forever.

As I have returned over the years, I have watched the School change and grow as Darina has become one of the most prominent voices in Irish food politics, and a vital leader in the Slow Food movement. Last year, at Ballymaloe's first ever Literary Festival of Food and Wine, she invited the greatest chefs, authors, and voices in food to gather and exchange ideas, from Stephanie Alexander to Madhur Jaffrey, Claudia Roden, David Thompson, David Tanis, and so many more. Darina is interested in the big picture of culture, forever challenging herself and others to expand the conversation about food into something deeper and more meaningful.

I think of Ballymaloe Cookery School as the very best sort of cooking school, and I send as many people to it as I possibly can. It is so exquisitely beautiful—you are always close to nature, digging your hands into the dirt, smelling the salt air. This is the sort of hands-on, immersive experience of cooking that is so important to impress upon people right now in order for them to understand the broader context of sustainability. I love how Darina takes her family and friends to have breakfast on the rocks down by the sea—bringing bacon, eggs, jam and marmalade she's made, and freshly baked bread—and everyone sits down on the big, soft grass by the side of the ocean and eats together. How can a young person—or an older one, for that matter!—not be seduced by that vision? I believe almost everyone who visits Ballymaloe Cookery School comes to think of it as a home away from home, much as I have—it is impossible not to fall in love with the way of life there. Ballymaloe's great and powerful message is not just about bringing back an appreciation of food and taste, but an understanding of the culture of food, and of Ireland: a culture of stewardship of the land, tradition, hospitality, and, above all, beauty.

Introduction

The Ballymaloe Cookery School opened on September 5, 1983 in converted farm buildings in the courtyard behind our house on the farm in Kinoith. I cofounded the School with my brother Rory O'Connell, and it was the culmination of several years of planning and soul-searching.

I first came to work in the kitchens at Ballymaloe House fresh from the School of Hospitality Management and Tourism on Cathal Brugha Street, Dublin, on June 16, 1968. I had heard about Myrtle Allen, a farmer's wife down in East Cork, who had opened a restaurant in her rambling old country house in the midst of a farm in Shanagarry, close to the little fishing village of Ballycotton. The menu was written every day depending on what was in season and available on the farm and in the gardens. Fish and shellfish came from Ballycotton and were added to the menu when the fresh catch was landed in the late afternoon. This was extraordinary at a time when most restaurants wrote their menu when they opened and it remained the same ten years later.

The food at Ballymaloe House was made from scratch every day. We shelled broad beans and peas and made ice cream from the fresh Jersey milk and cream. Veal, or rather baby beef, came from the male calves, fresh pork from the pigs in the farmyard, freshly laid eggs from the hens who fed on the food scraps from the restaurant, watercress from local streams. Local children foraged for blackberries, damsons, sloes, and wild mushrooms and brought them to the kitchen door; Myrtle paid them generously and incorporated the fruits of their efforts into the menu. An older generation brought wild bilberries from the Knockmealdown Mountains and harvested carrageen moss from the little rocks in Ballyandreen after the spring tides. Berries and fruit came from the walled garden; tomatoes, cucumbers, and lettuce came from the greenhouses in Shanagarry. In autumn over 15 varieties of apple came from the orchards around Kinoith, and in May baskets full of asparagus came from the sandy field near the beach in Ballynamona.

I worked side by side with Myrtle and soaked up everything she said like a sponge; she was a gentle and patient teacher with an unerring belief in the importance of good raw materials. I soon realized that if you start off with fresh, naturally produced local food in season, then it is easy to create something utterly delicious, whereas mass-produced, denatured ingredients require a magician to make them taste good—that's where those fancy sauces and twiddles on top are needed to compensate for the flavor that is not there originally.

In October 1970 I became a member of the Allen family by the simple expedient of marrying Myrtle's eldest son Tim. We inherited Kinoith, the beautiful Regency house we now live in, and the surrounding farm and thriving horticultural enterprise, which included five acres of greenhouse, a mushroom farm, and 65 acres of apple orchards. Since 1968 Myrtle had been giving cooking classes at Ballymaloe House to help to fill the bedrooms during the winter. She sweetly asked me to help; I weighed the ingredients and gave my opinion when asked. In 1981 she decided to take over the management of a restaurant in Paris to showcase Irish food: La Ferme Irlandaise. Her involvement in this restaurant meant that she was too busy to give classes at Ballymaloe House, but people continued to enquire, so she encouraged me to go ahead on my own. I thought no one would come to my classes because my name was totally unknown. But we really needed the money, so I plucked up the courage to put an ad in *The Cork Examiner* (now the *Irish Examiner*) for a series of eight Saturday morning classes. I taught them in the kitchen of the White Cottage, which had been converted into a vacation rental property. A local carpenter built a little dais for chairs, which I put in front of the window so guests could have a clear view of proceedings. My mischievous children used to come along to the window and stick out their tongues and make funny faces behind people's backs, which I had to pretend not to see.

For me the first class was the most scary. People arrived in their little fur jackets and BMWs. We hid our rusty old Renault

Right: In the vegetable garden at the Ballymaloe Cookery School.

4L behind the house and welcomed them with freshly ground coffee and homemade cookies. The response to the class was overwhelmingly positive—I suddenly realized that this was something I could actually do. Some things that I found easy and imagined everybody must know how to do, others seemed to find difficult and were really impressed by! I started to think about more classes, and my dear friend Pauline O'Kennedy suggested starting a residential cooking school, like the Cordon Bleu in London or Paris. Irish people were sending their children abroad to learn to cook, so why not open a cooking school here? I thought about it off and on, but all the while I was cooking at home and occasionally at Ballymaloe House, as well as looking after a young family.

At the same time I longed to learn more about Italian food, and, as luck would have it, Jane Montant, then editor-in-chief of *Gourmet* magazine in New York, came to stay at Ballymaloe House. Myrtle introduced us and Jane told me about an Italian cook, Marcella Hazan, who gave classes in Bologna, which included trips to markets, local bakeries, cheesemakers, vineyards, and restaurants. I wrote away for details—it cost £650, a fortune in those days. I longed to go, so Tim went to the bank, took out the last money we had, and enrolled me on the course as a present. It proved to be the best investment he ever made. It was a wonderful week. The group was all American, and I was the only Irish student; they were intrigued that an Irish farmer's wife had signed up.

When we visited the markets the produce was beautiful and fresh but I realized that it was no better than that at home in our garden and greenhouses. The week passed in a happy blur. On the last evening there was to be a celebration farewell dinner in a seafood restaurant in Cesenatico, the town where Marcella was born. The restaurant, La Gambara, was right on the beach and supposedly had the freshest, most wonderful seafood one could imagine. The fish dishes were indeed delicious, but no more so than the stunning fresh fish landed by our local fishermen in Ballycotton. Suddenly I truly, deeply understood what Myrtle had known all along—that fresh Irish produce is unsurpassed anywhere. I realized that the answer to my dilemma was staring me straight in the face. The solution was under my feet, a cooking school in the middle of our farm, close to the sea in Ireland—what could be more obvious? I came home with renewed determination to start a cookery school.

From the beginning we operated all year, coinciding with the school schedule; I still had small children and so had many of my teachers, so I needed to be free during the school vacations. We offered two 12-week courses a year (this has now increased to

Left (top): The Cookery School, which was converted from an old apple barn designed by Henry Hill, Myrtle's father, who was one of a long line of renowned Hill architects in Cork City.

Left (bottom): The interior of the Pink Cottage, which was originally a cow barn with stalls for milking the cows. We converted it in the late 1970s, first into simple accommodation for a local potter, then a Farm Shop and subsequently a vacation rental cottage. It has been used as student accommodation from the start of the School. Originally furnished with traditional old dressers and benches, which we begged, borrowed, and swapped, it is now rather more luxurious.

Above: The Pink Wash laundry, which overlooks Lydia's Garden, and which the students use to do their laundry during the 12-week course; a skill some students learn for the first time, much to their parents' delight!

three) intended to teach students a wide range of skills to equip them for a career in food, plus a whole series of short courses covering entertaining, vegetarian food, pub grub, and cooking with fresh herbs, which were still unfamiliar to many. I also taught a new trends course every year, which had a loyal following. During the nouvelle cuisine era, I included a series of classes covering that topic as well as a course entitled a Taste of Italy, France, Spain, Mexico or Morocco, depending on where I traveled.

The School has expanded over the years and on September 11, 1989, we found ourselves expecting 36 students from all over the world for the 12-week course, including five different nationalities: Irish, English, Scottish, American, and Australian. Our numbers had doubled from 18 to 36 students between June and September so we needed to expand the School buildings to accommodate them. Our local builders were beyond heroic; they literally worked through the night for the last 3–4 days. I ran up and down the ladders with freshly baked scones, topped with raspberry jam and cream, to keep them going. It really was a race against time. When the first students arrived on Saturday and Sunday, the School still wasn't finished, so we brought them into the conservatory in our house and welcomed them with homemade cakes and cookies in the midst of the red geraniums, summer jasmine, and plumbago.

We gave them a tour of the gardens, greenhouses, and the farm, but we had to keep them well away from the School or they would probably have bolted, convinced that it couldn't possibly be ready by 10 a.m. the next morning. They would have reckoned without Will Kenneally and his ace gang of builders, carpenters, electricians, plumbers, and painters, plus a whole team of cleaners who whipped the place into shape the moment the others finished. I remember the quarry-tiled floor in the hall was still damp as we brought the students into the newly expanded School on Monday morning. The heating in the dining room wasn't connected for another week, but fortunately the early September weather that year wasn't too cold!

The School has grown in size from a small kitchen adjacent to our house, to a beautifully converted apple store complete with demonstration kitchens, four hands-on student kitchens, dining rooms, prep rooms, and a shop. The Cookery School Shop sells preserves, chutneys, breads, cakes, raw milk from our Jersey cows, and cooking-related items and gifts. Each year has lead to a new venture, and we have developed the gardens one after the other over the past 30 years, adding a berry and currant garden to the original fruit garden and expanding the herb and vegetable gardens. In 1997 we even started the ambitious planting of a Celtic Maze in yew over a ¾-acre site (a costly enterprise which was conceived in 1991, the Year of the Maze). Then 1998 saw the completion of a colorful, airy new restaurant called the Garden Café next to the Cookery School, equipped with furniture made by our nephew Sacha Whelan and hand-painted by Nicky Krussman.

We grow most of our own fruit, vegetables, and herbs for both Ballymaloe House and the Cookery School. When we started the School, we didn't have anything like the range of vegetables and fruit we have today. Tomatoes, cucumbers, lettuces, zucchini, peppers, and the like were abundant in season but in the winter months we relied on the produce from the walled garden at Ballymaloe House—leeks, broccolini, Brussels sprouts, and parsnips, all grown by Mick Cullinane, who produced superb winter vegetables and

Far left: Antony Worrall Thompson has been a guest chef at the School on several occasions since the early 1990s. The students have always loved his eclectic food, self-deprecating wit, and the mischievous twinkle in his eye! He used to regularly propose to my teachers and he eventually married Jay, one of our past students, who assisted him at a demonstration at the Cookery School.

Left: Jane Grigson was always a food hero of mine, and one of my greatest pleasures was when Jane was able to teach a guest-chef course at the School. Her daughter Sophie came with Jane on other occasions and also to teach a course of her own in 1993.

Above: Students enjoying a hands-on cooking session in Kitchen Two. The photographer gathered all the students together from Kitchens One and Two (the main kitchens) for this busy picture, but we would usually have fewer students. There are four hands-on kitchens in total, which vary in size from 4–6 students in two, to 18 and 20 in the others. In each kitchen we have at least one teacher to every six students.

herbs for over 60 years. We now grow over 80 different crops on the farm, in the garden and greenhouses, albeit in small quantities. It is just possible that our 100-acre farm now has a more diverse range of crops than any other farm in Ireland.

In the mid-1980s, when we could no longer get the sweet, juicy pork I remembered as a child, I decided to get pigs and bought two weanlings from a smallholder in West Cork while I was filming one of my *Simply Delicious* TV series. When our local butcher Michael Cuddigan retired in 2000, we decided to raise a few cattle to have our own beef. I got advice from Michael on what to buy in terms of traditional breeds, and we now have Dexter, Angus, Shorthorn, Kerry and Jersey cows. The rest of our meat is supplied by local farmers, and fish is bought directly from the boats in Ballycotton, a stone's throw from the School. Whenever possible we try to source organic, local produce. The five Jersey cows provide milk and cream for the School from which the students learn to make butter, cheese, and yogurt. Eggs come from our own chickens and are collected every morning by the students on a rota basis.

JOAN SCOBEY PHOTOS

Ballymaloe House in Shanagarry.

Festive delights along Ireland's south coast

By Joan Scobey
Special to The Globe

A lot more than potatoes and Irish stew are cooking along the southern coast of Ireland. Inventive chefs are turning the natural bounty of seafood and fresh farm produce into a new light Irish cuisine; an international cooking school affiliated with one of Ireland's best-loved inns has been established; Ireland's only wine-producing vineyard has celebrated its first vintage; and the annual Gourmet Festival always adds a dollop of Gaelic hilarity to the newly-serious business of food.

This is an enticing menu for visitors to the area around Cork, who come to swim, sail and fish at coastal resorts, canoe and hike the river valleys, and explore old and new Cork, whose history goes back to the Vikings. The Republic's second city is celebrating the 800th anniversary of its charter, and the Irish will be celebrating through the year. What visitors might not expect is some of the best eating in Ireland.

At Kinsale, for instance, the picturesque resort and fishing village 18 miles south of Cork, a remarkable number of small chef-owned restaurants offer distinctive cuisines, most of them utilizing the superb local seafood. "Fish swim in the front door," says Brian Cronin, the tall, red-haired, genial proprietor and chef of The Blue Haven, a lively seafood restaurant.

Cronin is also the spokesman for the Good Food Circle, an informal group of 10 young restaurateurs that sponsors the Kinsale Gourmet Festival, a 4-day gastronomic extravaganza the first weekend in October.

"The Festival is fun, not at all serious," says Cronin. It opens with a champagne reception where you can sample fare from the participating restaurants and, after demonstrations by chefs and food and wine receptions on any pretext whatever, it ends with a special contest. One tried recently, for example, was a cocktail-shaking competition in which the winner used 27 ingredients.

Harbor view at Kinsale

If you get to Kinsale and need help with this culinary bonanza, head for the Harbour Bar in Scilly. Sit on the patio overlooking the harbor and study the menus of Kinsale over a drink; the proprietor will call your order in to the restaurant of choice.

Between meals, Kinsale, an international sailing and angling center, offers a variety of diversions. You can fish the wreck of the Lusitania lying 20 miles off shore, visit the 17th century fortifications that guard the harbor, wander the cobbled streets past the quays, the ramparts and well-tended Georgian homes. You can visit the museum (formerly the courthouse where the Lusitania inquest was held). Or you can browse the picturesque shops of Market Street that supply fish, produce and meat to Kinsale's restaurants.

If you want to play country ladies and gentlemen, settle in at Longueville, a Georgian mansion in the beautiful Blackwater River Valley in Mallow, 22 miles north of Cork. Longueville is known for its cuisine, its setting along the "Irish Rhine," and its romantic past that includes its forfeit to Cromwell and its rescue, 300 years later, by the original land owners.

The 500-acre estate furnishes virtually all provisions, from garden vegetables, salmon and trout (you can fish for your own) to the hundred sheep that graze on the front lawn under towering oaks.

Darina Allen of the cookery school.

A lot more than potatoes and Irish stew are cooking along the southern coast of Ireland. Inventive chefs are turning the natural bounty of seafood and fresh farm produce into a new light Irish cuisine.

Even the vintner is in danger of being replaced because proprietor Michael O'Callaghan recently uncorked the first vintage of "Longueville," a sweet Riesling grown and bottled on the estate.

A French-style cuisine

The kitchen is supervised by O'Callaghan's wife, Jane, who periodically goes to France to refresh her imaginative and elegant country French-style cuisine. In keeping with manorial life, you'll dine in front of a white marble Adams fireplace under the portraits of the presidents of Ireland. The typical fare will be Longueville lamb, or Blackwater salmon and trout, always garnished with vegetables fresh from the garden.

Longueville has a fine wine cellar, but you won't be discouraged from trying the house wine. After a sweet from the trolley, you'll retire to the gracious high-ceilinged drawing room for coffee, truffles and perhaps a brandy. The fixed-price dinner is $18.

O'Callaghan claims the only vineyard in Ireland. In 1978, he planted his former rose garden with a variety of German Riesling, which thrives in a climate similar to Ireland's and hung "Vineyard" on the iron fence. How now cultivates 3 acres.

Vinification at Longueville has a certain insouciance. The whole family, including his 90-year-old mother, picked the grapes, crushed them in a motorized laundry mangle, then pressed them into oak barrels imported from France.

The Longueville label claims a particularly inventive wine review: "Every night I gave my pregnant wife, Jane, a glass of Longueville, but it didn't agree with her at all," said Michael. "I thought, 'Oh, dear, what did I get wrong?' and took her to the obstetrician. He gave her a Medoc, and everything was fine. He gave her a Burgundy, no problem. Then he gave her a glass of Longueville, and the

rumbling started again. He sent her to X-ray – and there was the baby clapping!"

If life at Longueville and Kinsale has a continental air, Ballymaloe is all Irish, and celebrated for the special style of Myrtle Allen. "It's the tradition of Irish country house food with local ingredients of high quality – prime, fresh, simply cooked," she said.

Surrounded by acres of serene farmland and grazing sheep, Ballymaloe is the pastoral country house-hotel of Myrtle and Ivan Allen in Shanagarry, 23 miles southeast of Cork. Here, her cooking is served up with easygoing hospitality in the Yeats Room, named for its paintings by Jack Yeats, brother of poet William Butler Yeats.

The Sunday evening buffet is the best time to sample some of the specialties that have won Myrtle Allen culinary recognition from Michelin, Egon Ronay, and Gault-Millau: fish soups, pates, sea urchin, fresh oysters and mussels, spiced beef and rib roasts, Ballymaloe's famous brown bread, and sweets that are likely to include caramel mousse and gooseberry fool. The fixed-price meals are $19.

Life at Ballymaloe is unhurried. You might stroll down to the nearby fishing village of Ballycotton and watch the day's catch unloaded, or drive to Waterford. Perhaps play tennis or swim, or read on the front lawn. You'll feel like family, waiting for the next meal.

Truly a family enterprise

Ballymaloe is very much a family enterprise. Myrtle Allen developed her recipes over the years, testing them with her husband and six children. One son runs the surrounding 400-acre farm that provides the dairy products, lamb, pork and bacon for the kitchen; another supplies vegetables and fruit from his 100-acre neighboring produce market; their wives help run the kitchen and the hotel. Ivan Allen buys the wine for the outstanding cellar, and one son-in-law manages the Allens' Paris restaurant, La Ferme Irlandaise.

In 1983, daughter-in-law Darina started The Ballymaloe Cookery School, which teaches Myrtle Allen's "Ballymaloe style." Darina describes it as "using the natural produce of the area, which combines rich farmland and an abundance of seafood." The school, set in a lovely Regency House in the middle of orchards and gardens, offers several 1-week courses, 3- and 4-day sessions, and afternoon demonstrations, in addition to the 12-week certificate course. The school is open from September to mid-May; for details, write to Darina Allen, The Ballymaloe Cookery School, Kinoith, Shanagarry, Co. Cork, Ireland (021-646785).

Joan Scobey is a free-lance writer from New York.

Over the years I've noticed students becoming more and more detached from the reality of how food is produced, so I decided to begin each 12-week course by introducing the gardeners and farm manager to the students. On the first morning we start with a welcoming cup of coffee, and then I introduce the students to Haulie Walsh and Eileen O'Donovan. We then make our way to the fruit garden, where I have a wheelbarrow full of compost ready. This has been made from the food scraps and organic matter from the 12-week course a year earlier. I talk to the students about the importance of sourcing good ingredients, how all good food comes from good earth, and that we all depend on the few inches of topsoil around the globe for our survival. I discuss the emerging food security concerns and remind them that there is no more than 90 days of food available in the world at any one time. I run my hands through the soil and tell them about the extraordinary bacteria, enzymes, minerals, trace elements, and magic earthworms in the soil. Without rich, fertile soil we won't have clean water or good food. All of this gets a rather baffled and confused response as they stand around in a polite circle, clearly thinking, "Crazy, aged hippy! It didn't say anything about this is the brochure!"—but by the end of the course they are every bit as passionate as I am.

Then we wander through the gardens, past the herbs, vegetables, and fruits, through the wildflower meadow, and down to the greenhouses, where Susan Turner, our consultant head gardener, is waiting to show them how to sow a seed. For me this is a very important first lesson of the course, because for many people food is something that comes wrapped in plastic off a supermarket shelf. In their busy lives they have little time to think about where it comes from or how it is produced, not to mention the breed or the variety. I know of no better way to give people a respect for food and those who produce it than to show them how to sow a seed and for them to watch it grow. We give each student a vegetable—it could be broccoli, scallions, or even lettuce, depending on the season—to put into the ground. They write their name on a popsicle stick and watch their vegetable's progress over the three months of the course. The responsibility for caring for their plant is a real revelation, as is the understanding that it can take the full 12 weeks of the course for their corn or broccoli to be ready to eat. This also brings home the precariousness of our food system, as they begin to realize that

Left: An early article about the School, which appeared in The Boston Globe *on June 16, 1985.*

you can't just plant a vegetable and expect it to be ready to eat next week. Students suddenly appreciate the sheer work and dedication that goes into producing delicious ingredients, and realize that plants have to be regularly watered and animals need to be fed and cared for every day. It also ensures that they treat produce with more care and respect in the kitchen. Students are so excited when they harvest and cook the vegetables that they have grown and want to share this with the rest of their class.

Students on the 12-week course come from all over the world. There is a teacher for every six students, and the day is structured so that they all get an opportunity to cook several of the dishes they have watched being demonstrated the previous afternoon. The afternoon demonstrations often cover as many as 25 recipes illustrating variations on the same techniques, ingredients, and themes. By the end of the course, these recipes are a comprehensive anthology of everything the course has covered. These sessions are open to the public as well as the 12-week students.

The day officially starts at 9 a.m. but many students begin at 8 a.m. or earlier if they want to learn how to milk the cows. Duties are split by rotas and include picking salad and vegetables, making butter, preparing stock, weighing ingredients, and general kitchen tasks that need to be done before the pressure of the morning starts. Students work in pairs, although everyone cooks their own dishes. Once they have completed their dishes, we have a tutor tasting, where the teachers mark each recipe. Continual assessment gives us the chance to gauge progress. Halfway through the course, there is a midterm test. At the end, there is a full examination, which together with the assessment marks, goes toward the 12-week course certificate.

The age range is as diverse as the nationalities and backgrounds of the students. There are a number of gap year students, 30-year-olds embarking on a career change, mothers whose children have left home, people working in the food business who want training and a qualification, B&B owners, food writers, and food lovers from all walks of life.

When I joined the International Association of Culinary Professionals (IACP) in 1986, I met many iconic cooks, chefs, food writers, and teachers and invited them to teach at the School. One of the earliest guest teachers in 1985 was Ada Parasiliti from Milan, and Anne Willan, who ran the highly regarded Ecole de Cuisine La Varenne in Paris, came in 1991. John Desmond, who has worked in many three-starred Michelin restaurants, came annually for many years—an excellent teacher, he and his wife Ellmary own Island Cottage Restaurant on Hare (or Heir) Island off Baltimore, in Ireland. Each chef has added to our knowledge and their recipes have become favorites in our repertoire over the years.

Ever hungry and curious for knowledge and new ideas, I also incorporated what I learned from my travels into the courses. Fortunately food and agriculture are my passions, so each trip I had was a delicious experience, with a perfect excuse to eat for Ireland, all in the name of research. I introduced Mexican recipes after my trips to Oaxaca, Michoacán, and Teotitlán del Valle; Asia provided further inspiration as dishes from Thailand, Singapore, Malaysia, and Cambodia have been added to our curriculum. These experiences bring my classes to life as I paint word pictures of Vietnam, India, Laos, Europe, and the US and their food for the students. After my first visit to California I was so excited that I have tried to return to the West coast at least biannually. The IACP Conference is held somewhere on the North American continent every year, which has given me the opportunity to visit many US cities including Denver, San Francisco, Dallas, Houston, Seattle, Chicago, and New York. Slow Food has brought me to Salone del Gusto and Terra Madre in Turin, a life-changing experience.

When I first visited Galle in Sri Lanka in 2010, everyone was agog with excitement about the Galle Literary Festival. We caught the end of it and had fun with Louis de Bernières, author of *Captain Corelli's Mandolin*, Skye Gyngell, Nick Lander, and Jancis Robinson, all participants in the festival, who had stayed on for a few days to enjoy beautiful Sri Lanka. The festival's wildly creative director Geoffrey Dobbs suggested that we think about having a literary festival at Ballymaloe, and so the concept was born.

It took three years for The Ballymaloe Literary Festival of Food and Wine (or LitFest) to become reality. With the Ballymaloe connection it seemed natural to celebrate the work of iconic food and wine writers from around the world. When the decision was made to go ahead, I picked up the phone and invited friends from all over the world to come to Ballymaloe on the May Bank holiday weekend, and all, apart from two people who were already committed, said yes. Alice Waters and Stephanie Alexander, who are both committed to edible food education, were top of my list. Grandes dames of the food world Madhur Jaffrey and Claudia Roden, guest chefs in earlier years, agreed to return. David Thompson came from Bangkok to talk about Thai and Asian street food. Claus Meyer, cofounder of Noma, agreed to talk about the Nordic food revolution. David Tanis, prominent American chef from Chez Panisse, and David Prior, journalist for various publications

Above (clockwise, from top left): Matthew Fort moderates a panel of Donal Skehan, Rachel Allen, Stevie Parle, and Thomasina Miers giving a talk on New Voices in Food; my nephew, Sacha Whelan, expertly hand-carving a pata negra at the LitFest—in real life he makes beautiful custom wooden furniture and the hardwood cutting boards we use at the School; iced cookies sold at the LitFest by past student Gail Porter; me and Madhur Jaffrey giving a cooking demonstration from her book Curry Nation; our line-up of 42 speakers at the LitFest included Sandor Katz, who drew people from all over the world, including a fan from Japan, and David Thompson, who gave a riveting demonstration on Asian street food; Rosie Campbell and Dennis McCarthy demonstrate falconry with the birds from their Animal Magic Wildlife Rescue Centre.

including *The New York Times*, both said an enthusiastic yes, as did "King of Fermentation" Sandor Ellix Katz. Thomasina Miers, Stevie Parle, Claire Ptak, Donal Skehan, Rachel Allen (all past students), and Skye Gyngell represented the new young voices in food. Joanna Blythman, Suzanne Campbell, and Ella McSweeney gave a workshop on Digesting Unsavory Truths. Bill Yosses, the White House pastry chef, came to tell us about Michelle Obama's vegetable garden.

There were food historians, bloggers, foragers, and restaurant critics attending literary dinners and readings, question and answer sessions, and talks covering topics such as food writing for the digital generation. There was a strong Irish presence and a huge wine element organized by Colm McCan, sommelier at Ballymaloe House, who also teaches a number of wine courses at the School. People traveled from around the world to hear Jancis Robinson, MW, speak on wine grapes and her husband Nick Lander, restaurant correspondent for the *Financial Times*, speak on the Art of the Restaurateur.

The LitFest took place at Ballymaloe House, the Grainstore at Ballymaloe and the Ballymaloe Cookery School. There were back-to-back cooking demonstrations at the School plus Saturday Pizzas and Sunday Roasts from the wood-burning oven in the Garden Café. The huge fringe festival in the Big Shed at Ballymaloe took on a life of its own. It had a makeover with recycled furniture made from lots of pallets and was decorated with graffiti and a chandelier made from old whisky barrels.

We had hoped for 2,500–3,000 people over the weekend; instead more than 8,000 visitors poured in, creating a continuous bustle of people roaming around the farmers' market stalls and enjoying the many free fringe events. The festival received write-ups in *The New York Times*, *International Herald Tribune*, *The Malaysian Times* as well as the *Guardian* and over 100 other publications. It trended several times on Twitter in Ireland and Europe over the weekend, an amazing achievement. Plans have started for the festival in 2014 and it looks like it may be an annual, or at least biannual, event over the next few years.

When Rory and I started the school in 1983, I was aware of only one other cooking school in Ireland, Alix Gardner's school in Ballsbridge, Dublin. Now there are around 40-plus, many of which are very successfully run by my ex-students. So we have created our own competition, which is great because it not only keeps us on our toes but also spreads the word and teaches more and more people to cook—a skill badly needed in a society, which, like many

Above (top): Skye Gyngell has returned to teach at the School on many occasions. Here she is making a green salad and adding her own twist by grating lemon zest and Parmesan over it at the last minute before tossing. She loves to fill the salad bowl with freshly picked greens grown here at Ballymaloe.
Above (middle): Sam Clark from Moro taught at the School in 2002, sharing the food that has made Moro and, more recently, Morito famous.
Above (bottom): Jacob Kenedy of Bocca di Lupo, another of my food heroes, visited the School in 2013 and showed us how to make artichokes a la giudia and a shaved radish salad, among other delicious dishes.

in the Western world, has placed greater emphasis on the value of academic rather than practical skills for the past two or three generations. Consequently, a high percentage of the population are no longer equipped with the basic skills needed to feed themselves properly. For many, anything more than slitting the top of a packet or reheating a precooked meal in a microwave is a mystery. I love teaching people how to cook and feel fortunate that food is my subject. The look of pride on the students' faces when they take their first loaf of bread out of the oven gives me a feeling of excitement every time.

Over the past few years I've become more and more concerned about the quality of the food we eat. Food is the fuel for our bodies; if you don't put good gas in the tank, the "car" won't perform properly. It's ironic that so many of us care for our cars and motorcycles much better than ourselves. We wouldn't dream of putting inferior oil or gas in them, yet we shovel any kind of old rubbish into our bodies and then wonder why we are low in energy, sluggish, or lacking in concentration. For most people, the only criterion when choosing food is price; never before have we spent so small a percentage of our income on food. The truth is that very few people connect the food they eat with how they feel. If we did, we would make it a greater priority.

At this point in time I have no intention of retiring and plan to keep teaching as long as I have the energy and strength. I am eternally curious and love learning as much as my students. Food, wine, and farming give me the opportunity to add to my knowledge and meet fascinating, inspirational people—both here at Ballymaloe and on my travels across the globe—who are every bit

as passionate as I am about delicious, nourishing food, sustainable farming, and looking after the soil that nourishes us all. Ballymaloe Cookery School students now work all over the world cooking and teaching and are involved in food in a myriad of ways, from manning stalls at farmers' markets to running farm shops and their own cooking schools, writing cookbooks and blogs, to cooking on yachts, oil rigs, in the Outback, or in pubs, cafés, and food trucks. They work in food manufacturing, artisanal food production, cake shops, delicatessens, bakeries, and at food camps. Some give pop-up dinners, teach kids' cooking classes, run dining clubs, and make homemade chocolates. Others have careers as cooks and chefs, TV presenters, cheesemakers, or organize food conferences and symposiums. They use their skills foraging, preserving, pickling, brewing, butchering, and making charcuterie. It doesn't matter where in the world I go now, from Asian airports to Sri Lankan beaches, gastropubs to cafés and food fairs, an ex-student will pop up, calling my name.

I love what I do and feel blessed to be teaching a subject that not only excites people but also gives them the skills and confidence that will enhance the quality of their day-to-day lives.

Above (left): Jeremy Lee from Quo Vadis in London is a wildly entertaining teacher—this image captures a serious moment among the usual hilarity. When the students taste the food of our guest chefs, they immediately add the chef's restaurant to their "London list" and plan to book a table and taste more when in town.
Above (right): Rory O'Connell teaching in the newly renovated demonstration kitchen in the summer of 2013.

Art around the School

The collection of art around the School is eclectic to say the least; a mixture of contemporary paintings, mixed media pieces, oils, etchings, and watercolors of the gardens, plus some early portraits painted by our daughter Lydia while she was at art school in Florence. Poetry by Seamus Heaney and the Deer's Cry (also known as St. Patrick's Breastplate), a beautiful piece from the late 7th or early 8th century, adorn the walls in the reception area close to the blackboard where the "Food from the Farm Today" is written.

In 1987 the boxwood hedges in the herb garden were becoming more established. Rory and I had been working very hard setting up the Cookery School, so our caring physician Dr. Derry McCarthy ordered a rest, and I spent a lovely two weeks with my mother up in Cullohill. When I arrived back at the Cookery School, I was met by Tim in a suit and I knew something was afoot. I was led out to the garden blindfolded and up the rickety steps of the viewing platform made of recycled greenhouse timber and old apple stakes. Suddenly down below people burst into a rousing "Happy Birthday!" The herb garden was packed with friends gathered from all over the country and abroad—a surprise birthday party.

The family presented me with a beautiful stone sundial carved by Tanya Mosse, one of the multitalented Mosse family from Bennettsbridge in County Kilkenny. We have been collecting the drawings and paintings by her brother Paul since the mid-1990s; Nicholas Mosse's pottery has been a part our lives since he first opened his studio in 1976; and his brother Keith is a woodturner extraordinaire. The huge wooden bowl that holds the green salad in the Blue Dining Room at the Cookery School every day was turned by Keith from Irish elm in 1988. Oliver, the youngest member of this extraordinary Mosse family, is a horticulturalist and recently gave me a present of a truffle oak, which we hope will bear fruit in the not too distant future. Tanya's sundial, carved in Kilkenny limestone, incorporated four cherubs on the panels of the pedestal (representing our four children) bearing gifts of fruit, vegetables, flowers, and herbs. Owen Deignan, a member of the Royal National Lifeboat Institution (RNLI), made the actual sundial from brass. The piece is embedded in the gravel in the boxwood semicircle on the northeast side of the herb garden, close to the old potting shed and remains of Lydia Strangman's fernery.

In 1991, I commissioned sculptor Ken Thompson, of Ballytrasna, near Ballycotton, to made a bird bath for Tim for Christmas. It's a

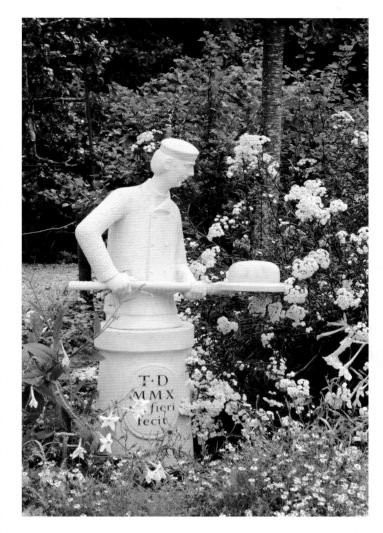

beautiful piece, also carved from a chunk of Kilkenny limestone, large enough to be a tabletop—4½ft in diameter and 3½in deep, but with a shallow water bath in the center. The inscription is a William Blake quote, which reads "He who binds to himself a joy/ Does the winged life destroy;/ But he who kisses the joy as it flies/ Lives in eternity's sunrise." On the inner circle is written "A Christmas gift from Darina to Tim 1991." It sits outside the main entrance to the Cookery School, surrounded by seats for the students to sit and chat around it every day in nice weather.

The Ballymaloe Baker (pictured above) is the newest addition to the grounds. This beautiful sculpture of a baker proudly taking a loaf of bread out of the oven on a paddle was also carved by Ken Thompson. Its inscription, in Latin, reads *T*D MMX mefieri fecit* and translated means "Tim and Darina caused me to be made in 2012." The students quickly christened it the "feck it" statue, an irreverent play on the Latin word *fecit*.

The First 12-week Course

When my brother Rory O'Connell and I started the Cookery School in 1983, I was aware of only one other in Ireland: Alix Gardner's school in Ballsbridge, Dublin. However, in the 30 years since then, over 40 cooking schools have opened across the country, many of which are very successfully run by my ex-students.

When we decided to open a residential cooking school, I decided to visit those with the best reputation and, wherever possible, enroll in an afternoon class. I was quite open with everyone about my own plans and was greeted warmly and generously by each and every school I visited.

Alix generously welcomed me at Ballsbridge to see how she operated her classes. In London, Caroline Waldegrave and Sally Proctor showed me around Prue Leith's and generously shared their experience with me, as did John and Beryl Childs at Tante Marie in Woking (now co-owned by Lyndy Redding, Andrew Maxwell, a past Ballymaloe student, and Gordon Ramsay). I went to see Sabine de Mirbeck's cooking school in Sussex, where I had a lovely convivial day, lunch with the students and teachers and a tour of the school's facilities and gardens. I also loved La Petite Cuisine in Richmond,

outside London, run by another superb chef and teacher, Lyn Hall. After the cooking demonstration I introduced myself to Lyn, and I always remember her words as I enthusiastically told her about my plans: "Well, be prepared to work 11 hours a day and then it'll be great!" She wasn't far off the mark.

The bank manager had turned down our original application for a loan to open a cooking school—in fact, he was quite amused by the idea. My parents-in-law Ivan and Myrtle Allen generously acted as guarantors for us. So, as soon as Tim and I received the bank loan we needed, we started the process of converting some farm buildings into a school and extra accommodation. The builders and carpenters worked nonstop for several months to get the kitchen-cum-demonstration area and dining room into shape. (The latter had been the children's playroom plus an extra bedroom where we took overflow from Ballymaloe House on a B&B basis during the summer months.) The new kitchen was 21ft x 22ft with a peaked roof. We decided to put a long, narrow window along the front, overlooking the orchard, and inserted some skylights into the roof. The walls of the building were about 2ft thick, so we were able to have a wide windowsill for pots of herbs and edible flowers, including sweet geranium, and of course space to cool bread. I've always loved the image of a loaf of soda bread cooling on a wire rack by an open window in the traditional way.

The kitchen cupboards and shelves were made from white deal pine. Barry O'Keeffe, our local carpenter, made them and fortunately unpainted wood was just becoming fashionable. The counter and shelves were easy-to-clean white formica—I had always liked the look of it. The original plan had been to use hardwood, but that proved to be outside our budget.

We framed a couple of Tessa Traeger's *Vogue* food posters and hung them on the walls. A few red wire grids to hang utensils completed the country-chic look. The floor was tiled with beautiful terra-cotta quarry tiles imported from Spain by Stephen Pearce, our potter friend from the village of Shanagarry. The softly plastered walls were whitewashed with burnt lime in the traditional way.

Above: The interior of the apple barn with the apples piled high (left) and the apple grader (right). Architects find this building of interest because it was designed with very tall windows to let in the maximum amount of light. These long, tall windows are still part of Kitchens One and Two at the School. The barn was designed using the minimum amount of timber needed to support the roof structure because it was built at the end of World War II when timber was scarce. These images show the farm buildings before their conversion into the Cookery School, with the Pink Cottage in its original state as a cow barn. It had a galvanized roof, which we later replaced with slate and timber windows and doors. The White Cottage (bottom right) was where the original School was and this was where the students were taught for the first classes in 1983.

Left: A very much younger version of my brother Rory and me demonstrating together in the early days of the Cookery School. Right: Very intense pictures of me from the early days of School, looking like I could do with a hearty steak and good night's sleep! From the beginning we used the gardens at the School to provide fresh produce for the students' cooking. In the image on the top right I can be seen slathering butter onto chicken liver pâté—very of its time.

A little corridor between the kitchen and dining room with a work surface and shelves on each side was our weighing area, where the preparation of ingredients for the cooking demonstrations was done. At the other side there was a bathroom and pantry and an office-cum-library on the balcony overhead. This busy little office overlooking the dining room was where my secretary, Rosalie Dunne, worked when she joined us in February 1984. The phone was answered, enquiries and bookings dealt with, and recipes typed and printed. Anyone visiting the School was greeted from up here and immediately looked after. My cookbook collection was housed on shelves up under the eaves and the students were allowed to browse and borrow. Over the years the cookbook collection grew and grew and is now in the region of 3,000 copies and still expanding!

The dining room had a couple of round tables, just over 6.5ft in diameter, with a large wooden revolving lazy Susan in the center, from which the dishes were accessible. I love round tables; they seem very welcoming and somehow there's always room for another person. We used blue-and-white gingham tablecloths, beautifully laid with a little vase of flowers from the garden, small bowls of sea salt, and pepper mills, unusual in 1983. From the beginning the students and teachers sat down together to relax, enjoy the company, and discuss the results of the morning's cooking, always a very convivial time. This interaction between students and teachers and sharing the results of the students' labors is not a common feature in all cooking schools but something we really value at Ballymaloe. The students and teachers are often joined by a few guests, perhaps friends or family of the students, who are always welcome to join us.

While the building was taking shape, Tim, Rory, and I were grappling with another decision—what should we call the school? Shanagarry Cooking School? Darina Allen Cooking School? At that stage my name was totally unknown. However, the name Ballymaloe already stood for integrity and quality; Ivan and Myrtle Allen's hotel and restaurant, Ballymaloe House, was highly regarded, with top ratings in the *Good Food Guide* and *Egon Ronay Guides* for the quality of its food. We didn't dare propose it, but my parents-in-law suggested we call it Ballymaloe Cookery School. This was an incredible boost and a show of faith in us. A friend who had been in advertising helped us design a simple brochure. We put an ad in the national newspaper *The Irish Times* and the local *Cork Examiner*, and waited for the mailman to come and the phone to ring. By now we were deeply in debt—it simply had to work, so we decided to operate all year round during the normal school year.

There was NO money for extra advertising. We decided to charge similar fees to the Cordon Bleu and Prue Leith Cooking Schools in London—I was determined that if we were going to run a cooking school it would be as good as, if not better than, anywhere else in the world. So we needed to charge enough to do it really well with a margin for generosity. If someone burned their bread or made a mess of something, I wanted to be able to give them more ingredients without feeling resentful. I was determined that everyone who came should feel that they had at least gotten value for money and, preferably, much, much more.

As I planned the menus for the first 12-week course in 1983, it suddenly occurred to me that I needed to incorporate a wine

Above (top): Rory and me with the students of one of the first 12-week classes.
(middle): The mirror we had above the demonstration area from the beginning provided a view directly into the saucepans for the students, which intrigued people when they first came but is now a common sight in many cooking schools.
(bottom): This was initially a dual-purpose room; in the morning the students cooked in a hands-on session, and in the afternoons we brought chairs into the center of the room to create a demonstration area.

element into the course. It was almost unthinkable to enjoy a good meal without a glass or two of wine. In the early 1980s, many people's knowledge of wine was very limited. Most houses would have had a little sherry and whisky, maybe a bottle of port in a cabinet in the living room, but it was another decade at least before one could buy wine as easily as we do today. Consequently, many found wine an intimidating subject—they felt they ought to know a bit more about it but weren't sure how to go about learning. There weren't all that many books on wine and few wine retailers.

I decided to incorporate some wine lectures into our first 12-week course, and from then on I took every opportunity to learn as much as I could about the subject. I was very anxious to take the mystery out of wine, to equip the students with enough knowledge to make them comfortable about the subject in any social situation, and to give them the necessary confidence, know-how, and contacts to assemble a wine list in a restaurant.

My father-in-law, Ivan Allen, also came to my rescue, giving the wine lectures for the first couple of years, and since then we've had a series of wonderful wine lecturers, including the late John O'Connell, Kevin Parsons, Tom Doorley, Sacha Whelan, and Colm McCan (head sommelier at Ballymaloe House for many years).

Tim and I swapped roles; he looked after the children, getting them to school and cooking for them, so that I could concentrate on getting the School up and running. We started on September 5, 1983 with 11 students on a 12-week certificate course that aimed to equip them with the basic culinary knowledge and skills to earn their living from their cooking. My brother, Rory O'Connell (who had been a chef at Ballymaloe House), and I did absolutely everything—wrote the recipes, which were then typed with an electric typewriter onto stencils and printed off on a Gestetner printing machine (this was before the days of word processors, computers, and laser jet printers), demonstrated, taught hands-on classes, washed the dishes, and answered queries.

On the first 12-week certificate course we had ten girls and one lucky chap—all Irish. Several came from their own family-run businesses, either hotels or restaurants, and a couple of others were anxious to do the course so that they could cook and entertain with confidence and panache. Caroline Casey from Blackrock in Cork had always had a great interest in cooking. Her ambition was to start her own catering business doing lunches, private dinner parties, etc. She intended to go to London to do a course in cooking, but when she heard about the new diploma course at Ballymaloe she decided to enroll. Susan Cummins from Dublin wanted to concentrate on getting into the catering business in Ireland. Mary Cotter from County Cork already worked in the hotel trade locally and enrolled on the course to further her knowledge of cooking. Clodagh McAlinden worked in the Adam and Eve Restaurant in Cork but wanted to gain experience in cooking and to get new ideas for her job. Anna Sheehan, of Charleville, was also involved in the hotel business. She worked in her family hotel and, like Clodagh, wanted to gain the experience and confidence to cope with staff and the running of a hotel kitchen. Tim Rooney from Sligo had spent several years at sea, fishing. He had also done a business course, but discovered that his real love was cooking and that he yearned to work in a kitchen. Several of our first batch of students have continued in the restaurant business.

We taught an extensive range of cooking techniques: butchery, fish filleting, preserving, freezing, ethnic cooking, and so on. There were lectures on menu planning, food costing, food hygiene, and career advice. We still cover all these topics and, over the years, have added in more information and expanded students' learning opportunities.

Gradually, news of Ballymaloe Cookery School spread, mainly through word of mouth. Once we had settled in and things were up and running smoothly, we decided to have an official opening on November 14, 1983. We chose that date because we wanted to have the opening before the current class started their exams, and before Ballymaloe House was getting busy for the Christmas season. It was also a good way of generating publicity for the next course, which was to start in January 1984. We invited Michael MacNulty, Chief Executive of Bord Fáilte (Irish Tourist Board); Minister for Agriculture Paddy Hegarty; Pat McDonagh of Bord Bainne (Dairy Board); Maeve Bracken of CBF (The Irish Meat Board); and many friends and members of the press. Ever generous, my parents-in-law invited them all to Ballymaloe House. The new students cooked and proudly served a delicious afternoon tea at the Cookery School: little scones with homemade jam and cream, raspberry and almond tartlets, praline cake, gingerbread, and a traditional Irish fruit cake called a barmbrack. There were speeches and much well wishing—I remember being amused and a little overwhelmed when I heard my friend Pauline O'Kennedy, who had always encouraged me, remark to my mother: "History is being made today."

Above: Teaching a class in the original Cookery School, wearing what became my trademark red glasses.

Equipping the School

When I started the School, I was determined to equip the kitchens with the best and most beautiful equipment. For me that was Le Pentole ICM saucepans, which I had bought one by one over the years for my own house from David Mellor's lovely shop in Sloane Square, London. Simply designed, beautiful, stainless-steel saucepans, they have solid three-layer bases (copper, steel, and alloy) to conduct the heat. It was a big investment, but one that has proved to be worth every penny. I also chose David Mellor's range of Provençale cutlery for the dining room, which we still use and enjoy.

Rory and I made a trip to Dehillerin in Paris, an old-fashioned kitchen shop on the corner of rue Coquillière and rue Jean-Jacques Rousseau. It is a cook's heaven. Dehillerin has been owned by the same family for over 200 years and is known for selecting items for quality, not just price. Kitchen utensils are piled high from floor to ceiling on (sometimes dusty) wooden shelves. It is primarily for the professional chef, but you are just as likely to see American and Japanese tourists rummaging through the cramped and crowded aisles of this unique and historic store to find obscure utensils—all are welcome. I bought a nest of stainless steel bowls for every section in the School's kitchen, and they are still in use 30 years later.

I also bought some madeleine and genoise pans and a couple of rum baba molds, which would have been difficult to find in Ireland at the time.

French Peasant Soup

This is a very substantial soup—it has "eating and drinking" in it and would certainly be a meal in itself, particularly if some grated Cheddar cheese was scattered over the top. We have added different variations to the soup over the years, sometimes including cooked beans, such as kidney beans, to the soup to make a more substantial meal, or a drizzle of kale pesto during the winter. When Myrtle Allen ran La Ferme Irlandaise in Paris, serving Irish country food, she changed the name of this soup to Connemara Broth— the French loved it.

Serves 6

6oz unsmoked slab bacon (in one piece)
1 tablespoon olive or sunflower oil
1 cup peeled potatoes, cut into ¼in dice
½ cup finely chopped onions
1 small garlic clove, peeled and finely chopped (optional)
1lb very ripe tomatoes, peeled and diced or
1 x 14oz can of diced tomatoes and their juice
sea salt and freshly ground black pepper
½–1 teaspoon sugar
3 cups homemade chicken or vegetable stock
¾ cup finely chopped cabbage (Savoy is best)

To serve
flat-leaf parsley, coarsely chopped

Remove the rind from the bacon if necessary and cut the bacon into approx. ¼in strips. Blanch the bacon in cold water by bringing it to a boil over high heat to remove some of the salt and nitrates, if present. Drain off the frothy water and dry the bacon on paper towels.

In a frying pan, sauté the bacon in the olive or sunflower oil until the fat runs and the bacon is crisp and golden. Add the potatoes, onions, and garlic, if using, sweat for 10 minutes, and then add the diced tomatoes along with any juice. Season with salt, pepper, and sugar to taste. Pour in the stock, bring to a boil, and simmer for 5 minutes. Add the finely chopped cabbage and continue to simmer just until the cabbage is cooked. Taste and correct the seasoning, if necessary. Sprinkle with lots of chopped parsley and serve.

This basic soup has been a Ballymaloe staple since the beginning of the School. It teaches students how to slice and dice and how to blanch and refresh, as well as how to extract salt from the bacon.

Glazed Loin of Bacon

We sometimes serve the bacon with spiced plums or peperonata; in the earlier days the usual accompaniments were tomato fondue and champ (an Irish dish of mashed potatoes with scallions). We use loin of bacon off the bone.

Serves 12–15

4–5lb loin of bacon, either smoked or unsmoked
approx. 20–30 whole cloves
1¾ cups demerara sugar (not soft brown sugar)
approx. 3–4 tablespoons pineapple juice

Put the bacon in a large saucepan, cover with cold water, and bring slowly to a boil. If the bacon is very salty, there will be a white froth on top of the water and, if this is the case, it is preferable to discard this water. It may be necessary to change the water several times, depending on the saltiness of the bacon. Finally cover with hot water and simmer until almost cooked, allowing approx. 20 minutes to the lb.

Preheat the oven to 475°F. Remove the bacon from the pan and cut off the rind. Cut the fat into a diamond pattern and stud with cloves. Blend the demerara sugar into a thick paste with a little pineapple juice, being careful not to make it too liquid. Spread this over the bacon. Bake in the preheated oven for approx. 20–30 minutes or until the top has caramelized. Remove from the oven and put on a carving dish. Carve in thick slices lengthwise so each slice includes some of the eye of the loin and streaky bacon.

Fork Cookies

We've been making these simple cookies since the beginning; originally they were plain, but we now have fun doing many variations on the theme. Try Jette Virdi's Cumin Cookies (see Variations); the spice proved to be a really good addition.

Makes approx. 45–50

16 tablespoons (2 sticks) butter, softened
½ cup superfine sugar
2¼ cups self-rising flour, sifted
grated zest of 1 lemon or orange
vanilla sugar, to sprinkle

Preheat the oven to 350°F and line two baking sheets with parchment paper.

Cream the butter and add in the sugar, sifted flour, and grated lemon or orange zest, and mix until it all comes together. Alternatively, put all four ingredients in the bowl of a food processor and mix slowly until all the ingredients come together. (At this stage, the dough can be put in the freezer or kept in the fridge for up to a week.)

When required, bring up to room temperature, and form into small balls the size of a walnut. Flatten them out onto the prepared baking sheets using the back of a fork dipped in cold water. Allow plenty of room for expansion.

Bake in the preheated oven for approx. 10 minutes. Sprinkle with the vanilla sugar and leave to cool. When cold, store in an airtight container.

Variations

For Jette Virdi's Cumin Cookies, add 2 teaspoons of freshly roasted and ground cumin seeds and the freshly squeezed juice of 2 lemons to the basic mixture.

For cinnamon, ginger, or chocolate cookies, add 2 teaspoons ground cinnamon or ginger or 2–3oz chopped chocolate to the basic mixture.

Almond Tart or Tartlets with Raspberries or Loganberries

These little tarts are still made at Ballymaloe House and are also a favorite here at the Cookery School. Students can't believe how easy they are to make and how many variations they can explore with seasonal toppings—kumquats, rhubarb, raspberries, strawberries, blueberries… I have a particular soft spot for this recipe, apart from the fact that it is super-delicious. Years ago, when I was a student at Cathal Brugha Street College in Dublin, I went to an afternoon tea party with my boyfriend. Among the dainties on offer were little almond tartlets with homemade raspberry jam and a blob of cream. I loved them and ventured to ask for the recipe. The hostess was flattered but flatly refused; it was her secret. When I arrived at Ballymaloe a few weeks later, Myrtle had these little tartlets on the dessert cart and she not only shared the recipe but showed me exactly how to make them.

Preheat the oven to 350°F. To make the pastry, cream the butter really well and then stir in the sugar and almond flour. (Don't overbeat the mixture or the oil will leak out of the almond flour as the pastry cooks.) Divide the mixture between 24 shallow 2½in tartlet pans or two 7in layer cake pans. Bake in the preheated oven until golden brown—approx. 10–12 minutes for the tartlets or 20–30 minutes for the tarts.

Meanwhile, make the red currant glaze. Melt the red currant jelly with the water in a small stainless steel saucepan. Stir gently, but do not whisk or it will become cloudy. Simmer for 1–2 minutes, no longer or the jelly will darken.

Remove the tartlets or tarts from the oven and set aside to cool in their pans for 5 minutes before turning them out. Do not allow them to set hard or the butter will solidify and the pastry will stick to the pans. If this happens, pop the pans back into the oven for a few minutes so the butter melts, and then they will come out easily. Set aside to cool.

Just before serving, arrange the whole raspberries or loganberries on the base. Briefly reheat the red currant glaze and brush over the fruit. Decorate with rosettes of cream and tiny mint or sweet cicely leaves.

Serves 12 (Makes 24 tartlets, 2 medium tarts, or 1 tart and 12 tartlets)

For the pastry
8 tablespoons (1 stick) unsalted butter, softened
½ cup superfine sugar
1 heaping cup almond flour

For the red currant glaze (1¼ cups)
1½ cups red currant jelly
approx. 1 tablespoon water (if necessary)

For the filling
1lb fresh raspberries or loganberries
1¼ cups whipped cream

To serve
mint or sweet cicely leaves

Red Currant Jelly

2lb red currants
2lb (4½ cups) granulated sugar

Remove the strings from the red currants either by hand or with a fork. Put the currants and sugar into a wide, stainless-steel saucepan. Heat and stir continuously until they come to a boil. Boil for exactly 8 minutes, stirring only if they appear to be sticking to the base. Skim carefully. Turn into a nylon sieve and leave to drip through—do not push the pulp through or the jelly will be cloudy. You can stir gently once or twice just to free the bottom of the sieve of pulp.

Pour the jelly into sterilized jars immediately. Cover and store in a cool, dry place. Red currants are very high in pectin, so the jelly will begin to set just as soon as it begins to cool.

Local Artisan Producers

I recently heard a new term for a type of food sadly on the increase: "catalog cooking." Not exactly a complimentary term, it refers to an ever-increasing number of establishments where the chef picks up the phone and orders virtually everything from a catering catalog. Much of it is pre-prepared, portioned, and already garnished. At the Cookery School we seem to be the polar opposite of that; we source our produce from well over 150 food suppliers, mostly Irish. Some are tiny, others slightly larger, but the majority are local artisans, small farmers, fishermen, farmhouse cheesemakers, and foragers; we know them all and the list continues to grow. I was lucky that Myrtle had built up a loyal network of suppliers at Ballymaloe House so that when I started the School, I was able to tap into her contacts list and gradually add to it. This is a vitally important element of the Ballymaloe Cookery School and the restaurant at Ballymaloe House. It is not an exaggeration to say that we are totally indebted to all these passionate people who produce the beautiful raw materials that make it possible for us to make delicious food. We have a "Wall of Fame" in the Blue Dining Room with photos of many of our food heroes, framed for all to see.

Many of our producers have been supplying us since the day we opened; some have retired, others have come on stream. Nora Aherne has been sending tasty, plump Aylesbury ducks to both Ballymaloe House and the School for many years. Ballycotton Seafood has for a long time been a source of fresh fish, and one of our more recent suppliers, Brenda O'Riordan, sells the fresh catch from the boats in our local fishing village, Ballycotton, from her Love Fish van. Patrick and Mary Walsh from the farm across the road grow rhubarb, potatoes, juicy strawberries, and other soft fruit. Jane Murphy makes several goat cheeses, including the mild and gentle Ardsallagh, and, like many other farmhouse cheesemakers, comes to talk to the students and tell her story. Michael Woulfe from Midleton supplied us with honey from the early days and helped us set up hives in the apple orchard for our own bees. He still gives us advice on all bee matters and supports our new young beekeeper, Gary O'Keeffe.

Left: Geese grazing.
Above: The humble mackerel, discounted by many, is my favorite sea fish, but it has to be super fresh. In coastal communities there is a saying that the sun should never set on a mackerel, so it is best eaten within hours of being caught. We get fresh mackerel from Ballycotton in the summer. Word spreads through the village when the mackerel arrive in shoals. Anyone with a rod and reel runs down to the pier, and the fishermen take to their boats to take advantage of their presence.

Left: Michael Cuddigan's butcher's shop in the shadow of St Colman's Cathedral in Cloyne, County Cork, with Michael working at his beautiful wooden butcher's block and meat hanging at ambient temperature from the meat hooks in the background. Michael originally wrapped his meat in time-honored fashion in parchment and brown paper, tied with butcher's string. Here he is explaining different cuts of beef and the importance of hanging and dry-aging.

A local butcher, Michael Cuddigan, supplied the Cookery School with superb beef and lamb for 17 years until he retired in 2000. He had been supplying meat to Ivan and Myrtle Allen at Ballymaloe House since 1948, initially to the family and then to the Yeats Room restaurant when they opened in 1964.

Michael, a third-generation artisan butcher, always bought his meat "on the hoof" (live cattle) directly from the local farmers he knew and trusted. He kept the animals on his own farm until such time as he judged them in prime condition for slaughter. Some of his land had never been tilled in living memory—virgin soil, full of wildflowers and a wide variety of grasses and herbs for the cattle to feast on. He knew all the farmers who raised the animals and what they had been fed on; this is real traceability, local food for local people.

Michael (and I completely agree with him) favored the traditional breeds, like Aberdeen Angus, or Aberdeen Angus crossed with Shorthorn or Pol Angus, Strawberry Roan Shorthorn, or Hereford. They are suited to our terrain and can be completely fattened on grass rather than grain for premium flavor. Recently, several farmers have started to rear Dexter cattle again. Dexter are a small, hardy breed of cattle that originated in the southwest of Ireland; they are good dual-purpose cattle, suitable for producing both beef and milk. The cuts of meat from this breed are small but the flavor is superb. Ireland's climate is ideally suited to grass-growing, and the cattle may be kept outdoors for much of the year.

Buying this meat keeps the traditional breeds thriving, and I was heartened to hear that the Irish Rare Breeds Society, which had become dormant due to the Foot and Mouth outbreak in 2001, is being reactivated by people interested in supporting our traditional native breeds. Sadly, many of the heritage breeds can be difficult to find nowadays because of the general shift toward continental breeds, such as Belgian Blue, Simmental, Charolais, and Limousin. They have a larger, leaner carcass, which makes them popular in a market that is increasingly paranoid about fat. At the School we love the fat, and I stress over and over again to the students that without the fat, the meat would not be juicy and succulent. I emphasize that only two vitamins are water soluble; all the rest are fat soluble, so unless we eat some fat we cannot absorb all the nutrients from our food—yet another reason why a low-fat diet is not necessarily the healthiest choice. If you really would rather not eat the fat, leave it on the edge of your plate, but the flavor of the meat will be infinitely better if it is cooked with the fat on.

Like many other local butchers, Michael killed maiden heifer grass-fed beef and hung it for about 14 days. These younger animals produce more tender meat, and hanging greatly enhances the flavor and texture. Meat loses weight while hanging and therefore costs a bit more, but the result, worth every penny, was tender, with a rich, beefy flavor—delicious. His simple butcher's shop was in the village of Cloyne, County Cork, close to St Colman's 13th-century cathedral and the 11th-century Round Tower. Like many family butchers, he knew his customers and their needs, and sometimes even what they wanted for dinner. Once when I was in the shop, a little local lad ran in and just asked for chops "for the dinner."

Michael didn't even hesitate; he took down a loin of lamb from the hook and cut the chops on the ancient wooden butcher's block. He seemed to know exactly how many would need dinner in that house and exactly what type of chop they'd expect—now that's service for you!

Now that Michael has retired, we buy from several other local butchers, including Frank Murphy, a third-generation butcher on the Main Street in Midleton, who also has his own slaughterhouse. His son Brian has now come into the business, proudly continuing the legacy of his father, grandfather, and great-grandfather before him. We are fortunate in Ireland to have over 550 artisan butchers around the country; many of these are family-run businesses where the skills have been passed down from generation to generation. There's a growing realization of the importance of tradition and the value of having small slaughterhouses. These butchers buy their animals from the local market or from farmers with whom they have built up relationships over many years. They know how the animals are reared, the quality of the feed, the breed, and the values of the farmer. Some, like Michael, have their own farms and bring the animals to the stage where they are ready for butchering (known as finishing) on their own pasture—this is the ultimate standard. We introduce our butchers to the students and encourage them to seek out and build up a relationship with their local butcher and to highlight the provenance of the meat on their menus when they have restaurants of their own.

In 2001 we introduced the Producer of the Week concept to the 12-week course, inviting a farmer or food producer to come to the School to join us for lunch and afterwards to tell the students their story. For example, when we are using bacon, we might invite pig farmers Martin and Noreen Conroy from Woodside Farm in Ballincurrig, East Cork, who rear and cure the heritage saddleback pigs. The students love to be able to put a face to the name and they certainly handle the produce with more care and respect after they have heard the story of how it is produced. We have a network of suppliers, local and small producers, from whom we buy throughout the year. We encourage students to link up with local farmers and to establish a similar network when they set up their own businesses. We emphasize that buying everything locally checks all the desirable boxes: you build up a good relationship and a bond of trust with your producer, with the added bonus that the fresh, seasonal produce invariably tastes better. Buying locally also keeps the money in the local economy, which helps everyone. Also, if you run out of some vital supplies over the weekend, it's always easier to call someone you know to come to the rescue!

Right: I've always loved offal and variety meats and loved the succulent dishes that you can tease out by slowly cooking lesser cuts. Frank Murphy, our local artisan butcher, brought a range of inexpensive cuts and offal including sweetbreads, hearts, liver, kidneys, oxtail, and tripe to a Slow Food event we held at the School for students and members of the public. He explained the cuts and I then provided recipes and lots of suggestions for how to cook them.

The Farm Shop

We first started a farm shop in June 1982 after we decided, for economic reasons, to stop growing tomatoes commercially. The idea developed from selling apples directly from the farm; we thought that we could expand on that kind of thing, so both Tim and I traveled to England to get an idea of how they went about it, because farm shops were a more established tradition there.

On our return, we converted the old mushroom-packing shed into a farm shop. Our Ballymaloe carpenter, Danny Power, made some sloping stands to hold the traditional wicker baskets. We filled them with fresh vegetables, and we also sold homemade jams, marmalade, chutneys, and a beautiful collection of cakes and cookies, free-range chickens and salamis, and beans. I went down to the end of the road and put up a sandwich board with a chalk sign for Shanagarry Farm Shop and Garden Café, and waited for the curious passersby to come up the lane. We put little ads in the *Cork Examiner* and later put some proper signs up in the village.

Within a few weeks of opening, we took on three extra people to work in the Farm Shop. We employed a highly skilled organic gardener named Jill Gairdner to help us set up a pick-your-own fruit and vegetable area to complement the Farm Shop. Jill joined us in May 1982, having replied to an advertisement for a Head Gardener in *The Grower* magazine.

The Farm Shop, probably the first in the country, was much-loved by local people, summer residents of the nearby campsites, and other visitors, and the Corkonians, who drove out from the city to buy fresh vegetables and fruit and to eat at the little Garden Café behind the shop. All day long we baked to replenish the selection of our cakes and cookies. I remember one day Florrie Bolger (now Florrie Cullinane and a senior tutor at the Ballymaloe Cookery School), who had come from County Wexford to work with us that summer, and I baked six batches of scones during the day. Imagine—we sold 120 scones from a galvanized shed, albeit a very pretty one, with long window boxes full of geraniums. The bases of the tables in the little café were made from Singer sewing machine bases, the chairs a motley borrowed collection, blue-and-white gingham cloths here and there—all very retro chic, but this was out of necessity, long before the term was coined. Those were the days when you could decide to get up and do something and just do it. There was far less regulation and red tape involved in getting an enterprise off the ground.

We charged a price halfway between wholesale and retail costs. We also gave away unfamiliar vegetables for free—zucchini, eggplant, peppers, artichokes—plus simple but delicious recipes for people to experiment with. By the end of the summer, many of our customers had become much more adventurous in their cooking habits.

The Farm Shop operated for three years, seven days a week, but we realized by the end of summer 1984 that our energies would be better spent concentrating on the Cookery School. This was getting much busier, generating quite a bit of interest and beginning to attract students from abroad.

Smoked Gubbeen Cheese and Pearl Barley Salad with Toasted Almonds, Apple, and Pomegranate Seeds

The Ferguson family at Gubbeen in West Cork make the famous Gubbeen washed rind cheese. Their smoked Gubbeen is not as well known, but it is equally delicious and might be available at a specialty cheese shop. Their son Fingal makes an ever-increasing range of charcuterie, and their lovely daughter Clovisse has created a garden of Eden from whence she sells salad leaves and organic vegetables to local restaurants and friends.

Recently there's been a tremendous revival of interest in cheap and cheerful barley, an almost forgotten grain with lots of flavor and a rich complement of vitamins and minerals, including iron and some calcium. It's also a source of protein and natural fiber.

Put the barley and water into a saucepan and add the salt. Bring to a boil and simmer gently for approx. 20 minutes. Drain well.

To make the dressing, whisk the extra virgin olive oil, vinegar, and garlic together. Season to taste with salt and pepper.

Place the drained barley in a mixing bowl, spoon in half the dressing, and toss while still warm. Spread out to cool.

Meanwhile, quarter and dice the apples. Put in a mixing bowl, squeeze in a little lemon juice, and add the pomegranate seeds, toasted almonds, and diced smoked Gubbeen cheese. Add the remainder of the dressing. Toss gently and combine with the barley. Taste and correct the seasoning if necessary. Transfer to a serving dish and allow the flavors to meld for an hour or so. Scatter with parsley leaves and serve.

Serves 4 as a main course or 8 as an appetizer

1 cup pearled barley
6½ cups water
1 teaspoon salt

For the dressing
½ cup extra virgin olive oil
3 tablespoons Forum Chardonnay vinegar, or
    another good-quality white wine vinegar
1 garlic clove, peeled and finely chopped
sea salt and freshly ground black pepper

2 eating apples, such as Gala, cored
freshly squeezed lemon juice
seeds from ½–1 pomegranate, depending on size
½ cup toasted almonds, coarsely chopped
4–6oz Smoked Gubbeen cheese, diced
flat-leaf parsley leaves, to serve

Salad of Lamb, Green Beans, and Fennel with Tomato and Chile Jam

Our local butcher for many years, Michael Cuddigan, had his own fields of pasture, some of which had never been turned in living memory. The texture and the flavor of the meat reflected the variety of grasses and wildflowers in the pasture where the lambs grazed. Irish lamb in general has a sweet flavor, which varies from one area to another and changes whether it comes from the hills or lowlands. It's fun to experiment—look out for Wicklow, Connemara, Kerry, and Mayo lamb; each has its own unique flavor.

This salad may be served in a wide serving bowl, family style, or in individual portions for a summer lunch.

Bring a saucepan of water to a boil. Add the green beans and the salt, and blanch for 2 minutes. Drain, refresh under cold running water, drain again, and set aside. (If the beans are large, cut them on an angle and blanch for a little longer.)

Slice the fennel very finely with a sharp knife or Japanese mandoline and put into a bowl of cold water. Add the lemon juice to prevent discoloration.

Preheat a grill pan over medium heat. Season the meat generously with sea salt and freshly ground black pepper, and then drizzle with extra virgin olive oil. Put the lamb onto the hot pan and cook for 4–5 minutes on one side without moving. Then turn and cook for another 4–5 minutes on the other side. Remove from the heat, transfer to a hot plate, cover loosely with foil, and allow to rest for 15 minutes. The lamb should still be pink in the center but not too rare.

Meanwhile, wash and dry the salad leaves.

To make the dressing, put the lemon zest into a bowl. Add the freshly squeezed lemon juice and whisk in the extra virgin olive oil. Season to taste with a little sea salt and some freshly ground black pepper.

Just before serving, drain the fennel and dry on paper towels. Put the salad leaves in a bowl, whisk the dressing once again, and drizzle over the leaves. Sprinkle with the grated Parmesan (or Desmond or Gabriel cheese) and toss gently. Carve the lamb on the diagonal into slices, approx. ½in thick.

To serve, arrange the salad on individual plates and layer with the fennel slices, beans, and warm lamb. Drizzle a spoonful of Tomato and Chile Jam on top. Scatter with some tiny olives and a few cubes of feta or other sheep's milk cheese (if using). Serve immediately.

Serves 6

8oz fine green beans, topped and tailed
3 teaspoons salt
1 large or 2 small fennel bulbs, tough outer layer removed
freshly squeezed juice of ½ lemon
2 boned, short racks of lamb, we use eye of the loin
  (total weight approx. 2lb)
extra virgin olive oil, for drizzling
6 handfuls of mixed salad leaves

For the dressing
freshly squeezed juice of ½ lemon, plus 1 teaspoon finely grated zest
sea salt and freshly ground black pepper
½ cup extra virgin olive oil

To serve
2 tablespoons freshly grated Parmesan or Desmond or Gabriel cheese
4 tablespoons Tomato and Chile Jam (see page 266)
18 tiny black Niçoise olives (optional)
¾ cup (4oz) feta or Knockalara Sheep's Cheese (optional)

Watercress, Blood Orange and Toons Bridge Mozzarella Salad

We are overjoyed to have Irish mozzarella at last, made from the milk of happy grass-fed buffalo. The rich West Cork pasture that the buffalo feed on gives the Toons Bridge mozzarella its quintessentially Irish taste. In this salad, a few beautiful, fresh ingredients put together simply make an irresistible starter. If watercress is not an option, arugula works well also.

Serves 4

a bunch of fresh watercress
2–3 balls of fresh mozzarella
2 blood oranges
2–3 tablespoons local honey
a good drizzle of extra virgin olive oil
coarsely ground black pepper
8–10 toasted almonds (optional)

Scatter a few watercress leaves over the base of each plate, and slice or tear some fresh mozzarella over the top. Using a sharp knife, remove the peel and pith from the blood oranges and cut them into slices, ¼in thick. Tuck the orange slices here and there in between the watercress and mozzarella. Drizzle with honey and really good extra virgin olive oil. Sprinkle with a little coarsely ground fresh black pepper and serve.

I love a few slivers of toasted almonds over the top as an extra treat.

Claudia Roden

" When Darina called me, almost thirty years ago, to ask me to do a course on Middle Eastern food at Ballymaloe Cookery School, I was intrigued. Ireland was hardly known for its cuisine or interest in food, and neither was Britain at that time. Although nouvelle cuisine had created excitement about the new French approach to cooking and presentation, going out to restaurants was still a rare activity, reserved for events like birthdays. Chefs had no status, and cooking schools catered for well-to-do girls waiting to be married. They, like hotel and catering schools for professionals, taught only French classic cuisine according to the rules set by Auguste Escoffier.

Middle Eastern cooking was thought of as strange, and the ingredients were hard to find. I wondered whether Irish people would be interested in what I had to offer. I made out a very long list of recipes I could demonstrate for Darina to choose a few from. When she came to see me in London, I was impressed by the intense, fast-talking, serious young woman—she looked at the list, asked me to describe the dishes, and said we could do a lot more. I was used to schools demonstrating at most six dishes a day but she said "Don't worry, I'll be there cooking with you" and that she would be getting all the ingredients—the filo and kadaif, the bulgur and couscous, the tamarind, pomegranate syrup and tahini, and the spices.

I was entirely charmed by Ballymaloe—the house, the Allen family, Myrtle, the landscape, the way the School operated, the way Darina and Rory taught. We cooked a dazzling number of dishes—tagines and pilafs, spicy mezzes, cool yogurt salads, desserts scented with rose and orange blossom water. During a break, Darina suddenly said, "Let's do another fish," and we went off to Ballycotton and bought a monkfish from a fisherman, which we skinned and cooked with a Moroccan chermoula sauce. The smells and tastes in the demonstration kitchen and the methods of cooking were entirely strange to the students, but Darina's enthusiasm was contagious and they were enchanted. I could see I was with a live wire with boundless energy and an extraordinary passion for food, who had a hunger for discovering everything that was good to eat and a desire to pass it on. The School was serious and very professional, but what made it unique was the special enthusiasm and affectionate warm spirit that radiated from Darina, Rory, Tim, and the extended Allen family. I stayed at Myrtle and Ivan's Ballymaloe House. The idyllic setting and Myrtle's cooking made it a memorable experience.

It has been a joy over the years to see the School and its organic farm expand into a formidable center of gastronomy that attracts people from all over Ireland and all over the world. It has trained chefs in classic French cuisine and given them a real knowledge of Italian, Indian, Thai, Middle Eastern, and North African, among other cuisines, and the chefs have gone on to cook all over the world. By honoring Irish products and cuisine, by supporting local farmers, fishermen, and artisans, by inspiring home cooks and restaurateurs, Myrtle, Darina, and now also Rachel have transformed Ireland from a food wasteland into a vibrant and exciting destination for food lovers. You can see their influence in the splendid English Market in Cork, at the farmers' markets and on restaurant menus all over Ireland. At one farmers' market I was thrilled to find people selling their home-cooked Middle Eastern foods. One said she used recipes I had demonstrated at Ballymaloe.

I brought my family over for my seventieth birthday lunch. They were enthralled by the ducks and geese, the pigs and cattle, and the fabulous greenhouse and market garden. The School, with its organic farm, holistic approach, and outreach activities, is a utopian food empire whose example and influence is felt well beyond Ireland. It is an international phenomenon. The spirit and the magic was still there at the Ballymaloe Literary Festival of Food and Wine in April 2013, which attracted gastronomic luminaries from all over the world. It was unique among festivals in the way it examined the problems of food in the world as it celebrated the pleasures of cooking and eating and the joy of bonding over food. **"**

Upper right: I had long admired Claudia Roden and pored over her book on Middle Eastern food, so was thrilled to be able to invite her as a guest chef. Her first course introduced us to Middle Eastern cooking—at that time even hummus and tabbouleh were unusual and exotic recipes. Many of the ingredients Claudia used would have been unfamiliar to the majority of students, although I was fortunately able to source most of what she needed from Mr Bell's stall at the English Market in Cork City.

Moroccan Lamb Pita Wrap with Hummus

We offer one, and sometimes several, barbecue or grilling courses every summer. The first was in 1991 when over eighty people turned up, predominantly men. Since then Irish people have really taken to grilling, and there's scarcely a household that doesn't have one, or in some cases several, types of barbecue. Everyone has become much more adventurous and are having fun with flavors from Mexico, Asia, India, the Middle East, the Mediterranean…

Serves 4

For the Hummus
¾ cup raw chickpeas, soaked in cold water overnight
freshly squeezed juice of 2–3 lemons, or to taste
2–3 garlic cloves, peeled and crushed
⅓ cup tahini
1 teaspoon ground cumin
salt

For the pita bread
1oz fresh yeast
1⅓ cups lukewarm water
3⅔ cups all-purpose flour, plus extra for dusting
1 teaspoon salt
sunflower oil, for greasing

1 lb 2oz boneless lamb (shoulder or leg), cut into
    1½in cubes

For the marinade
1½ teaspoons roasted and ground coriander seeds
½ teaspoon roasted and ground cumin seeds
¼ teaspoon ground allspice
¼ teaspoon ground cinnamon
2 tablespoons freshly squeezed lemon juice
4 tablespoons extra virgin olive oil
½ medium onion, finely chopped
2 garlic cloves, peeled and finely chopped

To serve
4 handfuls of shredded Boston or Romaine lettuce
4 ripe tomatoes, cut into wedges and seasoned
16 fresh mint leaves
sea salt and freshly ground black pepper

Start with the hummus. Drain the soaked chickpeas, cover with fresh water, and cook until tender, approx. 30–60 minutes, depending on the quality.

Meanwhile, make the pita bread. Crumble the yeast into ½ cup of the water and set aside for 10 minutes until the yeast has dissolved.

Sift the flour and salt into a large mixing bowl. Add the yeast along with the rest of the water, and mix well—the dough should not be too dry. Turn out onto a lightly floured work surface and knead until smooth and elastic, approx. 5–6 minutes. If the dough is a bit sticky, add a little extra flour while kneading.

Transfer the dough to a lightly oiled bowl and turn the dough so that the whole surface is oiled. Cover with plastic wrap, and set aside in a warm place to rise for 1–1½ hours or until the dough has at least doubled in volume.

Meanwhile, whisk all the ingredients for the marinade together in a large bowl to make a purée. Add the cubed lamb and toss well to coat evenly. Cover and set aside to marinate in the fridge for 1 hour.

Turn the dough out onto a floured work surface and knead again until smooth, approx. 2 minutes. Roll into a thick log and divide into 8–10 equal-sized pieces. Roll each piece into a smooth ball. Put on a floured surface, cover with a clean kitchen towel, and set aside to rise for approx. 30 minutes or until doubled in size again.

Preheat the oven to 450°F and heat two baking sheets.

Light the barbecue and finish the hummus. Drain the chickpeas, reserving the cooking liquid. Process the cooked chickpeas in a food processor with the freshly squeezed lemon juice and a little of the reserved cooking liquid if necessary. Add the garlic, tahini, cumin, and salt to taste. Blend to a soft, creamy paste. Taste and continue to add lemon juice and salt until you are happy with the flavor.

Roll out the dough balls into circles, approx. 6in in diameter and ¼in thick. Bake two at a time on a hot baking sheet for approx. 3 minutes or until just brown and puffed. If not using immediately, leave to cool on wire racks.

Thread the lamb onto wooden skewers, which have been soaked in water for 30 minutes, and grill over medium-hot embers, turning every couple of minutes until well browned but still juicy and slightly pink inside, approx. 7–8 minutes. Alternatively, cook on a hot grill pan—but make sure you open the windows, since it creates quite a bit of smoke! Split each pita into two pieces and put directly onto the grill to warm through.

To serve, fill the pita bread with the grilled lamb, top with the shredded lettuce and tomato wedges, and scatter with the mint leaves. Drizzle with the hummus, sprinkle with sea salt and freshly ground black pepper, and serve immediately while the lamb is still warm.

Claudia Roden's Flan de Naranja—Orange Flan

❧

Claudia Roden came back to teach at the Ballymaloe Litfest of Food and Wine in May 2013. She cooked for three hours and every recipe had a story—she had the audience transfixed. Claudia suggests that this refreshing, creamy, slightly sharp flan is just what you need to end a rich meal. You must use the freshly squeezed juice of oranges or clementines—it's best if you squeeze the fruit yourself.

Serves 8

2½ cups freshly squeezed orange or clementine juice
⅔ cup superfine sugar
2 large organic eggs plus 10 yolks

To serve
oranges, clementines, fresh mint leaves and orange blossom water

Preheat the oven to 300°F.

Heat the citrus juice with the sugar over low heat and stir to dissolve the sugar.

Beat the egg yolks and the whole eggs lightly with a fork in a large bowl, then gradually beat in the citrus juice. Ladle the mixture into 8 x 6oz ramekins. Put them in a shallow roasting pan and pour in enough boiling water to come halfway up the sides of ramekins (it is called a bain-marie). Bake in the preheated oven for 30 minutes or until the custard sets. It needs to be cooked at a low temperature to get a perfectly smooth texture without bubbles.

Take the ramekins out of the pan and allow to cool. Cover with plastic wrap and transfer to the fridge to chill. Serve chilled on its own, or with a little citrus salad of oranges, clementines, and perhaps a few fresh mint leaves and a couple of drops of orange blossom water.

Syrian Laymoun bi-na na Fresh Lemonade with Mint

❧

We had a memorable holiday in Syria in 2009. The food was wonderful and the people were friendly and welcoming. Freshly squeezed juices were widely available everywhere in Damascus and Aleppo, in restaurants and at street stalls (lots of orange and pomegranate of course), but we particularly enjoyed this refreshing lemon and mint drink. It's a brilliant way to use up an abundance of fresh mint.

Serves 6

juice of 6 lemons
1¼ cups simple syrup (see below)
1¼ cups chilled water
2 handfuls of fresh mint leaves

Squeeze the lemons and pour the juice into a blender. Add the syrup, chilled water, and fresh mint leaves, and blend until the mint is finely chopped and the drink is frothy. Pour into tall glasses and drink through a straw while still fresh—divine.

Simple Syrup

Makes 3½ cups

2¼ cups sugar
2½ cups water

Dissolve the sugar in the water and bring to a boil. Boil for 2 minutes, then allow to cool. Store in the fridge until needed.

The Herb Garden

Fresh herbs have excited cooks for not just hundreds but thousands of years, even as far back as the late 4th and early 5th centuries, when *Apicius*, a collection of Roman cooking and recipes, also known as *De re coquinaria* (On the Subject of Cooking) was compiled, containing numerous recipes for dishes flavored with herbs. Notwithstanding that, I would hazard a guess that never at any period during history has there been such a universal interest in herbs as in recent times, both for healing and culinary purposes. I don't know what we would do without herbs; our cooking at Ballymaloe is laced with them, and big bunches come from the garden and greenhouses every day.

When the Ballymaloe Cookery School opened in 1983, for most people, fresh herbs other than parsley, chives, thyme, and mint were exotic—it was five or six years before basil was widely available. In the early years of the School I ran several courses on how to use fresh herbs to add magic to your cooking; I introduced students to new flavors and demonstrated how familiar dishes could be made more exciting by adding a variety of fresh herbs. The first course, entitled Cooking with Herbs, was held in July 1991. The students loved the Onion and Thyme Leaf Soup, Roast Chicken with Summer Herbs, Cod with Cream and Bay Leaves, Lemon Sorbet with Borage Flowers, Lavender and Honey Ice Cream, and Summer Fruit Salad with Rose Geranium leaves. I chose about 15 fresh herbs, some reasonably common, e.g. mint, sage, and rosemary, and others, like angelica, lovage, and hyssop, less well known, and gave recipes to showcase each one, mostly in culinary terms, but also mentioning medicinal uses.

My abundant use of herbs led to the construction of our very own formal herb garden with boxwood-edged beds, inspired by a visit to the potager vegetable gardens at Villandry in the Loire

Left: Lavender and fennel growing in the herb garden in the early morning light. We crystallize lavender at the bud stage to decorate cakes and also use it to flavor honey and make lavender ice cream and syrups.
Right (above): A view of the formal herb garden and potting shed from the treehouse, which overlooks them. The beech hedge, one plant deep, is estimated to be about 180 years old and considered by many gardeners to be the most remarkable in Ireland.
Right (below): The herb garden in winter. Because of the formal structure of the garden with its boxwood hedges, it looks lovely even in the snow. In the center is the Myrtus ugni, which I planted as the axis of the garden as a homage to my mother-in-law, Myrtle Allen.

Valley. In 1986 we found a perfect site in the middle of the old gardens in Kinoith, enclosed by 20ft beech hedges and overlooked by the old potting shed. The initial plans were drawn, as every inspired design should be, on the back of an envelope! Over 70 different herbs are now to be found in this garden, including lemon balm, bronze fennel, purple sage, lovage, summer savory, sweet cicely, parsley, garlic, chives, angelica, and 6–8 types of mint and thyme, planted in sculpted beds. These are laid out parterre style in a formal pattern of beds, edged with boxwood and set in gravel paths. We like to grow from organic seeds whenever possible as we find that the plants are invariably hardier and healthier. Organic seeds come from plants that have been grown organically and have not been treated with chemicals during their life cycle and have therefore built up their own resistance to disease.

Each bed is planted with three or four herbs, to provide a contrast of texture, leaf shape, color, and height—for example, a bed may be edged with chives, then golden marjoram, with angelica or fennel planted in the center for height. We try to ensure that we choose herbs that flower at different times in the same bed to provide

Above: An early picture of me in the herb garden.

a variety of textures and continuity of color and perfume in the garden. Some herbs, for example green or bronze fennel, grow into a glorious feathery clump about 5ft high, while others, such as parsley, are scarcely 6in tall.

Bees, so vital for pollination, love borage, both white and blue, so it attracts them into the garden. We use the pretty flowers to decorate cakes and to scatter into salads. Bees also love comfrey, another important medicinal herb useful for drawing out infection; it's the main ingredient in comfrey cream and we use the leaves for fritters. One can also make "comfrey tea," a potent plant food and fertilizer. It is a valuable addition to the compost heap, and the pigs love it. Sweet cicely is a lesser-known perennial, with a feathery fernlike leaf, which we use in fruit compotes to reduce the sugar and frequently for garnishing sweet dishes. The young leaves of salad burnet are delicious in salads, and hyssop is particularly tasty when dried; few are aware that this is the same as the herb used to make the Middle Eastern herb mix za'atar, which has become so popular over recent years.

We grow both curly and flat-leaf parsley and chives. Chives are brilliant because they are perennial and are "cut and come again." Parsley plants will usually last for a year or more, so I like to have lots. More recently I've also introduced the flat-leaved garlic chive. Over the years we've expanded the thyme bed with five varieties: common, creeping, lemon, lavender, orange, and pizza. (Not a misprint, this last variety is low-growing with rich, deep purple flowers, pity about the name!)

There are about a dozen varieties of mint, including ginger, mojito, after eight (tastes just like the chocolates), lemon, banana, basil, orange, limette, strawberry, Kentucky Colonel, spearmint, and peppermint—spearmint or Bowles's mint are best for general use. We also grow French tarragon, not to be confused with Russian tarragon; the French have here, as in most things, the gastronomic edge as far as flavor is concerned. I started with one sage—the common green variety—to jazz up stuffings and combine with pasta, but we now grow purple sage, pineapple sage, and Russian sage. Lemon verbena is grown alongside lemon balm plants, both of which we add to herb butter or float in jugs of iced water at lunchtime—a lovely refreshing flavor instead of the hackneyed lemon wedge.

All these are perennial, but there are a few annuals that are essential basics in my kitchen, which I urge students to grow if space permits. My absolute favorite annual is marjoram or oregano; there are several varieties here, but the annual variety is by far the most fragrant. I also love to have golden marjoram to include in green salad; plant in the shade since direct sunlight can burn the edges of the leaves. A few dill and chervil plants are also a must. Dill is essential for gravlax and chervil just goes with everything and deserves to be better known. Basil plants need plenty of rich soil and sunshine to nourish them. When they start to flower, we pinch off the growing point so they will throw out more shoots and produce a lusher plant. Finally, we are all hooked on cilantro—it can be a bit of an acquired taste but quickly becomes quite addictive—and it is essential for all Asian, Middle Eastern, Mexican, and South American food. All parts of the plant are edible and each has a different flavor. We use the roots for Thai curry pastes; the stalks can be added to salads, stews, and tagines; and of course the leaves are an invaluable addition to so many dishes—in fact cilantro is by far the most widely used herb in the world, much more so than parsley. We use the delicate white flowers in salads and appetizers and then the seeds are dried to provide the coriander spice, which we use on its own or in conjunction with cumin and other spices in a myriad of delicious ways.

We tend to use fresh herbs all year round, but a couple of herbs are worth drying, e.g. annual marjoram or oregano and perhaps thyme. In 2012 we bought a dehydrator, which lives in the pantry of the School and is brilliant for drying herbs, mushrooms, and chiles.

Two other wonderfully robust and gutsy herbs, which are hardier than any of those I have mentioned so far, are rosemary and bay. Both need space but are tremendously useful herbs for stews, pasta sauces, and roast vegetables. Bay grows easily, but for a real treasure try to plant a standard bay outside your kitchen door in a pot or as the axis of your new herb garden. We have six standard bays in the herb garden, which add height to the plantings, and because they are evergreen, as are the boxwood hedges, the herb garden looks brilliant both in winter and summer.

Most culinary herbs are perennial, so once you plant them they will re-emerge each year in early spring in nice fat clumps ready for picking. Each herb has several uses; the leaves can of course be chopped and used to flavor a huge variety of dishes in various combinations, but the flowers are also edible. Some are inconspicuous and not worth bothering with, but others, e.g. sage, make glorious garnishes and are quite delicious, and some are particularly good eaten raw in salads, for example chives, cilantro, chervil, mint, and tiny sprigs of tarragon and lovage. One can also collect and dry the seeds to use as a spice; fennel, dill, and coriander seeds are especially worthwhile. Fennel pollen, particularly magical,

Above: We have constant requests for internships at the School and organic farm gardens because of the range of experiences they have to offer. Here one of our interns, Sonya McGee, is holding a recycled can containing clary.

Left: Every morning the students go out with the gardeners on a rota basis to pick herbs for the morning's cooking. At the beginning of the course, the 12-week students are baffled by the range of herbs in the garden and greenhouses, but by the time they are six weeks in, when they have a herb recognition and technique exam, they can name them all as well as suggesting two ways to use each herb. In this photo you can see a flurry of excitement in the garden as they brush up on their knowledge before the exam.
Right: Alexis Cornu, a French intern, picking in the basil bed, where we grow 5–6 different varieties.

is one of the must-have cheffy ingredients right now. In August we show the students how to shake the pollen onto parchment paper and how to collect it. When the poppy and nigella seed heads dry in early autumn, the students collect them and learn how to shake out the seeds. They then use them to flavor cakes and sprinkle on breads.

Fresh herbs are so easy to grow, I feel everyone should have a herb garden—if not an actual garden, at least a few pots or tubs, or even a window box, brimming with parsley, thyme, and chives. It's not just the fact that a little sprinkling of fresh herbs can add magic to your cooking, there's also the buzz you get when you make a little foray into the garden to snip a few sprigs of rosemary, lemon balm, sweet cicely, or whatever it is you need. It is an easy and inexpensive way to garnish and add flavor to your food, and ring the changes with basic ingredients like potatoes and beans, which are greatly enhanced by a sprig of savory in the cooking water. It is this that I try to teach the students, especially those on the 12-week course who are able to watch the herbs grow and appreciate what is available seasonally. The reality is that, after spending a few days, not to mention 12 weeks, at Ballymaloe, they can scarcely imagine cooking without fresh herbs. During the May 12-week course, the students have the option to have a raised bed area or a patch of ground to plant herbs or vegetables, to create an edible

garden while they are with us. It doesn't appeal to everyone, but for those who are interested it is sheer magic and can trigger a lifetime passion for growing one's own food. Students go out on a rota basis with the gardeners every morning to pick herbs for the cooking, and it is a great resource for them, a cook's paradise. Residential students can help themselves to herbs for their cooking, enjoy the herb garden in the evening or at weekends, and just sit and listen to the birds in the surrounding trees.

When we were designing the herb garden in 1986, I had a thought. I decided to plant a myrtle tree in the center bed as a tribute to Myrtle Allen, who has been an inspiration and constant support throughout the years. I ordered a *Myrtus luma* and planted it within a boxwood circle, then got on with planting the other beds with a mixture of contrasting herbs. As the year passed it grew, but rather oddly; eventually in June it was covered with pale pink flowers, as opposed to the pretty white flowers of *Myrtus luma*. My good friend and renowned gardener, Jim Reynolds, inspected it and pronounced it to be a different cultivar, *Myrtus ugni*. He predicted that it would be covered with wine-colored myrtle berries in autumn, and so it was. I was thrilled; I had inadvertently planted a variety that produced delicious berries, what a quirk of fate. We look forward to nibbling them in the autumn, and scatter them into salads; they are also delicious with game.

Shrimp Salad with Rice Noodles and Prawn Crackers

The whole world of noodles was quite a revelation to me—nothing beats slithery fresh rice noodles in Thai or Vietnamese dishes, but noodles of all types are a must-have for my pantry. There are a million delicious noodle salads you can make, but they are also great added to soup or as an extra something in spring rolls.

Although we have become more familiar with cilantro over the past 30 years, some people are determined it is a herb that they don't like. I try hard to convince them to change their minds, since it is a key ingredient in so many Asian, South American, and Middle Eastern dishes.

Note: We use Ballycotton shrimp, which vary in size but are roughly one-third of the size of an Asian shrimp. If using extra-large shrimp, these may need to be cut into 2–3 pieces, depending on size. We don't use Asian shrimp unless we can source sustainable organic ones.

First, deep-fry the prawn crackers. Heat some oil in a deep-fat fryer or frying pan, and fry the prawn crackers, two or three at a time, for approx. 30 seconds until puffed up and golden. Drain the crackers on paper towels.

Put the noodles into a bowl. Cover with boiling water and set aside for 4–5 minutes until just tender but still a little al dente.

Meanwhile, make the dressing. Combine all the ingredients in a bowl and stir until the sugar has dissolved.

Pour the softened noodles into a colander, rinse briefly under cold running water, and drain well. Transfer the noodles to a serving bowl and toss lightly in the dressing while still warm.

Cut the cucumber in half lengthwise, scoop out the seeds with a melon baller or a sharp spoon, and discard (or feed to your hens). Cut the cucumber into ¼in slices at a long angle. Add the cucumber to the noodles along with the shrimp, scallions, cilantro, and mint leaves. Toss well, taste, and correct the seasoning if necessary. Scatter with the peanuts or cashew nuts, and serve with lime wedges and lots of fresh cilantro. Accompany with the prawn crackers.

Serves 8

For the Prawn Crackers
approx. 24 prawn crackers, uncooked (available from specialty Asian markets)
sunflower oil, for deep-frying

8oz thin flat rice noodles

For the dressing
½ cup soy sauce
¼ cup rice or cider vinegar
¼ cup extra virgin olive oil
1 red chile, thinly sliced
1 teaspoon freshly grated ginger
2 tablespoons brown sugar or palm sugar

1 small organic cucumber
48 shrimp or 32 extra-large shrimp (see note), cooked and peeled
8 scallions, finely sliced at a long angle into ¾in lengths
2 tablespoons fresh cilantro leaves
2 tablespoons fresh mint leaves
sea salt and freshly ground black pepper
¾ cup chopped peanuts or cashew nuts, roasted

To serve
lime wedges
fresh cilantro leaves

Pickled Carrots with Star Anise

Scott Walsh, a talented chef from Ballymaloe House, came up with this recipe. We serve it as part of the selection of salads on the Sunday night Ballymaloe buffet, but you can imagine how delicious it is in other salad combinations.

Serves 10–15, depending on how it is served

10 carrots (approx. 2¼lb), peeled and sliced thinly lengthwise
on a mandoline
2½ cups unsweetened carrot juice
½ cup superfine sugar
¾ cup white wine
¾ cup white wine vinegar
¾ cup water
1 cup extra virgin olive oil
bunch each of tarragon and thyme
8 star anise
2 tablespoons coriander seeds
10 black peppercorns

Put all the ingredients into a wide, stainless steel sauté pan. Bring to a boil, and then simmer gently for 10 minutes until the carrots are soft. Set aside to cool before serving. Serve with some of the spiced liquid.

I can't imagine cooking without fresh herbs and spices. It doesn't matter where you are, all you need to grow your own herbs are a few containers, water, and light. You won't believe it until you grow your own, but the flavor is vastly superior to anything you can buy.

Spatchcocked Chicken with Rosemary and Chile Oil

Spatchcocking enables the bird to cook much faster; there will be lots of crispy skin, and it will be really easy to carve. All poultry can be cooked in this way—you can vary the seasoning and spices if you have to give Mexican, Moroccan, or Asian flavors.

First spatchcock the chicken. Remove the wishbone from the neck end (keep it for the stockpot). Insert a heavy knife into the cavity of the chicken from the back end to the neck. Press down sharply to cut through the backbone. Alternatively, put the chicken breast-side down on a cutting board and use poultry shears to cut along the entire length of the backbone as close to the center as possible. Open out the bird.

Preheat the oven to 350°F or light the barbecue. To make the marinade, combine the rosemary, garlic, pepper, red pepper flakes, lemon juice, and extra virgin olive oil in a bowl. Just before cooking, brush the chicken—both inside and out—with the marinade. Sprinkle with sea salt.

If cooking in the oven, lay the chicken skin-side up on a rack inside a roasting pan and roast in the hot oven for 40 minutes. Alternatively barbecue for approx. 40 minutes, 8–9in from the coals, turning halfway through. Make sure the chicken is fully cooked through before serving.

Accompany with a good green salad and wedges of avocado.

Serves 6 or more

1 x 4–5lb organic chicken
1 teaspoon sea salt

For the marinade
1 tablespoon freshly chopped rosemary
4 garlic cloves, peeled and finely chopped
1 teaspoon freshly ground black pepper
½ teaspoon red pepper flakes
1 tablespoon freshly squeezed lemon juice
4 tablespoons extra virgin olive oil

To serve
fresh green salad
2–3 avocados, cut into wedges

Variation

Spatchcocked Quail with Rosemary and Chile Oil
Spatchcock the quail as above and brush with the marinade. Cook under a moderately hot broiler or on the barbecue for approx. 8 minutes on the bone side and then approx. 5 minutes on the skin side. Quail vary a lot in size; the birds we get tend to be quite small, approx. 5oz in weight.

Fresh Herb Tisanes

❧≈❧

We've just planted a tisane garden outside the Garden Café with our favorite fresh herbs. Herb teas and tisanes are best made with freshly snipped herbs, so plant them close to your kitchen door.

All you need to do is pop a few leaves into a teapot and pour in boiling water—the result is infinitely more delicious than using dried herb tea bags.

I'm very wary about ordering herb tea in a restaurant, but a Paris restaurant I dined in recently served herb infusions in the most delightful way. The waiter came to the table with several china bowls of fresh herbs on a silver salver. With tiny silver tongs, he put the guest's chosen herb into a little china teapot, poured in boiling water, and served it with a flourish. Exquisite.

We use fresh leaves from the garden to make herb teas and infusions, both in the Cookery School and at Ballymaloe House. The leaves can also be put directly into a cup if you just want to make one infusion. Students and friends are sometimes surprised at first when they are served a virtually colorless liquid that is so clear and fresh tasting. They are often amazed at how easy it is to make.

Use lemon verbena, rosemary, sweet geranium, lemon balm, spearmint, peppermint… the choice is endless.

Bring fresh cold water to a boil. Warm a china teapot with boiling water then empty it, take a handful of fresh herb leaves, and crush them gently. The quantity will depend on the strength of the herb and how intense an infusion you enjoy. Put them into the warmed teapot. Pour boiling water over the leaves, cover the teapot, and set aside to infuse for 3–4 minutes. Serve immediately in china teacups rather than mugs.

Ginger Tea

Put 3–4 slices of fresh ginger (each approx. ¼in thick) into a cup. Cover with boiling water and infuse for 3–4 minutes. Sip after dinner for a calming effect and to aid digestion.

Lemon Posset with Rose Geranium

❧≈❧

This lemon posset recipe has done the rounds—it is always lip-smackingly good, but it was Skye Gyngell who introduced us to this version scented with sweet geranium leaves (*Pelargonium graveolens*). She in turn attributed it to Jeremy Lee, so on it goes… Anyway, it is sublime, so thank you all.

Serves 4

1⅔ cups heavy cream
½ cup superfine sugar
5 rose- or sweet-scented geranium leaves
¼ cup lemon juice

To garnish
tiny rose- or sweet-scented geranium leaves

Place the cream, sugar, and geranium leaves in a heavy saucepan and bring to a simmer. Reduce the heat to low and cook, stirring often, for 5 minutes. Remove the pan from the heat, squeeze in the lemon juice, strain, and allow to cool, discarding the leaves. Pour the posset into small, tall glasses, cover with plastic wrap, and chill overnight.

Serve garnished with a tiny scented geranium leaf.

Game

Dealing with game can certainly seem intimidating when you are faced with a brace of pheasant in the feather for the first time—where to start? We've been offering game courses here at the School consistently for the past 30 years, and it's been so much fun demystifying the subject. The first game course was started in 1987 by George Gossip from Ballinderry Park in County Galway. George is a family friend and the best game cook I know and, 30 years later, he still teaches the occasional class. George has been shooting since he was a child and has a great love and respect for, as well understanding of, the countryside and the harmonious balance of nature. He is a brilliantly entertaining teacher with lots of stories—told in a booming baritone and interspersed with colorful language—everyone loves his lessons. Over the years he has built up a wonderful repertoire of game recipes; we especially love the Game Pie, Game Terrine, Roast Loin of Venison, Roast Wild Mallard with Jerusalem Artichokes, and the Carpaccio of Rabbit.

When George introduced the first game course at the School, people thought it was normal to be taught how to pluck, skin, and gut poultry or game. However, by the mid-to-late 1990s, attitudes had changed. Students on the 12-week course would turn their noses up in disgust and ask me in incredulous tones: "You can't seriously expect me to clean out this chicken?" People obviously expected to be presented with an oven-ready bird and were not interested in learning how to gut a chicken or skin and prepare game.

However, in recent years there's been a huge revival of interest in game and, surprise, surprise, it's become trendy again. I think it must partly be the Hugh Fearnley-Whittingstall effect. Hugh has done a series of television programs from River Cottage, in Dorset, England, extolling the virtues of self-sufficiency and showing people how to use and cook game. These have proved extremely popular and have encouraged many people to take an interest and even give it a try for themselves.

In my opinion, game is fantastic to cook with. It's all natural, for a start, and free-range and organic. None of it is endangered; in fact you're often doing farmers a huge favor by saving their precious

Left: A brace of pheasant hanging by the neck in the feather. It is best to hang them in a cool place, ideally individually, especially in humid weather. Most people, even if they aren't very keen on game, will have tasted pheasant. I like a rich, gamey flavor, which is achieved by hanging the birds for longer.

Above: George Gossip with two of his faithful gun dogs, Badger and Treacle, hunting at Birr, County Offaly. He has taught game courses at the School since its beginning, covering all aspects of game and introducing us to his favorite recipes.

crops from rabbits and deer. Furthermore, it's cheap and nutritious and a much healthier alternative to red meat. Wild game tends to be very lean due to the animal's active lifestyle and natural diet. Their meat is lower in saturated fat than red meat and contains a higher proportion of polyunsaturated fatty acids, so they are naturally low in fat, but with just as much texture and flavor as red meat—a very attractive prospect for many people.

It's gratifying to see how the times are changing. These days, our 12-week students almost always want to learn about game, and not just how to cook a mallard or a pheasant, but how to pluck, eviscerate, and remove the sinews. This isn't just a job for the boys—the girls, too, want to learn how to skin a rabbit or truss a woodcook or snipe with its beak in the traditional way.

At Ballymaloe, we're fortunate to have a local game enthusiast, Tom Duane, who supplies us with a wide selection of game. From late autumn through Christmas, he brings us birds, rabbits, and pigeons, and an occasional hare, which I love because they make a fantastic stew or jugged hare and also the best sauce for pasta. In the summer, out of game season, Tom brings in his beautiful collection of stuffed birds to show the 12-week students, plus a few frozen birds so he can demonstrate how to pluck and prepare them.

Tom shares his in-depth knowledge with the students. There are about ten varieties of pheasants in Ireland and he points out the subtle differences between each one. He shows how you can

distinguish the age of a pheasant by the length of its spur and also how to tell the difference between wild birds and those from a driven shoot.

Students learn the different types of wild duck: mallard, teal, widgeon, shoveler, and the rarer pintail. They hear that grouse, now so rare in Ireland, was the only indigenous game bird and that the large red deer is native to Ireland, unlike the sika and fallow deer. Fallow deer were introduced into game parks in Ireland around 1169. However, sika deer were not introduced into the Powerscourt Estate in County Wicklow until 1860. Tom also teaches students about the game season and about hanging times and techniques—such as the fact that game birds are best hung in the feather by the head and furred game by the back legs.

Learning about game connects the students with the countryside in a very direct way. Some who live in cities or big towns don't necessarily feel a connection to the place where they live, or to their neighbors or local community, nor to the earth, trees and birds. They are living their own lives in their own space, independently of everyone and everything around them. Spending time at Ballymaloe therefore often opens them up to the countryside around them and our essential interdependence with our environment.

Deh-Ta Hsiung

Deh-Ta Hsiung, author of (among other books) *Chinese Regional Cooking* and *The Chinese Kitchen*, was the first guest chef to come to the School in 1984 and returned again a couple of years later. Several friends, including local potter Stephen Pearce and Declan Ryan, chef/owner at that time of Arbutus Lodge Restaurant in Cork and now a renowned artisanal baker and owner of Arbutus Breads, had a wish list of guest chefs and topics, and Chinese food was high on the list. Ken Hom had a television series at the time, and they wanted to learn the secrets of some simple dishes such as fish with bean sauce, Jiaozi (Beijing dumplings), chow mein, wontons, and special fried rice. I did some research, and friends from London heartily recommended Deh-Ta Hsiung, who had just written the first book on Chinese cooking for Marks & Spencer.

Deh-Ta is pint-sized with a wonderful chuckle. A few weeks before the course, I arranged to meet him in London so that together we could buy the right cooking utensils and ingredients. Our shopping expedition was a wonderful experience: Deh-Ta took me into huge, strange-smelling Chinese supermarkets in Soho where we bought woks, steamers, chopsticks, ladles, and huge spiders (perforated wire spoons) and lots of then-unfamiliar ingredients, such as wood ear and shiitake mushrooms, Chinese brown rice vinegar, Shaoxing rice wine, sesame oil, black bean paste, and different types of soy sauce.

When we were finished, Deh-Ta took me to one of his favorite Chinese restaurants and ordered all kinds of weird and wonderful dumplings, steamed buns, tofu, and crispy duck and showed me how to assemble a Peking duck pancake. I ordered chicken's feet, and the waiter was so impressed that I was given my lunch for free—he said I was the first Westerner ever to order chicken's feet! I love them—they are soft and gelatinous with lots of little bones to be elegantly disposed of.

Deh-Ta and his lovely wife Paula came to Ballymaloe on several occasions and fell totally in love with Irish produce. Deh-Ta was so impressed by the superb gray sea mullet from Ballycotton that he almost moved to Ireland! In return, he took the mystery out of Chinese food for us and delighted the class participants.

Deh-Ta is a mere five foot two, so we provided him with a platform to stand on so he could be seen behind the counter. His courses were always great fun because not only is he a brilliant teacher but also a scholar. He explained that what distinguishes Chinese food from other cultures lies not only in the preparation and cooking,

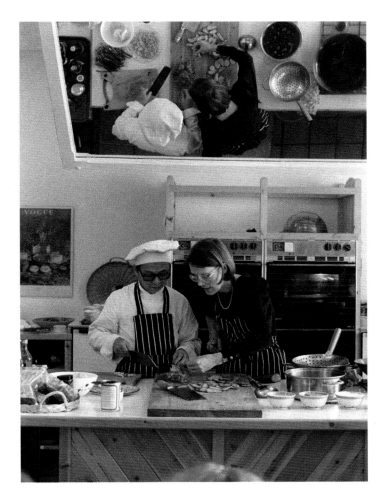

but also the way the food is eaten. A Chinese meal doesn't follow the conventional Western sequence of soup, fish, meat, cheese, and dessert. An everyday Chinese meal, served at home or in a restaurant, is like a buffet, with all the dishes (including soup) arranged together in the center of the table. Each person is given a bowl of rice and everyone must help themselves to whatever else they like, though not from every dish on the table, but from one or two at a time. Only on formal occasions are the dishes served course by course, and even then, they will appear in groups rather than singly, with soup the only course to be served in an individual dish.

Left: Tom Duane and Frank Mansell with their springer spaniels, in pursuit of pheasant for dinner.
Above: Deh-Ta Hsiung teaching a class at the School. He was a real gentleman and introduced us to authentic Chinese cooking as well as Chinese history, culture, and traditions.

Rabbit and Prune Terrine with Celeriac Remoulade

The students love rabbit. They get even more excited when we get a wild rabbit so they can skin, gut and prepare it themselves. This terrine, like many coarse-textured pâtés, improves after a day or two.

Preheat the oven to 350°F. Line a 5 x 8in terrine or loaf pan with most of the bacon, setting aside a quarter of it for the terrine.

Chop the reserved bacon into cubes and put it with the chopped livers in a large bowl, add the brandy and port, and season with lots of black pepper. Set aside to marinate while you prepare the other ingredients.

Heat the oil in a sauté pan, add the chopped onion and garlic, and sweat until soft but not colored. Set aside to cool.

Add the rabbit and pork to the marinated liver, and stir in the fresh herbs. Add the beaten egg and pistachio nuts, and season with salt and freshly ground pepper. Mix really well. Finally stir in the cooled onion mixture. Cook a small amount to taste and correct the seasoning if necessary.

Put half the mixture into the lined terrine, arrange a line of prunes down the center, and cover with the remaining mixture. Fold over the ends of the bacon, lay a bay leaf and a sprig of thyme on top, and cover with aluminum foil or a fitted lid. Seal the lid, if using, with luting paste—white flour and water mixed to a loose paste like play dough—if necessary.

Transfer the terrine to a roasting pan and pour in enough boiling water to come halfway up the sides. Bake in the preheated oven for 1¾–2 hours or until a skewer inserted into the mixture for 30 seconds feels hot to the touch when taken out. If you are still in doubt, remove the lid and check: the pâté should have shrunk away from the sides of the pan and the juices should run clear.

Transfer the terrine to a large plate, remove the lid, and weigh down the pâté with a scrubbed piece of wood or similar weight to form a compress. (Alternatively weigh down with the upturned lid and some weights.) Set aside to cool, and then transfer to the fridge to mature overnight.

To make the Celeriac Remoulade, trim the celeriac with a knife, peel off the skin, and coarsely grate the flesh into a bowl. Stir the Dijon mustard into the mayonnaise and add some to the celeriac (keep back a little in case not all is needed). The remoulade should be saucy but not too sloppy. Add freshly squeezed lemon juice to taste and a little more seasoning if necessary.

To serve, turn the terrine out onto a board and cut into slices, ½in thick. Accompany with a little celeriac remoulade, a salad of organic leaves and herbs, and some crusty bread.

Serves 10

For the terrine
1lb smoked bacon
5oz rabbit and chicken livers, trimmed and chopped into small pieces
2 tablespoons brandy
2 tablespoons port
sea salt and freshly ground black pepper
2–3 tablespoons extra virgin olive oil
1 cup finely chopped onion
2 garlic cloves, peeled and finely chopped
12oz rabbit meat, coarsely ground
14oz pork belly, chopped into small pieces
2 teaspoons freshly chopped thyme leaves
2 teaspoons freshly chopped marjoram
2 teaspoons freshly chopped oregano
1 organic egg, beaten
⅔ cup pistachio nuts
8 prunes, pits removed
1 bay leaf, to decorate
a sprig of thyme, to decorate

For the Celeriac Remoulade
1½lb celeriac
1 tablespoon Dijon mustard
1½ cups homemade mayonnaise (see page 72)
freshly squeezed lemon juice
sea salt and freshly ground black pepper

To serve
a salad of organic leaves and fresh herbs
crusty bread

Pheasant or Partridge with Savoy Cabbage, Cream and Bacon

Partridge are pretty scarce in Ireland, but a fine plump pheasant also works well here. George Gossip loves Madeira and quite rightly thinks it should make a more regular appearance in our kitchens!

Serves 2

1 whole pheasant or 2 whole partridges
sea salt and freshly ground black pepper
1–2 pats of salted butter (optional)
4oz smoked bacon or pancetta, cut in cubes
½ Savoy cabbage, finely shredded
½ cup heavy cream
a good splash of red wine or Madeira

Preheat the oven to 450°F. Season and truss the pheasant and roast in the preheated oven for 35 minutes according to taste. Alternatively roast two partridges, stuffed with a small pat of butter, for 15–20 minutes.

Meanwhile, cook the bacon or pancetta in a heavy saucepan until crisp, throw in the cabbage, and stir-fry for 1 minute. Add a glass of water, cover with a lid, and turn down the heat. Cook for 5–6 minutes until the cabbage has softened.

Once the cabbage has softened, remove the lid and boil away the remaining water in the pan. Add the cream and boil rapidly until it forms a thick sauce. Season with a little salt (you may not need much if the bacon is salty) and plenty of black pepper.

Remove the bird(s) from the oven and transfer them to a warm plate to rest while you deglaze the pan. Put the roasting pat over high heat, pour in the wine or Madeira, and bubble away to form a rich sauce. Season to taste with salt and pepper.

To serve, cut the birds in half and arrange on a bed of cabbage. Pour on the juices from the pan.

George Gossip's Venison Sausages with Colcannon

George likes a very coarse, meaty sausage with no extraneous ingredients: "We do not use oatmeal or rusk, and the addition of diced bananas or cranberries is definitely not for us. That said, we do like plenty of good Dijon mustard, and venison sausages are the perfect foil for spicy or fruity sauces and chutneys." They are a really delicious way to use shoulder or scraps of flank. Venison sausages make good sausage rolls and they are also great served cold for picnics.

Note: These sausages do not contain a preservative and should be eaten within 4–5 days unless you can vacuum-seal them, which will allow you to keep them a little longer. They freeze very well and are an ideal lunch or supper dish.

**Makes approx. 8 large sausages per 1lb meat,
128 sausages in total**

approx. 6ft natural sausage casings
12lb chopped venison (we used shoulder)
2lb pork fat (from a free-range heritage breed)
2lb lean pork meat (from a free-range heritage breed)
⅓ cup salt
1 teaspoon ground black pepper
1 teaspoon ground nutmeg
1 heaping teaspoon ground ginger
1 heaping teaspoon ground cloves
olive oil, for frying

For the Colcannon (Serves 6–8)
3lb potatoes, e.g. russets
sea salt and freshly ground black pepper
1lb kale, or Savoy or spring cabbage
approx. 4 tablespoons salted butter
approx. 1 cup milk
¼ cup finely sliced scallions (optional)

Soak the sausage casings in cold water overnight.

Next day, chop the meats, mix together, and grind in a meat grinder. Add the seasonings gradually and cook a small amount of the mixture to check that the flavoring is to your liking. Take great care not to over-salt. Keep everything very cool.

When you are happy with the taste, add sufficient water to make the mixture malleable. Fill the casings, twist and link the sausages, and hang them up in hanks to dry in a cold place overnight.

To cook the sausages, heat a little olive oil in a frying pan over medium heat. Cook the sausages for 3–4 minutes on each side, depending on the size. They should be golden in color and cooked through to the center.

To make the Colcannon, scrub the potatoes but leave them whole. Put them in a saucepan of cold water, add a good pinch of salt, and bring to a boil. Cook for approx. 15 minutes, and then strain off two-thirds of the water. Replace the lid and "steam" over low heat until fully cooked.

Meanwhile, remove the dark outer leaves from the kale or cabbage. Wash the rest and cut into quarters, remove the core, and cut finely across the grain. If using kale, remove the central rib. Cook the kale or cabbage in a little boiling salted water until tender. Drain, season with salt and freshly ground pepper, and mix in a small pat of the butter.

Once the potatoes are just cooked, pour them into a colander and set aside until they are cool enough to handle. Meanwhile, put the milk and scallions (if using) into a clean saucepan and bring to a boil. Pull the skins off the potatoes and discard. Mash the flesh quickly while it is still warm and beat in enough boiling milk to make a fluffy purée. Finally, stir in the cooked cabbage and taste for seasoning. For perfection, serve immediately in a hot dish with a pat of butter melting in the center, and the sausages on the side.

Colcannon may be prepared ahead and reheated later in a moderate oven at 350°F for 20–25 minutes. Cover while reheating so it doesn't get too crusty on top.

Irish Food

In 1986 I heard about and became a member of the International Association of Culinary Professionals (IACP), a hugely influential international organization for cooking school teachers and food writers. Many of the most prominent food people from all over the world were members, including Julia Child, Stephanie Alexander, Alice Waters, Ann Yonkers, Marion Cunningham, Nathalie Dupree, Francois Dionot, and Nancy Kirby Harris. It was a brilliant networking tool, and through it I met and exchanged ideas with people from the global culinary scene. The Annual Conference in the US was unmissable, and earlier presidents like Lauraine Jacobs from New Zealand, who was then editor of *Cuisine* magazine, Anne Willan, of Ecole de Cuisine La Varenne in France, and Paula Lambert ensured that the international viewpoint was well represented. It was at IACP that I had my first workshop on how to cook for the camera, several years after I started making television programs!

The Annual Conference is held in a different US city every year and I have been invited as a speaker on many occasions. A series of smaller regional conferences was later initiated, and this is a brilliant way to discover the culinary landscape of the host country. In October 1993 we attended a Regional Conference in Mexico organized by Marilyn Tausend, where I met Diana Kennedy, Rick Bayless, Mark Miller, and Maria Dolores Torres Yzabal, all recognized authorities on Mexican food. The event was based in Oaxaca, and this began my lifelong love affair with Mexico and its food. In winter 2012, I visited Diana Kennedy on her farm in Michoacán and had a memorable couple of days with this extraordinary woman who has dedicated a great part of her lifetime to collecting and recording recipes from around Mexico. Diana was born in the UK but has lived in her adopted home since she moved there in 1957.

Other memorable regional meetings were in Norway with Ingrid Espelid Hovig (the Julia Child of Norway) and in Sicily with Anna Tasca Lanza of Regaleali. I ate spleen sandwiches and soft rolls with Parmesan in Palermo, watched hand-rolled couscous being made in Erice, and enjoyed some of the most delicious food I've ever eaten. I still make the Semifreddo di Mandorle from the recipes I was given in Erice. I also remember eating a Timballo with macaroni, as described in *The Leopard* by Giuseppe Tomasi di Lampedusa.

In June 1985 we offered the first Cook's Holiday in Ireland, intended to promote Irish produce and change people's perceptions of the country's cuisine. This was a vacation program for people like myself who love to combine travel with an opportunity to learn about the food and produce of another land. The week-long schedule included cooking classes at the School, visits to markets, bakeries, farmhouse cheesemakers, a fish smoker, a visit to Cork's English Market, dinner in private houses, and a talk on Irish food history. We met the fishing boats coming into Ballycotton, foraged for shellfish on Shanagarry beach, and listened to traditional Irish music in the pub. I realized that we could offer a truly wonderful Irish experience and help to change people's image of Ireland. We ran these courses every summer from 1985–1989.

In 1988 we hosted an IACP regional conference at Ballymaloe. Delegates came to Shanagarry from Italy, France, Holland, the US, and UK for four days. I was anxious to change the image of Ireland as the land of corned beef and cabbage. The delegates loved Myrtle's cooking at Ballymaloe House and the cooking class at the Cookery School. They were delighted by the emerging food movement and particularly loved the Irish farmhouse cheeses that had begun to earn international recognition for their quality.

On the Friday of the visit they walked with me through the English Market in Cork, where they were mightily impressed by the selection of fruit, vegetables, meat, poultry, game, and fish. They were also intrigued by the local specialties of tripe and drisheen. Among the visitors was the late Jan Weimer from the influential Los Angeles-based *Bon Appetit* magazine, who commented to a local journalist: "I must admit that I didn't really think of Ireland as an international gourmet center, but what we have seen at Ballymaloe has changed many of our opinions. We are very impressed with the way the Allen family have been able to use the natural resources."

From the beginning of the first 12-week course in 1983, we have always taken the students on a tour to help them to appreciate the wealth of produce in Ireland. The object of the exercise is not just a jolly "skite," although we always have a fun day, but for them to see for themselves the variety of enterprises; the different ways of adding value to a product like milk, e.g. farmhouse cheesemaking, and to understand the effort and skill that goes into producing these delicious ingredients. The "Shanagarry Express" pulls out of the Ballymaloe Cookery School parking lot at 7 a.m., complete with bleary-eyed students and a picnic including coffee machines, plus baskets of homemade jam and pickles as presents for the artisans and farmhouse cheesemakers we will visit during the day.

We choose the mix of venues very carefully in order to introduce the students to as many diverse food operations as possible. We always visit a farmers' market, usually at Mahon Point on a Thursday morning—a superb mix of local farmers, fishermen,

Above: Foraging on the seashore with Myrtle Allen. Ireland has 1,448 miles of coastline, so we have a wealth of wild produce on offer with rich pickings of seaweed and shellfish, including mussels, sea urchins, limpets, razor clams, and cockles. When foraging for these wild foods, you need to ensure that the water is clean and unpolluted and also that you harvest sustainably: for example, seaweed should be snipped and the holdfast left attached to the rock.

and food producers (several of whom are former students making their living from the food skills and techniques they learned at the Cookery School). The produce on offer ranges from desserts and confectionery to jams and pickles, sauces, salads, cake pops, sushi, homemade lemonades and cordials, plus gluten-free baked goods. We often include an artisanal smoker on the trip; perhaps Bill Casey who smokes fish on our farm, or Frank Hederman from Belvelly near Cobh, who does both cold- and hot-smoked fish, as well as more unusual produce such as smoked garlic, oatmeal, and butter. A visit to a farmhouse cheesemaker is a highlight of the day. We have visited Milleens, Gubbeen, Ardrahan, Durrus, Cashel Blue, Coolea, Bay Lough, St. Tola, Desmond and Gabriel, Fermoy, Carrigaline, Inagh, Hegarty's, Ardsallagh (goat cheese), Toons Bridge (buffalo cheese), and Knockalara (sheep cheese)—a who's who of the Irish cheesemaking world. This gives the students the opportunity not only to meet the cheesemakers and experience their passion but also to visit the farms and see the process, in some cases from beginning to end. They see the rich pastures that the cows, goats, sheep, or buffalo feed on to produce the top-quality milk needed to produce superb cheese, and they begin to understand and appreciate the phenomenal amount of work and tender loving care that goes into making these handmade cheeses. With this understanding, they rarely complain about the price ever again. Instead they are hugely impressed by the dedication and skill of the artisans and the passion they have for their produce.

We may have our picnic there on the farm, sharing it with our hosts and enjoying their cheese with the students' homemade bread. A visit to a café, tea shop, and restaurant or country house hotel is also part of the experience. If there's time we visit a craft brewer, the whiskey distillery in Midleton, or a pub that does good food. We might visit a garden, an old orchard, or an apple farm to see how apple juice and cider are made and explore the ways of adding value to an apple crop, such as jams, jellies, and apple cheese. Each experience highlights opportunities in food production.

As well as giving our students an appreciation of and pride in our Irish produce and ingredients, we also acknowledge and stress the importance of preserving and encouraging Irish culinary traditions. In the early 1990s I recognized that, with the passing of one more generation, a whole culinary tradition, with its considerable range of curious regional variations, was in imminent danger of being lost. That was the starting point for my book *Irish Traditional Cooking* and writing it was a labor of salvage as well as one of love.

Following a huge response to my requests for recipes in the regional papers, I set off on a voyage of discovery. In Ballyheigue in County Kerry, I spent a memorable day with John Guerin and his mother Bridget, learning how to collect *bairneachs* (barnacles) off the rocks to make traditional Irish Good Friday soup. In County Monaghan, Granny Toye, well into her eighties, described in vivid detail how to make the boxty pancakes of her youth. As my collection of recipes built up, I realized how common the misconception is, even among Irish people, that Ireland has no culinary tradition to speak of. There is much more to it than bacon and cabbage and Irish stew, delicious as they are.

Ireland's farming heritage has given a variety of methods for cooking meat, poultry, and eggs. The potato, so central to Irish subsistence (half an acre of cultivated ground could feed a family for a year), is the main ingredient in an array of dishes with infinite regional variations. Oatmeal has always been important, too, used in many interesting ways. Most exciting, perhaps, is Ireland's strong tradition of home baking, with its encyclopedic range of breads and cakes traditionally made with flour from home-grown wheat. Again, regional differences are noteworthy, with the North an especially rich source of recipes. From the dining rooms of grand houses to the kitchens of the poorest cabins, Ireland has had a strong tradition of generous hospitality from pagan times right up to the present day.

The time is certainly ripe for a revival of interest in traditional Irish cooking—the wholesome, comforting food that nourished our ancestors for generations and is just as delicious today. The next step must be for more young Irish chefs to include it in their menus and to cook these dishes with pride. We can all learn a great deal from a gastronomic tradition that is based around fresh local ingredients, simply and succulently cooked. Sadly, the reality is that many Irish people don't really believe that we have a food culture to be proud of.

2013 was the year of the "Gathering" here in Ireland, a tourist initiative that encouraged all of us to invite many of our family and friends to return to Ireland and bring their friends to introduce them to what Ireland has to offer—not just warm, friendly, welcoming people and a beautiful ever-changing landscape, but the renaissance in food and the emergence of an artisanal food culture. I've been encouraging chefs, restaurateurs, pubs, cafés, and caterers to proudly feature at least one Irish traditional recipe on their menu every week. To facilitate this, in 2013 I created a website, www.irishrecipes.ie, of well-tested traditional recipes for people to access easily.

Homemade Mayonnaise

I know it is very tempting to reach for a jar of the well-known brand, but homemade mayonnaise can be made in 5 minutes, even by hand. If you decide to use a food processor, it's even faster and so worth the effort. As ever, the quality of the eggs really matters. Use the best organic eggs you can find and really good-quality sunflower and olive oil and wine vinegar.

Makes 1¼ cups

2 organic egg yolks
¼ teaspoon salt
¼ teaspoon Dijon mustard or pinch of English mustard powder
1 teaspoon white wine vinegar
1 cup oil (7 parts sunflower to 1 part olive oil or 6 parts peanut to 2 parts olive oil)

Put the egg yolks into a medium-sized glass bowl with the salt, mustard, and white wine vinegar. Pour the oil into a measuring cup. Take a whisk in one hand and the oil in the other and drip the oil into the egg yolks, drop by drop, whisking at the same time. (If using a food processor, you need to double the recipe and use a minimum of four egg yolks or the blades won't be able to catch the egg at first and the mixture may curdle.) Within a minute you will notice that the mixture is beginning to thicken. When this happens you can add the oil a little faster, but don't get too confident or it will suddenly curdle because the egg yolks can only absorb the oil at a certain pace. Taste and add a little more seasoning and vinegar, if necessary.

If the mayonnaise curdles, it will suddenly become quite thin and, if left sitting, the oil will start to float to the top of the sauce. Should this happen you can quite easily rectify the situation by putting another egg yolk or 1–2 tablespoons boiling water into a clean bowl, and then whisking in the curdled mayonnaise, a half teaspoon at a time, until it re-emulsifies.

Any leftover mayonnaise can be stored in a sterilized jar in the fridge for a week to ten days.

Variation—Dill Mayonnaise
Add 2–3 tablespoons finely chopped fresh dill to the basic mixture, folding it in at the end. If you add fresh herbs to mayonnaise, this shortens its shelf life, so any left over will keep at its best for only a couple of days.

Ballycotton Shrimp Whole in their Shells with Watercress and Dill Mayonnaise

Not cheap, but always a wow. You may be able to buy langoustines already cooked from your fish store, but they are very simple to cook at home. Homemade mayonnaise is a must to embellish these beautiful fresh langoustines or shrimp. Make sure you open their heads and scoop out the soft tomalley. Provide a nutcracker to crack the claws so you can extract every last sweet morsel, then save the shells for a shrimp bisque; chefs often make more money from the bisque than they do from the shrimp. Shrimp and langoustines are very expensive and, believe me, there is a world of difference between really fresh shrimp and shrimp that have been "dipped" in sodium bisulfite or sodium tripolyphosphate to extend their shelf-life. Ask the fish store if the shrimp have been dipped—if they have, don't waste your money.

First cook the shrimp or langoustines. Bring the water to a boil and add the salt (it may sound a lot, but this is the secret of real flavor when cooking shrimp). Do not be tempted to cook too many together, or they may overcook before the water even comes back to a boil; cook them in two or three batches.

Put the shrimp into the boiling salted water and, as soon as the water returns to a rolling boil, test one to see if it is cooked. It should be firm and white, not opaque or mushy. If cooked, remove the shrimp or langoustines immediately with a slotted spoon. Very large shrimp may take 30 seconds–1 minute more. Set aside to cool in a single layer on a baking sheet. Uncurl the tails.

To serve, arrange five or six cooked whole shrimp on each plate. Spoon a tablespoon or two of homemade Dill Mayonnaise into a little bowl or oyster shell on the side of the plate. Pop a wedge of lemon on the plate, garnish with some fresh wild watercress, and serve with fresh crusty brown soda bread and Irish butter.

Serves 8

40–48 large, very fresh shrimp—preferably Ballycotton langoustines in their shells
4 quarts water
3 generous tablespoons salt

To serve
4–8 tablespoons homemade Dill Mayonnaise (see opposite)
4 lemon wedges
a handful of watercress leaves
crusty brown soda bread and Irish butter

Tripe with Tomatoes

Tripe is the lining of a cow's stomach. The stomach is divided into two parts, and there are three distinct types of tripe: plain tripe, which comes from the first stomach chamber; honeycomb tripe, which comes from the second stomach chamber; and packet tripe, which comes from the far end of the second stomach chamber. Honeycomb tripe is by far the most tender and flavorful and is my preferred option.

Serves 6

For the tripe
2lb honeycomb tripe
1 tablespoon salt
1¾ cups roughly chopped carrots
1 medium onion, quartered
2 bay leaves
2 sprigs of thyme
2 sprigs of flat-leaf parsley
6 black peppercorns
2 tablespoons white wine vinegar

For the sauce
2 tablespoons extra virgin olive oil
5 garlic cloves, peeled and sliced
1 red chile, seeded and sliced
2 medium onions, sliced
3 celery ribs, cut into ½in dice
1 red pepper, cut into ½in dice
1 green pepper, cut into ½in dice
2 teaspoons sweet paprika
1 bay leaf
1 teaspoon thyme leaves
2 x 14oz cans of diced tomatoes
sea salt, freshly ground black pepper, and sugar
1¼ cups chicken stock

To serve
3–4 tablespoons roughly chopped flat-leaf parsley
potatoes or rice

First prepare the tripe. Wash the tripe very thoroughly in several changes of barely warm water. Drain and put in a bowl. Rub the salt into the tripe and set aside for 30 minutes. Drain and rinse well.

Put the tripe into a large saucepan with the carrot, onion, bay leaves, thyme, parsley, peppercorns, and white wine vinegar. Cover with cold water. Bring to a boil and simmer for 1½–2 hours or until the tripe is tender. Strain off the cooking liquid, discard, and cut the tripe into slices ½in thick and 2in long.

Meanwhile, prepare the sauce. Heat the olive oil in a saucepan, add the garlic, chile, onion, and celery, and cook over low heat without coloring for 5 minutes. Then add the red and green pepper and cook for another 5 minutes. Next add the paprika, bay leaf, and thyme, stir and cook for 1 minute. Add the canned tomatoes and cook, uncovered, for 10 minutes. Season with salt, pepper, and sugar. Add the sliced tripe and chicken stock and simmer gently for 10–15 minutes or until the sauce has reduced slightly. To serve, scatter with parsley and accompany with potatoes or rice.

Carrageen Moss Pudding with Poached Apricot and Sweet Geranium Compote

Carrageen is a small, scratchy seaweed that grows around the coast on the little rocks from which it takes its name in Gaelic. Traditionally, it was harvested after the Spring Tides every year. The purpley wine-colored seaweed was then spread out on the grass, to be washed by the rain and bleached in the sun, for about ten days, by which time it would be a very pale, almost translucent color. It can then be stored for many years and is a powerhouse of iodine, minerals, and trace elements. It is packed with natural gelatin and has many commercial uses, but we use it to make this delish Carrageen Moss Pudding to Myrtle Allen's recipe, which I think is the best I've ever come across. The challenge is to use little enough; carrageen is so light, it's difficult to weigh. In Ballymaloe, we serve it with a compote of seasonal fruit. It's possibly the most traditional of all the desserts we serve in Ballymaloe.

In the summer, when we take the students foraging, we show them how to harvest carrageen moss sustainably on Ballyandreen beach, to the west of Ballycotton.

Serves 6

¼oz cleaned, well-dried carrageen moss, a semi-closed handful; you can substitute gelatin
3½ cups whole milk
1 split vanilla pod or ½ teaspoon pure vanilla extract
1 organic egg
1 tablespoon superfine sugar

For the Poached Apricot and Sweet Geranium Compote
4–6 large sweet-scented geranium leaves (*Pelargonium graveolens*)
1 cup superfine sugar
1 cup cold water
1lb fresh apricots, left whole or cut in half and pitted

To serve
softly whipped cream

To make the pudding, soak the carrageen in a little bowl of tepid water for 10 minutes. It will swell and increase in size. Strain off the water and put the carrageen into a saucepan with the milk. If you are using a vanilla pod rather than extract, add it now. Bring to a boil and simmer very gently, covered, for 20 minutes. At that point, and not before, separate the egg. Put the yolk into a bowl, add the sugar and vanilla extract (if using), and whisk together for a few seconds. Pour the hot milk and carrageen through a strainer onto the egg yolk mixture, whisking all the time.

By now the carrageen remaining in the strainer will be swollen and exuding jelly. You need to press out as much of this jelly as possible through the strainer, and whisk the jelly into the egg and milk mixture. Test for a set by placing a teaspoon of the mixture on a cold saucer; it should hold its shape but still be a little wobbly. If it's too stiff, add a little more milk, and if it's too soft, push some more of the carrageen through the sieve. In a separate bowl, whisk the egg white until stiff, and fold or fluff it into the custard; it will rise to make a fluffy top. Divide the mixture between six 6oz ramekins and set aside to chill in the fridge for 7–8 hours or overnight.

To make the apricot compote, put the sweet geranium leaves into a saucepan with the sugar and water, and bring slowly to a boil. Drop in the apricots, cover with a lid, and simmer until the apricots are soft. Set aside to cool, and then transfer the compote to the fridge to chill.

Serve the carrageen moss pudding with the chilled apricot compote and softly whipped cream.

The Fruit Garden

In 1989 my friend, garden designer Jim Reynolds of Butterstream, Trim, County Meath, designed a fruit garden for us that was intended to be decorative as well as productive. It is situated in front of the Blue Dining Room at the Cookery School, with steps of Liscannor slate leading down into a gravelled area below the windows, where the students can choose to have lunch in the warmer months beneath the large umbrellas. The soil is good, having been enriched by farmyard manure, seaweed, and compost over the years. Jim designed a formal layout to accommodate a wide variety of fruit so the students could see many different types of fruit blossoming and growing and have the opportunity to pick their own and bring it into the kitchen and eat it. Many who are unfamilar with how fruit grows are intrigued to see how currants hang in clusters and gooseberries hide beneath the leaves and need to be topped and tailed before eating.

Strawberries, loganberries, tayberries, gooseberries, red and yellow raspberries, Worcesterberries, jostaberries, boysenberries, cranberries, blackberries, blueberries, red, black, and white currants and crab apples are all planted here. Greengages, plums, peaches, apricots, and rhubarb are planted around the perimeter. Pears and heirloom apples, including several old Irish varieties, are trained over metal arches. We also grow more unusual varieties, such as a delicious early apple called Irish Peach, which has been grown in Ireland for more than two centuries and is still appreciated and sought out by those who like flavorsome apples. We chose apple varieties no longer easily available in the shops and supermarkets: American Mother, Egremont Russet, Lane's Prince Albert, Pitmaston Pineapple, Arthur Turner, Beauty of Bath, and Lady Sudeley. We did this for two reasons: to have more choice than the predictable varieties available in the shops, and to preserve and reacquaint people with these almost forgotten flavors, many of which have a delicious, bittersweet taste.

The black mulberry in the center, underplanted with autumn crocuses, is just beginning to produce fruit at last. It was planted in 1989 and took over ten years to produce even a small crop.

Green Almonds

Timmy ambles in—I know by his non-committal expression that he has something exciting to announce!

"Have you looked at your almond tree recently?"

I need no more prompting; I race across the dining room out onto the steps overlooking the fruit garden. I don't believe it: my almond tree is covered with soft, furry, green almonds. I'm wild with excitement. Madhur Jaffrey told me how delicious they are eaten at this green stage. I eat one whole. Umm, I'm not sure if that is what she meant. Then I take a knife and cut through the protective outer green husk and taste the moist, white flesh of the green almond inside—delicious. In the Mediterranean countries where they grow, they are eaten, green husk and all, when they are young and tender. The Greeks love them sprinkled with lemon juice and sea salt. The French like to marinate green almonds in verjus. We now have a little almond feast every year. We eat them fresh off the tree in April or early May, sitting under the almond tree with a little paring knife.

Left: We have trained old varieties of apple over the arches in the fruit garden: for example, we grow Egremont Russet, Lane's Prince Albert, Arthur Turner, Beauty of Bath, Pitmaston Pineapple, and Irish Peach (yes, it is an apple!). This shows the view from the fruit garden, looking up toward the little woods and kitchen garden.

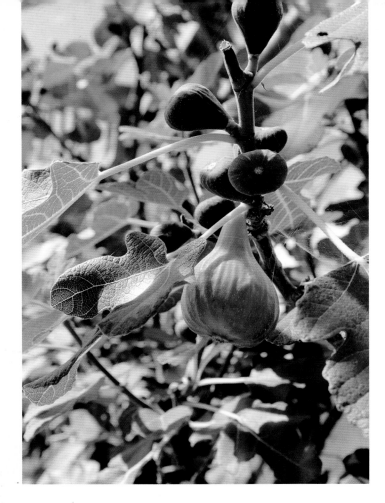

Left: Figs ripening on one of our fig trees.

Right: One of the many old varieties of apple that we grow in the fruit garden and the old orchard to introduce the students to the flavors and range of apples that are no longer available in supermarkets. Most don't realize that you can have apples almost all year round as some varieties such as the famous cooker, Bramley's Seedling, can be picked off underripe and stored in a cellar or cool garage for months on end.

The fruits resemble long, winey blackberries. Two weeping white mulberries frame a garden seat. The almond trees bear abundant furry fruits, which split to release the stones from which the sweet kernels can be extracted. Few students have seen almonds grow, so they are fascinated to see the furry green pods and to know they can be eaten at several stages.

One surprising success has been the Asian pear, or nashi; the trees have produced excellent, crisp fruits, which are apple-like with a heavy russet. The elders (*Sambucus nigra*) that grow along the stone wall to the south of the garden include Wildings and the dark purple-leaved cultivar named Guincho Purple. From the end of May, for about a month, we use an abundance of elder blossoms for cordial, lemonade, fritters and elderflower fizz, and the berries are used for jams and jellies in autumn. Figs grow against the wall of the Cookery School, and there is an olive tree, too, although sadly this does not produce enough fruit to make olive oil—still, it earns its place in the fruit garden, as students can see what an olive tree looks like.

The fruit garden is underplanted with spring bulbs, so it is especially joyful in spring when the Lenten roses and bulbs bloom—snowdrops, grape hyacinths, and countless crocuses, fritillaries, snowflakes, and tiny *Iris reticulata*. Here, too, in the shade of the elders, I replanted the Kinoith violets that Lydia Strangman and her brother Wilson, who were the last members of the Strangman family to live in our house at Kinoith (Lydia was also a keen watercolor artist), once picked and sent to London, in conjunction with a number of other farms in East Cork. The violets were tied into little bunches, wrapped in a violet leaf, and taken to Cork to be exported to London on the ship *Innisfallen*. Ladies wore them on their lapels and enjoyed the beautiful scent of the dark purple violets. The violets were bunched in the "Violet Loft," now a part of the Pink Cottage, which overlooks where Lydia's garden once was. The flowers are sweetly fragrant, and, while most abundant in winter and early spring, there are stray flowers in other seasons. Nowadays we use these fragrant flowers at the School and at Ballymaloe House to make pretty crystallized violets to decorate cakes and pastries.

In the mid-1990s we planted white peaches and apricots on the south-facing wall of the dining room. The white peaches, Peregrine, particularly love it there, and we usually have an abundant crop to enjoy. We use this glut to make bellinis and both sweet and savory salads. White peaches are meltingly sweet and juicy but bruise really easily. Ice-cream maker extraordinaire, Kitty Travers of La Grotta Ices, gave us a tip about peeling and dropping them into hot syrup first—this prevents them from discoloring, which they do immediately otherwise. We also show the students how to use the peach leaves in ratafias, panna cottas, and crème brûlées, and to make a simple peach leaf tea from fresh or dried leaves, which has many nutritional and therapeutic qualities—it is reputed to be good for cleansing the kidneys, and in the past peach leaves were used to treat worms, bronchitis, and whooping cough. Peaches are also among the first fruits to flower in the garden, appearing as early as April; the pink blossoms are a joy after the long, sullen winter.

The Beginning of Television

My first foray into television wasn't part of a master plan—it was almost accidental. Keith Floyd, who was extremely well-known on television in the UK, was a great friend of Ireland and had a house in Kinsale in West Cork for many years. Claudia Roden had told him about the School, so when he was visiting in 1986 with a film crew, he asked to do a short piece. Our first film crew—we were excited and terrified. He arrived hours late, which made me even more apprehensive. I'd never even seen a television camera up close before. I was nervous and felt really silly in front of my class.

The first take was all arranged—there would be a shot of me teaching the class, then suddenly I would catch a glimpse of Floyd reading the *Racing Times* at the back of the class, look shocked, and tell him to put the paper down and concentrate. The first take was perfect, but Floyd forgot my name. So we had to do it again and again and again. The more takes we did the worse I got, so Floyd had a brilliant idea. Let's stop and have a glass of wine! So we did, and everything went swimmingly after that. I don't remember what we cooked—I think it was Irish stew—but I just remember the relief when it was over.

Afterwards Floyd said to Tim, "You know, Darina should do TV, she's a natural." We all thought that was hilarious, considering I'd found it so nervewracking, and at that time I had no plans to do any more television. However, sometime early in 1987, a letter arrived in the post from the Irish broadcaster RTÉ's Head of Features Clare Duignan, asking whether Myrtle and I would be interested in doing a pilot of a cooking series. We decided to have a go, and the pilot was shot at the School in August 1987. It took a week to make an hour-long program. With just one camera, every scene had to be shot twice. There was no playback, unthinkable nowadays when most series are made with four cameras and spontaneous editing. Continuity was a nightmare but it was certainly a good way to "cut our teeth." Eventually RTÉ came back to us and said they would like to make a series. They wanted to shoot it in July and August 1988—a very difficult time for Myrtle, right in the middle of the tourist season—so she encouraged me to go ahead on my own.

I was dithering: what if it was a disaster, it's so easy to make a fool of oneself in front of the cameras. Eventually, I decided to go for it, preferring to live with the possibility that it wouldn't necessarily be a smash hit, rather than wondering what if I'd had a go!

Colette Farmer, a producer/director who had worked for many years on the *Late, Late Show* talk show with Gay Byrne, which was at that time an unmissable program for half of Ireland, was assigned to the program by Clare Duignan. We had a small crew of five, who soon became like family: Roy Bedell was the cameraman, Pat Johns was on sound, Sean Keville was the "sparks" (electrician), and Patricia Swan was the production assistant for the first series: she was followed by Mary Power and then Kevin Cummins ably took on the role for the following years.

I was adamant that the show should be shot here at the School, where I had a well-equipped kitchen and easy access to beautiful, fresh produce. We could also pick up evocative background shots of the farm, gardens, and local area. When I agreed to do the series, I explained that I had absolutely no idea how to go about it. Everyone promised to help, but the crew had never done a food program before either, so we were all learning together. Fortunately I remembered that Claudia Roden and Madhur Jaffrey, who had been guests chef at the School, had done many TV series, so I called them. They were wonderfully generous and put us in touch with their production teams who gave me practical advice, such as rehearsing first and measuring out three sets of ingredients.

For me, the aim of *Simply Delicious* was to take the mystery out of cooking and to incorporate technique into every program while keeping the food simple and delicious, just as I taught at the School. Colette and I argued constantly about the content of the episodes; I always wanted to squash more into each program. She wisely knew that less is more and also knew my limitations. My style and the format of the program were very different from cooking programs nowadays, which are geared more toward entertainment than tutorial. I was very earnest about the whole exercise and determined that people should really be able to learn from the programs, which they did.

Initially, it took a day and a half to make a 30 minute program. Floyd may have thought I was a natural but in reality I found it incredibly stressful, particularly the simple pieces to camera, which I always seemed to have to do over and over again. The series was eventually "in the can" and disappeared off to RTÉ Donnybrook to be edited. We waited with mixed emotions of excitement and apprehension.

At some stage while we were filming, it occurred to me that we would need a cookbook with the series. Colette didn't think it was necessary because the recipes would be published in the RTÉ Guide every week. But I could foresee people either mislaying the

Above: A publicity picture for the first series of Simply Delicious of me with a selection of dishes from the book, taken outside in the courtyard of the School. The series featured simple recipes such as Kerry Pie, Blackberry and Apple Tart, Bacon Chop and the classic Ballymaloe

Brown Yeast Bread. The presentation is certainly very of its time and rather different to how we would present dishes today. My trademark glasses are blue instead of red here, possibly in an attempt to co-ordinate with the apron!

guide or not buying it and just phoning me for the recipes instead. I was determined to do a book, but Colette was still hesitant since we would need lots more recipes than were in the series. This was no problem because we already had thousands of recipes in our files. Michael Gill of Gill & Macmillan publishers had approached me a few years earlier to ask if I'd do a book, but at that stage I wasn't quite ready. When approached by RTÉ, he jumped at the idea.

I had no idea how to go about writing a book, but Michael assigned me a wonderful editor, Dee Rennison, who explained matter of factly, "We need 90 recipes and a bit of blurb for each one before the deadline of March." We chose the content, and I tested, tested, and re-tested; I was determined that the recipes would work easily for all my new readers. My brother Rory O'Connell and I cooked all the food for the photos—Rory did most of the food styling as well. It was to be a paperback and the cover was gray (what was I thinking?!) with a (very predictable) photo of me in my apron complete with those dreadful huge red trademark glasses.

The first program was to be shown on Monday March 13, 1989, at 7.30 p.m. On the Saturday before, Gay Byrne invited me to be a guest on the *Late, Late Show*. This was a huge deal. Colette had asked him to introduce me and the series to the Irish people. I was never so scared of anything, before or since. This was *live*! We cooked a whole array of food to bring into the studio as an example of what I would be covering in the series. I needn't have worried, Gay was kind and supportive—I was launched. The following day my life changed forever; suddenly I was recognized as I walked along the street; the windows of Easons, Waterstone's, and Hodges Figgis were full of my cookbook. I found this surprisingly difficult to cope with and was relieved to be able to disappear back into the relative obscurity of my home in Shanagarry.

Soon after the series was aired, all hell broke loose—the books, which were reasonably priced, started to sell in huge numbers and people lined up around the corner when I did book signings in Dublin, Cork, Galway, Waterford, and Kilkenny. People called into RTÉ and radio stations and complained that there were

arguments in their house because *Simply Delicious* was aired at the same time as *Coronation Street*. This was the era when there was definitely only one television in most houses and no playback. RTÉ responded and put on a repeat of each program. Both RTÉ and Gill & Macmillan were amazed by the reaction to the program. Journalists kept calling for interviews. People kept telling me how much they were enjoying it; I was obviously very pleased, but had nothing to measure the reaction by and honestly didn't register quite what a phenomenon it seemed to be. Two things gave me an inkling: the first was from Kevin Myers, who wrote "An Irishman's Diary" in *The Irish Times* and published a piece in his column on April 26, 1989, on how Irish publishing history was being made by a cookbook, of all things. The second hint that it was creating a real stir was sometime in the late autumn—possibly October or November. I had just completed a book signing in Waterstone's in Cork and as we were leaving, the Gill & Macmillan representative met a colleague from another company who inquired how things were going, to which the Gill & Macmillan rep replied, "We're having a fantastic year, this woman's book *Simply Delicious* is selling in telephone numbers!" I thought, "Wow, that's my book they're talking about." When we got to the car, I asked for the first time how many books I had sold. The answer was over 60,000 copies. At that time successful cookbooks usually sold 3,000–5,000 copies.

Since then there has been the phenomenal rise of the celebrity television chef. Some are more decorative than functional, but others, like Jamie Oliver and Hugh Fearnley-Whittingstall, have a strong social mission and have used their platform to effect political change and raise food issues, such as the dismal quality of school lunches, the plight of intensively produced poultry, and overfishing, for which I admire them greatly. I feel strongly that those of us who are fortunate enough to have the opportunity to be television presenters have a responsibility to educate and contribute to the greater good, rather than merely filling airtime!

Despite the enormous increase in the number of cooking programs on TV, it is a matter of conjecture and some dispute as

An Irishman's Diary

POOR Darina Allen. The phone can't go down in Ballymaloe Cookery School in Co Cork without her leaping under a table, sitting on her head, putting her fingers in her ears and screeching: "I'm not in. I'm not in. I'm not in." Because the one thing that a cookery expert hates above all things has happened to her. There is a mistake in her recipe for Christmas pudding in her latest book, and what's worse, it's the recipe for her mother-in-law's Christmas pudding. Oh mercy. Myrtle's rolling pin coming down onto daughter-in-law's cranium.

The error is this. The recipe for the Christmas pudding contains all the normal goodies, but the error is a subtle one. It does not then suggest that you add 13 lb of quick-setting concrete, and bung in a half bucket of rusting nails, or season the mix with a half pint of ox blood and 20 finely ground cloves of garlic. You might, just might, have detected an error there, though I personally doubt it. My own experience of any cookery book suggests that the reader goes into a trance of kamikaze obedience, and would unquestionably chuck a kilo of lightly minced rats' eyelids into a vegetarian hotpot.

Believable Error

But, as I say, Darina's error, the one that has her screeching with horror every time the phone tinkles, is of a more subtle order. In the recipe entitled "Myrtle Allen's Christmas pudding", she has said that you should use 2 lb of bread crumbs. The insidious thing about this error is that it is believable.

The figure should not be 2 lb. It should be seven ounces. But all over the island people have been throwing 2 lb of bread crumbs into the mix. (And all over the island is no exaggeration. Darina is the Harold Robbins of cookery writing, though normally her recipes are not quite as fictional as this Christmas pudding one).

And they have then cooked their Christmas pudding, and some of them have already — oh impetuous souls — decided to eat some of it early. And there at the table husband has looked at wife and asked: "What did you say this is

Darina Allen . . . 2 lb of gremlins in her Christmas pudding recipe

called?" "Myrtle Allen's Christmas pudding," she has replied, with downcast eyes.

And the entire family has nibbled with polite decorum at what they think is Myrtle Allen's Christmas pudding; except, of course, it is not. For it tastes like sliced pan and may justifiably be called mother's pride. And this might even be the case on Christmas Day, in which case people will soundly curse the name of the Allen family, or, if they are suitably drunk, will blame the ozone layer, and will lament for the Christmasses of their youth, when there was snow and holly and Christmas pudding that tasted of Christmas pudding rather than the bread sauce that went with the turkey.

A Breaking Heart

The error, you see, is simple and subtle. You should put seven ounces of bread crumbs into your mix, not 2 lb, and that way you'll have the true Myrtle Allen pudding, the one she nourished all 30 (or whatever: it's something like that) of her children on.

And now you know, though that is little consolation for poor Darina. "It breaks your heart," she hissed homicidally, "putting all these recipes together and proof reading, going over the bloody thing endlessly, and then you get an error like this." She stamped a foot and put her heel through the floorboards, and then ground her teeth, loosening half a dozen molars. You know they're angry in Ballymaloe

when the word bloody finds its way into the list of expletives.

"And the infuriating thing is that they are absolutely super recipes. I've had an awful week, and I don't want people not to buy this book because they think it's full of errors."

And it's not. All the other recipes are right, though the recipe for St Stephen's Day pie neglects to point out that the amount of onions you will need is 12 oz, and Mary Joe's cookies should have a half pound, not 1 lb, of chocolate. What's the difference?"

"It's a hell of a lot richer," said Darina, grimly.

Fiendish Recipe

But that's it. The latest copies of the book have errata slips, and one of the features Darina is particularly fond of is the recipes for children. No, this is not a cannibal's cookery book. This is something infinitely more fiendish. It is a plan to introduce children and foodstuffs into the same kitchen simultaneously, and then let them at one another, the winner being first to claim three falls or a submission. Though ideally, an adult should be present, and the idea is for the children to make things like a chocolate Christmas tree, rather than to eat 15 lb of cooking chocolate, and then to proceed to make the only restitution that is in their power.

"I'm so fragile," whispered poor Darina. "You won't overemphasise that single error, will you?"

Wouldn't dream of it.

Melodic Numbers

Just as Darina is dodging telephones, Miriam Blennerhassett is dodging 'flu bugs, so that she is in good voice for her concert in St Anne's in Dawson Street in Dublin tomorrow at lunchtime. If she gets the cold the Diary has, she'll be known as Mucous Blennerhassett. Miriam has chosen a brilliantly melodic programme for this concert in which she is accompanied by Clive Shannon. Songs by Dowland, Faure, Mahler, Beckett, and virginal, hitherto unheard numbers by Michael McGlynn which Miriam will sing (or snuffle, as the case may be). 1.10 pm, St Anne's, all right?

KEVIN MYERS

to whether people are actually cooking more or simply sitting back on the sofa enjoying the show—indulging in a little "armchair cooking." I'm not sure how one can quantify this—certainly there's a lot of produce on supermarket shelves and at farmers' markets, so someone must be doing something with it.

The myriad of cooking programs on offer has had varying effects on attitudes to food. In my experience, series such as *Masterchef* have had two effects: either they intimidate total beginners, who feel that cooking is all too complicated to attempt; or they make others feel that cooking is all about water baths, siphons, foams, and gels. The latter often come to the Cookery School eager to learn complex skills and skip the basics; they are convinced that it is totally irrelevant to learn how to make a pâte à choux or silky béchamel. They are desperate to learn how to put skid marks on the plate before they have mastered knife skills, which can be a challenge!

Plum Pudding

Within the first few months of the publication of *Simply Delicious*, Michael Gill, owner of Gill & Macmillan, approached me and asked whether I could very quickly write a Christmas cookbook. I wanted to include recipes for both my mother's and Myrtle's plum puddings. The latter had been passed down the Allen family for several generations and called for a 2lb loaf for the bread crumbs.

Because of the rush to publish, Gill & Macmillan offered to do the recipe conversions for the book. However, the person who was charged with the task didn't realize that a 2lb loaf didn't mean 2lb of bread crumbs! (A 2lb loaf would normally produce approx. 7oz of breadcrumbs.) No one spotted the mistake until the book went into the shops, then about a week later the phones started to ring. I still remember the sinking feeling when my PA, Rosalie Dunne, called me to the phone to speak to an irate woman who told me the recipe was wrong; she had got five puddings instead of the three the recipe said and they were all "very bready."

My heart sank as it gradually dawned on me what had happened. We contacted Gill & Macmillan and explained the problem. They generously suggested that I blame the publishers but I was not prepared to leave it like that. Even in the short time that the School had operated and we'd made one *Simply Delicious* series, I had built up a bond of trust with my readers and they really were using my cookbooks.

Having chatted to Michael Gill, I was determined to go on the radio to explain and to try to stop other people from making the same mistake. I contacted Gay Byrne, and he had me on his morning radio show when I explained to the Irish people about the mistake in the recipe. It caused a whole spate of hilarious jokes and was even the subject of a cartoon in the *Sun*. They say that there's no such thing as bad publicity and after that interview and the subsequent newspaper coverage, the bookshops reported a surge of people pouring into their shops looking for the "book with the mistake in it"!

Fig, Bocconcini, and Mizuna Salad with Opal Basil

Not everyone can have a fig tree, but it's definitely worth considering. They grow happily in this climate, both outdoors against a warm south-facing wall (contain the roots), or in a greenhouse, where the fruit will ripen better. We also use the leaves on the cheeseboard and to wrap fish or to flavor raspberry granita, a trick shown to me by Kitty Travers of La Grotta Ices when she came to teach at the School.

It really isn't worth bothering with figs unless they are in season and freshly picked—otherwise use dried Turkish figs rather than under-ripe imported ones.

Serves 4

12 bocconcini or small balls of fresh mozzarella
1 bunch of mizuna or arugula
1 bunch of Thai basil or opal basil
⅓ cup extra virgin olive oil
6 fresh figs, preferably Turkey or Black Mission
freshly squeezed lemon juice
sea salt

Bring a saucepan of water to a boil. Drain the cheese and put the balls in a thick plastic bag.

Mix the mizuna or arugula leaves with the basil in a large salad bowl. Drizzle with some of the olive oil and toss gently to coat. Pile the salad leaves into the center of four plates. Trim the stem from each fig and gently pull each one in half with your thumbs. Lay the fig halves open-side up on the salad.

Drop the bag of bocconcini or mozzarella into the hot water for 2–3 minutes, then remove the cheese from the bag and scatter over the salad.

Drizzle with a little more olive oil, sprinkle with a few drops of freshly squeezed lemon juice, and sprinkle with a few flakes of sea salt.

Raspberry and Fig Leaf Granita

This recipe was shown to me by Kitty Travers when she taught an ice cream course in the summer of 2012. She introduced us to some delicious and unusual flavors such as Rhubarb and Angelica Sorbet and Nectarine Leaf Ice Cream. Look out for her cart at Maltby Street Market, London.

Serves 10

⅓ cup granulated sugar
1 cup water
3 fig leaves
4 cups (18oz) fresh raspberries

To serve
Crème Chantilly (see below)

Put the sugar and water into a medium saucepan, stir to dissolve the sugar, then bring up to a simmer.

Rinse the fig leaves under some running water and rip them into a few pieces if they are large. As soon as the sugar syrup reaches a simmer, add the fig leaves to the pan, remove from the heat, and cover with plastic wrap to infuse for 15 minutes. Strain the leaves, pressing gently on them to extract as much perfumed syrup as is possible.

Add the raspberries to the still warm syrup, and process with a stick blender. Strain the purée through a sieve to remove the seeds.

Pour the mixture into a shallow metal pan, cover with plastic wrap, and put flat on a freezer shelf. Stir with a fork after 1 hour, breaking up any large lumps of ice. Keep stirring every 45 minutes thereafter.

The desired end result is a beautiful heap of fine, snowy crystals. This ought to be achieved after 3–4 hours. Serve with homemade Crème Chantilly (see below).

Crème Chantilly

½–1 tablespoon confectioners' sugar
2–3 drops pure vanilla extract
1¼ cups softly whipped cream

Add the confectioners' sugar and vanilla extract to the cream and fold gently to mix.

Green Gooseberry and Elderflower Trifle

Our repertoire of trifles continues to grow—this green gooseberry and elderflower one is a fairly recent addition.

Serves 16–20

⅔ cup elderflower cordial

For the sponge cake
9 tablespoons butter, softened, plus extra for greasing
¾ cup superfine sugar
3 organic eggs
1½ cups all-purpose flour, plus extra for dusting
1 teaspoon baking powder
1 tablespoon milk

For the green gooseberry and elderflower compote
3–4 elderflower heads; or elderflower cordial to taste
2 cups superfine sugar
2½ cups cold water
2lb green gooseberries; you can substitute rhubarb
    if gooseberries are unavailable

For the egg custard
2 cups milk
⅔ cup heavy cream
1 vanilla pod, split lengthwise
3 organic eggs, plus 3 organic egg yolks
4–6 tablespoons superfine sugar

To serve
2½ cups softly whipped heavy cream
gooseberry leaves and sweet geranium flowers or
    fresh mint leaves and elderflowers, to decorate

Preheat the oven to 375°F. Grease two 7in cake pans with melted butter, dust with flour, and line the bases with parchment paper.

For the sponge cake, cream the butter, gradually add the sugar, and beat until soft and pale. Add the eggs one at a time, beating well between each addition. (If the butter and sugar are not creamed properly and you add the eggs too fast, the mixture will curdle, resulting in a heavy texture.) Sift the flour with the baking powder and fold in gradually. Mix all together lightly and add the milk.

Divide the mixture evenly between the two pans, hollowing it slightly in the center. Bake in the preheated oven for 20–25 minutes or until cooked—the cakes will shrink away slightly from the sides of the pan; the center of the cakes should feel exactly the same texture as around the edges. A skewer should come out clean when put into the center of the cake. Turn out onto a wire rack and set aside to cool.

Meanwhile, make the compote. Tie the elderflower heads in a little square of cheesecloth and put into a stainless steel or enamelled saucepan—alternatively, you can just put them in loose or use elderflower cordial in place of some of the water and sugar to taste. Add the sugar and water, bring slowly to a boil, and continue to boil for 2 minutes. Put in the gooseberries and simmer just until the fruit bursts. They must actually burst, otherwise the compote of fruit will be too bitter. Set aside to cool.

To make the egg custard, heat the milk and cream with the vanilla pod in a heavy-bottomed pan until it reaches the "shivery" stage. Meanwhile, whisk the whole eggs and egg yolks with the sugar until pale and frothy. Pour the hot milk and cream mixture into the egg mixture, whisking all the time. Return the custard to the pan and stir over low heat until the custard is thick enough to coat the back of the wooden spoon. Don't let it boil or it will curdle. Remove the custard from the heat and continue to stir as it cools. Remove the vanilla pod. Set aside to cool.

To assemble the trifles, spoon one-sixth of the custard into the base of two 3½ cup glass serving bowls, and top with one-sixth of the gooseberry compote. Split the cakes in half, place a layer of cake on top of the compote, and drizzle one-quarter of the elderflower cordial over each. Top each with another layer of custard, some more compote, the last layer of cake, and the rest of the elderflower cordial. Finish with the rest of the gooseberry compote and a final layer of custard. Cover each bowl with plastic wrap, and transfer the trifles to the fridge to settle, preferably overnight or for at least 2 hours.

To serve, spoon a layer of softly whipped cream over the top each trifle. Decorate with gooseberry leaves and sweet geranium flowers or simply fresh mint leaves and elderflowers.

Autumn Peach, Blueberry, and Raspberry Crumble Tart

Peach, blueberry, and raspberry makes a delicious combination of fruit, but this recipe can be used as a base and topping for many other tarts using whatever seasonal fruit is available. We find that people love simple, homely desserts like this and they are also a great attraction on a café menu.

First make the pastry. Sift the flour onto a work surface and rub in the butter. Add the sugar. Make a well in the center and break in the egg. Use your fingertips to gently bring the mixture together, pulling in more flour from the outside as you work. (If the mixture is very crumbly, you may need to add a few drops of water.) Knead with the heel of your hand, making three turns. You should end up with a silky smooth ball of dough. Wrap in plastic wrap and set aside in the fridge for at least 1 hour before using. (If not using the pastry right away, it will keep for a week in the fridge and it also freezes well.)

Preheat the oven to 350°F. Line a 9in tart pan with the pastry and then line with parchment paper and fill it to the top with dried beans to hold the paper in place. Bake for 20–25 minutes. Remove from the oven and set aside to cool slightly.

To make the crumble topping, put all the dry ingredients into a bowl and rub in the butter until the mixture resembles coarse flakes.

To make the filling, slice the peaches or nectarines into a bowl and carefully stir in the blueberries and raspberries (if using). Sprinkle in the cornstarch and mix well. Taste—if the fruit is unusually tart, you may need to add a little sugar.

To assemble the tart, spoon the fruit into the pastry shell and top with an even layer of crumble topping—a generous ½in thick.

Bake in the preheated oven for 45 minutes–1 hour or until the topping is crisp and the fruit is tender. The juices should bubble up around the edges.

Serve with softly whipped cream with lots of freshly chopped mint folded in.

Serves approx. 8

For the sweet shortcrust pastry
1½ cups all-purpose flour
5 tablespoons diced butter, softened
¼ cup superfine sugar
1 large organic egg, beaten

For the crumble topping
¼ cup all-purpose flour
¼ cup brown sugar
½ cup rolled oats, organic if possible
⅛ teaspoon freshly ground cinnamon
2 tablespoons butter

For the filling
1½lb peaches or nectarines
1½ cups (8oz) blueberries or half blueberries
    and half raspberries
1 tablespoon cornstarch

To serve
softly whipped cream
a small handful of fresh mint leaves, finely chopped

Keeping Cows

In 1990, Tom Ferguson of Gubbeen Cheese in Schull took me to see a beautiful herd of Kerry cows grazing on the hillside overlooking Roaring Water Bay in West Cork. Memories came flooding back of the little black Kerry house cow my family had in Cullohill and the delicious raw milk we had as children. (It was a tradition in Ireland to have a special cow to provide milk for the household, and the Kerry breed is known to have particularly delicious and nutritious milk.) Tom has a great fondness for the Kerry and the superior quality of their milk and had serious concerns about their dwindling numbers. I resolved there and then to buy a Kerry to enlarge the gene pool and to have access to raw milk once again, not just for myself, but also for my children and grandchildren.

I bought my first purebred Kerry cow, Fortagusta Natasha (Fortagusta was the name of the herd and farm, and she was already named Natasha), in 1990 from an organic farmer in Wexford named Ivan Ward, who didn't quite realize that he was going to have to provide years of "after-sale service" as I slowly learned the ropes. The Kerry is a dual-breed, which thrives even on poor or marginal soil and is used for both dairy and beef. We rear the male calves for beef—the meat is succulent and flavorful with a rich covering of yellow fat—while we keep the females to provide us with a range of dairy produce. Sadly, that first beautiful, elegant cow is no longer alive, but one of her daughters has given birth to seven healthy calves. We now have three Kerry cows and a herd of five Jersey cows, which we milk every day. We opted for Jersey because these lovely cows are gentle and docile, and the milk is sweet and delicious, the cream rich and unctuous.

I feel very strongly about the health-giving properties of raw milk from a small, well-managed herd of healthy cows. A growing body of epidemiological research is reinforcing this belief in the health-giving and anti-allergic properties of raw milk, which significantly protects against asthma, eczema, and hay fever.

There is a global resurgence of interest in this issue and growing demand for raw milk. In May 2011 the first international Raw Milk Conference was held in Prague on the Risks and Benefits of Raw Milk, and subsequent conferences have been held in 2012 and 2013 in Vancouver. Regulations vary from country to country, but Ireland is particularly famous for the quality of its dairy products.

Every shop and gas station in Ireland sells pasteurized, homogenized milk, but I feel strongly that people who wish to should be able to choose to buy raw milk. It would seem grossly unfair if Irish people were to be deprived of the opportunity to

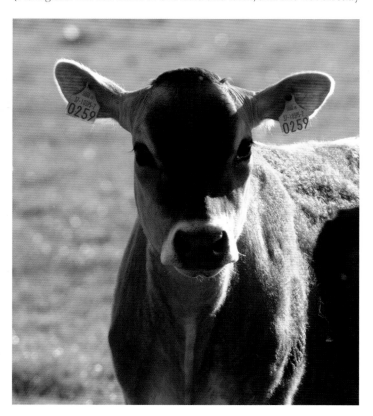

Left: One of our herd of five Jersey cows, which provide us with rich milk and cream to make butter, buttermilk, yogurt, and a number of cheeses, which then feature in many of the dishes that we make at the School. Right: Eileen O'Donovan bringing her beloved herd of cows in for the morning's milking.

Left: Our herd of black Kerry cows. Kerrys were almost an endangered species when I bought our first one in 1990.

choose. In 2011 the government announced its intention to ban the sale of raw milk to the public in the Republic of Ireland. There was a spirited campaign against an outright ban. We called for a geographical spread of farms around the country to be regulated in order to sell unpasteurized milk to the public who wish to have a choice. We argued that anyone who wants pasteurized, homogenized milk can buy it in any shop in Ireland, whereas those who feel strongly about raw milk have a right to choose.

At Ballymaloe we sell the fresh, unpasteurized Jersey milk and cream from a refrigerated unit in our Farm Shop to local people. Some customers drive up to 50 miles to buy it if their children have asthma or eczema and report dramatic improvement in their conditions. Ireland has the fourth highest prevalence of asthma in the world, and 18.9 percent of Irish 13–15 year olds have asthma.

Some customers just want to drink a glass of chilled milk in the shop. Interestingly, there is a small but growing demand for raw milk in the US and many European countries. Several milk bars have opened in New York alone, such as Momofuku and Ronnybrook, where customers can have a glass of pasteurized milk from a variety of breeds.

At the School we offer both pasteurized, organic milk and our own raw milk carefully labeled, so the students can make a choice. Many students are apprehensive at first, having being conditioned to be wary of raw milk. I remind them that milk was first pasteurized in Ireland in 1954 for a very good reason. During the 1950s there

was a serious problem with tuberculosis and brucellosis in cattle. Milk from many farms with varying degrees of hygiene was mixed together, so pasteurization was desirable. I explain both the risks and benefits of raw milk to our students, give them access to the papers from the Prague Conference on the subject and let them make up their own minds. When they taste the milk, they are usually hooked—raw milk from a small herd of healthy cows, which graze on rich and varied pasture, is a nourishing, health-giving food. Even some students who are convinced that they are lactose intolerant discover that they can eat our yogurt and drink our milk.

Learning how to milk a cow is an "extracurricular activity" in the 12-week course, but virtually every student grasps the opportunity to learn a skill that few are likely to need unless they want to impress a dairy farmer. We started to offer this activity when we built our new dairy in 2009 and were astonished by the positive response. Students experience firsthand just how milk is produced and are totally intrigued by the whole experience. They enjoy connecting to where their food comes from. It gives them yet another insight into how their food is produced and an appreciation of the work of a dairy farmer. They also realize that cows need to be milked twice a day, seven days a week, all year round and that includes weekends and holidays!

It has to be said this is not an opportunity students get at many cooking schools, and they love and really value the experience.

After they help to milk the cows, they see the milk being separated from the cream and take the Jersey cream up to the School to make butter and ice cream or to serve with dessert. Later they learn how to make thick, unctuous yogurt, labneh, ricotta, and several cheeses. The main type of cheese they learn to make is a hard Cheddar-like cheese; they must turn, salt, label, and care for their own cheese and they are free to take it home when they leave. Some overseas students take them, but Antipodean and American students leave them behind for us to enjoy because of import restrictions.

While few people will have the time, land, or money to keep their own cows to produce their own milk, there has been a significant rise in interest in making one's own simple dairy produce, e.g. butter, cheese, and yogurt. This is an interesting phenomenon, part of the craving to learn forgotten skills and to achieve a degree of self-sufficiency.

The artisanal milk and handmade butter movement is also really gathering momentum, and many top restaurants now proudly feature handmade raw butter on their tables. At last a growing number of dairy farmers are putting milk back into glass bottles, and some also sell organic milk and butter. I sense the same passion as in the artisanal brewing movement and a similar generosity of spirit. Tom and Sheila Butler have been making Cuinneog Irish country butter and buttermilk in Balla, County Mayo, since 1990. They won a coveted Great Taste Award in 2011.

Alan and Valerie Kingston from Drimoleague, West Cork, are also trailblazers, adding value to the beautiful milk from their Friesian and Jersey cows in a myriad of ways: yogurt, butter, traditional and clotted cream, strawberry smoothies, cheesecakes, lemon posset, and, of course, freshly pasteurized milk in quart glass bottles. At Mahon Point farmers' market, devotees fill their bottles with chilled pasteurized Glenilen milk or melt chocolate lollipops in hot milk. Using the milk from their herd of 55 cows in 1997, Alan and Valerie started to make cheesecakes for the local country markets; what started as a hobby continued to grow and has transformed their small farm into a hive of activity that now employs 34 people. They know that it all starts with the quality of the milk so "we treat our cows kindly allowing them to roam, keeping them warm in winter and never ever over-milk them"—a simple but crucial factor in their success. As well as letting students get a taste for producing their own dairy products at the School, we have also visited Glenilen Farm with them on our school tours so they can see how it is done elsewhere.

Shanagarry Jacob

In March 2013, Jacob Kenedy, of Bocca di Lupo in London, taught as a guest chef at the School. He was hugely excited about the produce, both wild and cultivated, on the farm, gardens and greenhouses, and hedgerows and cooked a wide variety of the dishes of the sort that have kept his customers returning over and over again. While he was with us, yet another calf was born, this time a male, so we honored him by naming the calf Shanagarry Jacob. Jacob was so pleased that he ordered a rib roast of rose veal for about five months time!

Virgin Jersey Butter

Now that we have five Jersey cows, we (and the students) make raw butter almost every day apart from weekends. Ever since I tasted the granular virgin butter at Noma in Copenhagen, which they proudly told us is made by Patrik Johansson with the cream from five goats in a castle near Gothenburg in Sweden, we have been making this virgin butter from the beautiful rich cream of our tiny Jersey herd—and everyone loves it.

The Jersey cream is very high in butterfat so it whips up in minutes and is a wonderful, rich, buttercup color. We serve it in little bowls. One can, of course, form it in blocks, rolls, or butter pats, if you prefer.

You don't absolutely need butter paddles to make butter, but they do make it much easier to shape the butter into blocks. They're more widely available than you might think, considering butter making is certainly an alternative enterprise—keep an eye out in antique shops and if you find some, snap them up. A good pair will bring you butter luck.

Unsalted butter should be eaten within a few days, but the addition of salt will preserve it for two to three weeks. You can make butter from any quantity of cream but the amount used in this recipe will keep you going for a week or so and give you enough to share with friends (though not in my house!).

Remember, sunlight taints butter (and milk) in a short time, so if you are serving butter outdoors, keep it covered.

Makes approx. 2¼ lb butter and 1 quart buttermilk

2½ quarts unpasteurized or pasteurized Jersey or heavy cream at room temperature
2 teaspoons dairy salt (optional)—omit if you would prefer unsalted butter

Pour the cream into a cold, sterilized mixing bowl. If you're using raw cream and want a more traditional taste, leave it to ripen in a cool place, where the temperature is approx. 46°F, for up to 48 hours.

Whisk the cream at a medium speed in an electric mixer with a whisk until it is thick. First it will be softly whipped, then stiffly whipped. Continue until the whipped cream collapses and separates into butterfat globules. The buttermilk will separate from the butter and slosh around the bowl.

Pour the mixture into a cold, spotlessly clean sieve and drain well. The butter remains in the sieve while the buttermilk drains into the bowl. The buttermilk can be used as a thirst-quenching drink (it will not taste sour at that point) or used to make soda bread.

Put the butter back into a clean bowl and beat with the whisk for another 30 seconds–1 minute to expel more buttermilk. Drain again and transfer to a bowl.

Fill the bowl containing the butter with very cold water. Use the butter paddles or your clean hands to knead the butter to force out as much buttermilk as possible. It's important to rinse out as much buttermilk as possible, because any buttermilk left in the butter will sour and the butter will deteriorate quickly. (If you handle the butter too much with warm hands, it will liquefy.)

Drain the water, cover and wash twice more, until the water is totally clear.

Weigh the butter—you will need to add 2 percent salt. Sprinkle half the salt over the crumbly butter, fork it in, and sprinkle the rest over the top. Allow to drain for 4–5 hours or overnight. Serve in chilled butter dishes or store in covered glass jars in the fridge until needed.

Rose Gray and Ruth Rogers

In 1987, I got a postcard from my friend Julia Wight in London saying: "I've found a wonderful place over in Hammersmith; they're serving beautiful, simple food made with exquisite fresh produce in the mode of Elizabeth David—come quickly."

When people realized that Rose Gray and Ruth Rogers at the River Café were interested in fresh, unusual, wild produce, they wanted to participate. People started to arrive at their kitchen door with all kinds of offerings. A woman from a local vegetable garden brought them surplus sorrel in the early spring. In April, a friend would pick nettles by the bagful on his farm in Hampshire. Other enthusiasts appeared with sea kale from the south coast beaches. Later in the year their contractor exchanged the huge puffball mushrooms that grew near his house for bottles of Chianti Classico. I rushed over and we had a memorable meal there—no silly frills or flounces, just really delicious food that sang on every plate.

When I came home, I immediately invited Rose and Ruth to the School as guest chefs and they came in July 1990. We had such fun; they loved the herb and vegetable gardens, the greenhouses, and the fresh fish from Ballycotton. They explained how their passion for vegetables and fruit in season has been at the heart of the River Café since they first opened in 1987. Their philosophy echoed our own, hence my eagerness to invite them here. They described how every day outside the kitchen they would pick from their organic garden many varieties of basil, marjoram, and mint, and interesting leaves such as purslane, cicoria, and treviso to use in their recipes. The recipes they taught at the School were heavily influenced by their love of Italy, their many visits over the years and their growing appreciation of the glorious variety of Italian food. These were not complicated recipes, and their message was simple: good cooking is about fresh seasonal ingredients, organic wherever possible, used thoughtfully. It is something the Italians and all good cooks have always known. Rose and Ruth suggested to the students that if you have a garden you should experiment with growing your own. If not, try farmers' markets, pick-your-own farms, and CSA plans. But, above all, develop a relationship with your grocer, urging him to supply interesting varieties.

Ruth's husband Richard Rogers, the acclaimed architect of the Pompidou Center in Paris, Lloyd's of London Headquarters, and the Millennium Dome, also came and mused over our miscellaneous barn conversions. Later that year I was able to spend a couple of days in the kitchens of the River Café and many of our students,

including well-known chefs Stevie Parle, Thomasina Miers, Jordan Bourke, and Gillian Hegarty (now joint head chef at Ballymaloe after being a teacher here for many years) have gone on to work there. We have always had an empathy with their philosophy and are deeply grateful to both Rose and Ruth for their inspiration.

Rose Blossom Panna Cotta with Crystallized Rose Petals

~≈⊱⊰≈~

Rose blossom water varies incredibly, so you may need to add a little more or less depending on strength. We also make a buttermilk panna cotta from our own buttermilk, which is less rich but equally delicious.

Lightly brush 6–8 x 3–4oz molds with the unscented oil, such as sunflower or peanut.

To make the panna cotta, put the cream into a heavy-bottomed saucepan with the vanilla pod and superfine sugar. Set over low heat and bring to the "shivery" stage. Meanwhile, "sponge" the gelatin: put the water in a bowl, sprinkle in the powdered gelatin, and set the bowl over a pan of simmering water until the gelatin has dissolved completely and turned transparent. Remove the vanilla pod from the cream. Add a little of the cream to the gelatin, mixing well, and then stir both mixtures together. Add the rose water and rose syrup, stir, and pour into the molds. Set aside to cool, and then cover the panna cottas with plastic wrap, and transfer them to the fridge to set, preferably overnight.

Meanwhile, make the crystallized rose petals. Break up the egg white slightly in a little bowl with a fork. Using a small paintbrush, paint the egg white very carefully over each petal and into every crevice. Pour the superfine sugar over the petals with a teaspoon. Arrange the crystallized petals carefully on parchment paper so that they retain a good shape. Leave to dry overnight in a warm, dry place. When properly crystallized, the rose petals will last for months, even years, provided they are kept dry. We store them in a pottery jar or a tin box.

To serve, turn out each rose blossom panna cotta onto a chilled serving plate. Garnish with crystallized rose petals and a few fresh raspberries, if available.

Serves 6–8

unscented oil such as sunflower or peanut, for brushing the molds

For the Panna Cotta
2½ cups heavy cream
1 vanilla pod, split lengthwise
¼ cup superfine sugar
2 tablespoons water
scant 2 teaspoons powdered gelatin
1 teaspoon rose water
1½ teaspoons rose syrup

For the Crystallized Rose Petals
organic egg white
rose petals (use the petals from fragrant roses)
superfine sugar—this must be completely dry (if necessary, spread it over a baking sheet and dry out in a low oven at 300°F for 30 minutes)

To garnish
fresh raspberries (optional)

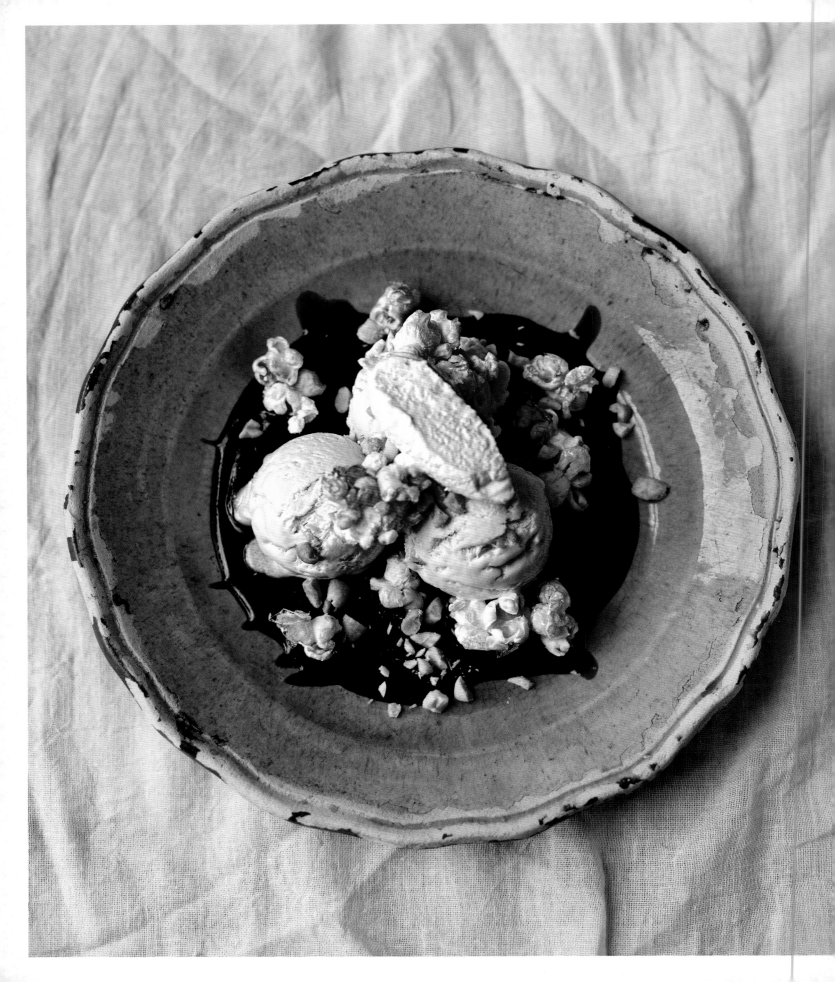

Caramel Ice Cream with Salted Peanuts, Caramel Popcorn, and Dark Chocolate Sauce

It's a bit of a mission to get all the elements together for this dessert, but the end result is so decadent that it is definitely worth the effort. This recipe, made using an Italian egg mousse base, is particularly good for home cooks because there's no need for an ice-cream maker since you just fold the cream into the basic mousse and pop it into the freezer. It's inspired by a dessert I enjoyed at ABC Restaurant in New York.

First make the ice cream. Put the egg yolks into a mixing bowl and whisk until light and fluffy (keep the whites for meringues). Combine the sugar and cold water in a small, heavy-bottomed saucepan. Stir over low heat until the sugar has completely dissolved, and then remove the spoon and boil until the syrup caramelizes to a chestnut brown. Quickly pour in the hot water. Do not stir. Boil gently until the caramel thickens to a smooth, thick syrup and reaches the "thread" stage: 223–236°F. It should look thick and syrupy when a spoon is dipped in. Pour this boiling syrup onto the egg yolks. Add the vanilla extract and whisk until the mixture forms a thick, creamy mousse. Fold the softly whipped cream into the mousse, pour into a bowl, cover, and freeze.

Meanwhile, make the caramel popcorn. Combine the sugar and cold water in a small heavy-bottomed saucepan. Stir over low heat until the sugar has completely dissolved, and then remove the spoon and boil until the syrup caramelizes to a chestnut brown. Spread out the popcorn on a silicone mat or oiled pan and drizzle the hot caramel over. Set aside to cool and harden.

To make the chocolate sauce, put the cream in a heavy-bottomed, preferably stainless steel saucepan and bring it almost to a boil. Remove from the heat and add the chopped chocolate. With a wooden spoon, stir the chocolate into the cream until it has completely melted. Add a little vanilla extract (or coffee or rum) to taste.

To serve, choose wide, shallow serving bowls. Pour approx. 3 tablespoons of hot chocolate sauce into the base of each bowl. Arrange three balls of Caramel Ice Cream on top, then sprinkle a couple of tablespoons of peanuts and some caramel popcorn around the base and some extra popcorn over the top. Shape a little ball of whipped cream and put it in the center to serve.

Serves 6–8

For the Caramel Ice Cream
2 organic egg yolks
¼ cup granulated sugar
½ cup cold water
½ cup hot water
½ teaspoon pure vanilla extract
2½ cups softly whipped cream

For the Caramel Popcorn
1 cup granulated sugar
½ cup cold water
oil, for greasing (optional)
8 cups popcorn

For the Dark Chocolate Sauce
1 cup heavy cream
8oz best-quality dark chocolate
a little pure vanilla extract (or coffee or dark rum)

To serve
¾ cup salted peanuts, lightly crushed
softly whipped cream, lightly sweetened with confectioners' sugar
  and flavored with a few drops of pure vanilla extract

Homemade ice cream has always been a feature of the dessert cart at Ballymaloe House.

Foraging

As children growing up in the country village of Cullohill, County Laois, in the Irish midlands, we were always foraging, except we didn't call it that. The year was punctuated by foraging expeditions. In early spring we went down the lane to the Chapel Meadows to pick wild watercress from the stream. We'd bring it home and have "salad" for an early supper. This consisted of hard-boiled eggs, tomatoes, scallions, watercress, and Chef Salad Cream. Later in the season, we picked cowslips, fresh nettle tops, primroses, wild garlic, elderflowers, and wood sorrel.

When I came to Ballymaloe in 1968, Myrtle made "butterfly sandwiches" for the children with the freshly picked watercress. In the autumn there was an abundance of berries, nuts, and fruit, including damsons, sloes, hazelnuts, elderberries, rose hips, and rowanberries. All these became part of the bounty of the year and were incorporated into jams, jellies, and miscellaneous dishes, and featured on the menu at Ballymaloe House.

On Fraughan Sunday, around the ancient Celtic festival of Lughnasa, we went on a fraughan-picking expedition up Cullohill Mountain. The tiny tart berries (also known as bilberries) were mashed and eaten with cream or piled onto a sponge cake. Served

with carrageen moss pudding, they were also part of our wedding feast at Ballymaloe House. So collecting wild foods was an integral part of our lives and something we very much took for granted.

In 1991 I traveled to Vancouver to attend and speak at the IACP (International Association of Culinary Professionals) Conference. The theme that year was "Pacific Encounters: West meets East." It was a revelation—I met Ron Zimmerman of The Herbfarm in Washington, and Dr. Sinclair Philip, whose menu at Sooke Harbour House was composed entirely of wild and foraged ingredients, organic local greens, edible flowers, and shellfish. I realized then that in the US there was a huge revival of interest in wild food, and that what we'd been doing all those years both at home and at Ballymaloe had a much cooler name—foraging. Not only that, but it was now very trendy, and top restaurants were incorporating wild foods into their menus. In the US, restaurants from coast to coast were employing foragers, full- or part-time, to gather wild foods to use in their dishes. I suddenly realized that the innate knowledge I had gleaned from my childhood forays was of immense value and should be passed on—so I thought it would be fun to incorporate foraging into the Cookery School schedule.

The Mushroom Hunt, which we ran from October 1993 (originally with Roger and Olivia Goodwillie from Lavistown in County Kilkenny), was the first in a whole series of Forgotten Skills courses. Some wild foods are very easy to recognize but with others, like wild mushrooms, one needs to more cautious, as some edible varieties are similar to poisonous species. It is prudent to go on a couple of guided mushroom hunts with skilled and knowledgeable botanists before you go mushroom hunting yourself. If in doubt, act with caution until you've got a trained botanist (or forager) to identify the species for you.

From late summer into autumn, one of our local foragers, Melissa Odendahl, regularly brings baskets of wild mushrooms to the School, starting with chanterelles or girolles (*Cantharellus cibarius*) in August followed by cauliflower mushrooms and porcini (*Sparassis* and *Boletus edulis*) and later yellow legs (*Cantharellus tubaeformis*). The students really love to learn how to recognize and cook these mushrooms. Wild fungi have disappeared from many intensive farms, but because the farm here at the School is organic we occasionally find field mushrooms on the lawn and on the path up to the Shell House when the weather is warm and moist in early autumn. Mushrooms invariably come up in the same place every year. But they can also be very erratic, depending on the weather. We often have a couple of giant puffballs (*Calvatia gigantea*) on the lawn which we enjoy in bread crumbs or in a stir-fry—that's if we

can get to them before my grandson Jasper decides to kick them into smithereens! A couple of shaggy parasols also pop up every year on the edge of the lane close to the back gate lodge in early October—they, too, are delicious while still young and are easy for the students to identify.

In September 1996 we ran our first foraging course: A Walk on the Wild Side with Darina Allen. The walk takes place around the farm and gardens and even in the greenhouses where wood sorrel (*Oxalis*) and bittercress (*Cardamine hirsuta*) flourish in the damp atmosphere. I begin the day's foraging literally outside the Cookery School door to emphasize to participants that there are edible wild plants everywhere around us during every month of the year, even in the depths of winter. It's an endless voyage of discovery. Just last year I discovered, in New York of all places, that the peeled stalks of the dreaded Japanese knotweed (*Fallopia japonica*) are delicious to eat. At Noma in Copenhagen I ate Iceland moss

Left: A selection of wild mushrooms foraged by our local mushroom expert, Melissa Odendahl. Over the last decade there has been a revival of interest in the wealth of wild mushrooms available. It is best to go on a guided walk with an expert to gain confidence because there are several varieties that look similar, but some can be toxic.
Above: Collecting sea urchins from the rock pools on the island of Inishmaan off the west coast of Ireland.

Above: A Walk on the Wild Side with Darina Allen. We now run this one-day course several times a year, and the numbers of participants continue to grow.

(*Cetraria islandica*) and several other wild foods, which I had never encountered before. When I returned home I searched around us here and found many, including sea (or shoreline) purslane (*Sesuvium portulacastrum*), beach mustard, and marsh samphire, also known as common glasswort (*Salicornia europaea*), some on our own land close to the seashore.

The reaction to our foraging courses is fascinating—people are really excited to discover that so many of the "weeds" around them are not only edible but delicious. There seems to be a real, almost primeval, excitement as people reconnect with their inner hunter/ gatherer. For many it's a life-changing experience, and going for a walk in the country or the park or by the seashore will never be the same again; where hitherto they saw weeds, now they see dinner—sea spinach soup, forager's salad, crystallized primroses, nettle pasta. From a nutritional point of view, there's a very convincing argument for incorporating wild foods into our diet. Unlike intensively produced and processed foods, they still have their full complement of vitamins, minerals, and trace elements, many of which are lacking in our modern diet and which can be accessed free in the wild when we know how to recognize and gather nature's bounty.

Foraging has also become an integral part of our 12-week certificate course. Wild and foraged foods are incorporated into the menus on a weekly basis, and the students are encouraged to learn about wild food, greens, plants, flowers, nuts, and berries, both on the land and by the seashore. The students have the opportunity to learn where and how to pick wild watercress and to distinguish between this and fool's watercress (*Apium nodiflorum*), which always grow side by side in the river. It's been a long tradition on each 12-week course to take the students down to the coast to show them how to gather periwinkles from the rock pools at low tide. We teach them how to tell the difference between periwinkles and the similar sea snail, which the locals call the "horse perry." The latter is easy to recognize due to its mother of pearl interior. Older people caution against eating it even though no one seems to be quite sure why. I have deep respect and pay attention to these *piseógs* of older people. Sometimes they are just superstitions, but it's better to be safe than sorry, so I tend to act on the precautionary principle until proven otherwise.

Slow Food has taken me to many remote places around the globe in search of ancient cultures and indigenous foods. On one memorable occasion I found myself in Sápmi (Samiland) in northern Sweden—the land of the midnight sun. Since time immemorial an indigenous race called the Sami (the reindeer people) have lived in an area called Sápmi that extends across four countries from the Kola Peninsula in Russia to northern Finland, Norway, and Sweden. Like all indigenous tribes they live in harmony with nature, including foraging with the seasons to survive.

Their diet consists of a lot of reindeer and elk meat, fresh, dried, salted, and smoked. In summer, they eat more fish and vegetables, in late summer and autumn a variety of berries, wild mushrooms, and fruit. Lingonberries and other wild berries are used for sauces, preserves, and desserts. One evening we had cloudberry jam with waffles and cream. Cloudberries look like yellow raspberries and grow in mossy areas and across the tundra. We also ate wild mushrooms in many guises: morels and delicious chanterelles in soup and little quiches and as a sauce with reindeer and arctic char—a pink fish with pale flesh not unlike trout. The wild mushrooms are dried during the season and are much loved.

Sami are expert at preserving their foraged finds—in the past their very survival depended on it. Originally they stored food in underground water holes, but now freezers are more common. In early spring they eat the young shoots of rowan and beech and make a soup from spruce leaves and a syrup from the needles. Angelica grows wild; the young stalks are peeled and eaten raw as a vegetable or candied as a sweet. They also pick buckets of wild sorrel in early summer and cook it in a little water until it wilts. Then it can be stored for months. The Sami women explained to me that the children love to eat bilberry flowers in early June. When I walked up the hill, I nibbled some; they tasted of sweet honey. As with many indigenous communities, they know the medicinal value of each plant and food.

Foraged foods are always fresh, always in season, and, better still, free, once you have the ability to recognize them. Most years almost all of this free bounty is left to rot because people don't know what to look for. In autumn I encourage people to organize blackberry picking expeditions because, whether you live in the city, town, or in the country, you won't have to travel far to find brambles laden with this prolific wild fruit. In recent years it's wonderful to see that foraging has virtually become mainstream. The Nordic food revolution, which started in Copenhagen with chefs like René Redzepi at Noma, has recently reinvigorated the trend and inspired others to celebrate the wild and foraged food of their local area and incorporate it into their menus. I ate a truly memorable meal in Noma in 2012 and was thrilled to see that René had my *Forgotten Skills of Cooking* book in his kitchen library!

Wild Things

Inside the door of the School, there's a blackboard where the gardeners write up what vegetables, fruit, and herbs from the farm are on the menu that day. Occasionally we have our own pork and beef as well. Even in winter the blackboard is full; in summer and early autumn it overflows onto several boards. Now that foraged foods have become a part of almost every day, we have recently added a Wild Things board to highlight the seasonal wild foods that grow in the fields, hedgerows and woods around us. Today, in February, we have wild watercress, bittercress, pennywort, wild sorrel, and Alexanders.

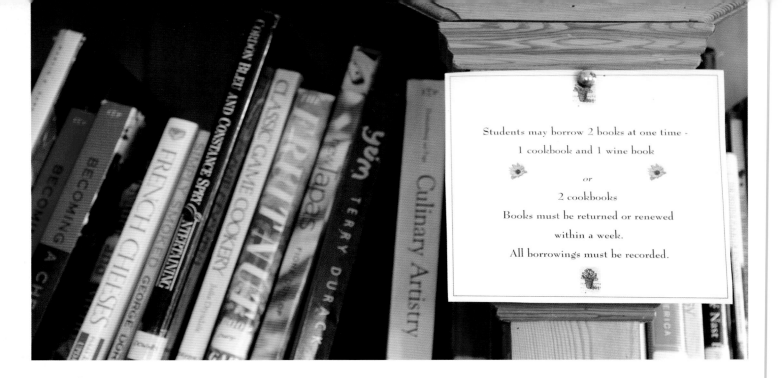

Students may borrow 2 books at one time -
1 cookbook and 1 wine book

or

2 cookbooks

Books must be returned or renewed
within a week.

All borrowings must be recorded.

The Ballymaloe Cookery School Library

The first cookbook library was situated under the roof beside my PA Rosalie's office, in the playroom where the original Cookery School started. There were about 20 books including Jane Grigson's *Good Things*; *The Conran Cookbook* by Terence Conran, Caroline Conran, and Simon Hopkinson; Margaret Costa's *Four Seasons Cookery Book*; Katie Stewart's *The Times Cookery Book*; *Mastering the Art of French Cooking* Vols. 1 and 2 by Julia Child, Louisette Bertholle, and Simone Beck; Marcella Hazan's *The Classic Italian Cookbook*; Jacques Pépin's *The Art of Cooking*, volumes 1 and 2 and *La Methode*; Harold McGee's *On Food and Cooking*; and then of course there was Roger Vergé's *Cuisine of the Sun* and *Cuisine Minceur* by Michel Guérard, the bibles of nouvelle cuisine, which we pored over in the 1970s and early 1980s.

In 1991 an English couple, Stephen Massil and Brenda Goldstein, enrolled on several cooking courses. After they left I got a letter; they had seen our little fledgling library and realized that we could do with a bit of guidance. They offered to catalogue it and put in a system; we gratefully accepted the offer and bartered a few cooking courses. We later discovered that Stephen was the keeper of the library at the Sir John Soane's Museum in London.

The library space has increased many times throughout the years, and we are once more bursting at the seams. Our latest library is beautiful—it stretches all along one wall of the upstairs office, in what was the apple barn. We started to convert it when we moved into the new School in 1989. The slightly classical shelves were made in 1990 by our local carpenter, Noel Barry. My collection of cookbooks has grown exponentially over the years and is now in excess of 2,000 tomes, with many treasures including *Honey from a Weed* by Patience Gray; Elizabeth David's *French Provincial Cooking* and *An Omelette and a Glass of Wine*; *The Way to Cook* by Julia Child; *Wild Food* and *Mushrooms* by Roger Phillips; Alan Davidson's *North Atlantic Seafood*; *First Catch Your Hare* by Hannah Glasse, and *Larousse Gastronomique*.

Whenever I travel to New York I pop into Kitchen Arts & Letters to check out the latest interesting cookbooks and invariably either carry or send a stack of the most exciting and topical volumes home. I always enjoy chatting to the sometimes grumpy owner, Nach Waxman, with whom I had a funny first encounter. On my first visit in 1990 I made a pilgrimage to the shop. Having walked for numerous blocks I eventually found it. It was firmly shut, but when I peered through the door I saw a gentleman working inside, so I knocked. He looked up and gestured for me to go away. I tried again and got the same response, but this time he was even more impatient. Eventually, he stormed toward the door and told me in no uncertain terms to go away; he was closed and busily trying to catch up on his work. I explained that I had come all the way from Ireland and asked if I could come in for a few minutes. He looked at me grumpily and said, "From Ireland, I don't suppose you can tell me how to get hold of that Ballymaloe girl's book I keep getting asked for?" To that I replied somewhat shyly, "I am Darina Allen!" "Well, in that case come in!"

The library is a brilliant resource for the students. Apart from cookbooks, there's a whole section of wine books and another on food issues alongside hundreds of food magazines, including copies of *Gourmet* from the 1980s. Taking pride of place are the cookbooks written by past students, now numbering over 40, which include:

Rachel Allen *Rachel's Favorite Food*; *Rachel's Favorite Food for Friends*; *Rachel's Favorite Food at Home*; *Rachel's Food for Living*; *Bake*; *Home Cooking*; *Entertaining at Home*; *Easy Meals*; *Cake*; *Rachel's Irish Family Food*; *Rachel's Everyday Kitchen*

Hugo Arnold with Leylie Hayes *Avoca Café Cookbook* and *Avoca Café Cookbook 2*

Gillian Berwick *Making Your Own Chocolates*

Jordan and Jessica Bourke *The Guilt-free Gourmet*

Prue Browne *Commonsense Catering*

Jez Felwick *The Bowler's Meatball Cookbook*

Catherine Fulvio *Eat Like an Italian*; *Catherine's Family Kitchen*; *Catherine's Italian Kitchen*; *The Weekend Chef*

Tiffany Goodall *From Pasta to Pancakes: The Ultimate Student Cookbook*; *First Flat Cookbook*

Emma Hannigan has written several novels:—*Designer Genes*; *Miss Conceived*; *The Pink Ladies Club*; *Keeping Mum*; *Driving Home for Christmas*; *Perfect Wives*—and her memoir called *Talk to the Headscarf*.

Lilly Higgins *Make, Bake, Love*; *Lilly's Dream Deli*

Rosemary Kearney with Darina Allen, *Healthy Gluten-free Eating*

Clodagh McKenna *The Irish Farmers' Market Cookbook*; *Fresh from the Sea*; *Homemade*; *Clodagh's Kitchen Diaries*

Thomasina Miers *Cook*; *The Wild Gourmets*; *Mexican Food Made Simple*; *Wahaca—Mexican Food at Home*

Sophie Morris *Sophie Kooks*

Ann Mulligan *The Irish B&B Cookbook*

Stevie Parle *My Kitchen: Real Food from Near and Far*; *Dock Kitchen Cookbook*; *Spice Trip*

James Ramsden *Small Adventures in Cooking*; *Do-Ahead Dinners*

Sam Stern *Cooking up a Storm*; *Real Food Real Fast*; *Get Cooking*; *Sam Stern's Student Cookbook*; *Sam Stern's Eat Vegetarian*; *Virgin to Veteran*

Maureen Tatlow *Back to Basics*

Eleanor Walsh and Michael Durkin *Eden Cookbook*

Barbecue Course

Our first one-day barbecue course ran in 1991—it was a huge success and so over-subscribed that we decided to run two the following year and have continued to do so every year since. We wanted to encourage people to widen their repertoire and produce something more exciting for what at that time was an occasional al fresco meal. The course explained the importance of good sauces and marinades and the unexpected thrills of the charcoal grill.

Over the years we've gone from teaching the absolute basics of how to light a barbecue and cook chicken breasts, sausages, and steaks to tackling just about anything on the grill. In 2001 we explored American regional grilling and barbecuing. This is not my particular area of expertise so I invited Elizabeth Karmel, who grew up in North Carolina and was raised on barbecues, to the School. To say that she has a passion for barbecue and grill is an understatement. She plays with fire virtually every day and cooks on a barbecue spring, summer, autumn, and winter—everything from hamburgers to suckling pig.

Since our first barbecue course people have become hugely skilled and adventurous. Where Irish barbecues were traditionally carnivorous affairs, with perhaps the odd green salad, now the menu can be far more sophisticated with multiethnic flavors and accompaniments. We encourage people to incorporate Mexican, Middle Eastern, Thai, and Indonesian flavors into their barbecuing. Those who own a Weber-style barbecue can attempt larger cuts of meat: duck, chicken, guinea fowl, even a turkey.

Once one grasps the simple principle and technique of grilling, the possibilities are endless. We love to have a vegetarian barbecue for a change, with delicious grilled vegetables, melted cheese parcels, bean, grain and lentil salads, freshly picked corn in the husk—not even the carnivores miss the meat.

Wild Garlic Custards

❧✦❧

This recipe comes from my brother Rory O'Connell. During the 5–6 weeks when wild garlic is in season, it is woven in and out of the menu at the School every day. There are two types of wild garlic: the wider-leafed *Allium ursinum*, which grows in shady places along the banks of streams and in undisturbed mossy woodland; and *Allium triquetrum*, with long thin leaves, which grows alongside roadsides and country lanes. The latter is also known as the three-cornered leek or snowbell because it resembles white bluebells.

Serves 8

melted butter, for greasing
1 cup heavy cream
1 cup milk
4 organic egg yolks
1 cup Parmesan or Coolea cheese, finely grated
sea salt and freshly ground black pepper
pinch of cayenne pepper
3 tablespoons finely chopped wild garlic

To serve
wild garlic flowers, to decorate (optional)
fingers of plain toast or triangles of Melba toast

Preheat the oven to 300°F and brush the inside of eight deep ovenproof cups or ramekins (approx. 3oz)—we use deep shot glasses—with melted butter.

In a mixing bowl, whisk the cream and milk with the egg yolks and the finely grated cheese. Season with salt, freshly ground pepper, and a pinch of cayenne pepper. Whisk again. Add the wild garlic to the custard at the last minute and immediately pour into the cups or ramekins.

Fill a roasting pan with hot water and put in the cups; the water should come about two-thirds of the way up the sides. Cover the tops with a sheet of parchment paper. Depending on the depth of the cups, bake for 30–45 minutes in the preheated oven or until the mixture has just set. A skewer inserted into the center should come out clean when they are ready.

Serve decorated with some wild garlic flowers, if using, and a few fingers of plain toast or triangles of Melba toast.

Buffalo Mozzarella with Spruce Syrup
and Wild Bitter Greens

This Noma-inspired salad uses spruce syrup, which was a revelation when I tasted it there. It initially took some courage for me to try the spruce tips off the trees around Ballymaloe, but they are delicious and tender and taste very much like spruce smells.

Serves 4

4 handfuls of wild bitter greens, e.g. wood sorrel, watercress, bittercress, dandelion, pennywort, etc.
extra virgin olive oil
sea salt and freshly ground black pepper
2 balls of fresh buffalo mozzarella (we use Toons Bridge)
2 tablespoons Spruce Syrup (see right)

To serve
crusty white bread

Toss the greens in the extra virgin olive oil, and season with sea salt and pepper. Strew on a plate, top with torn mozzarella, and drizzle with the spruce syrup. Serve with crusty white bread.

Spruce Syrup

We collect the spruce tips in April while they are soft and green. Any leftover syrup can be stored in the fridge for 1–2 months. Serve with cream cheese or soft goat cheese.

Makes 1¼ cups

3–4oz fresh spruce tips
⅔ cup cold water
1 cup granulated sugar
freshly squeezed juice of 1 lemon
pinch of salt

Chop the spruce tips in a food processor. Transfer to a saucepan with the cold water and sugar. Bring to a boil and simmer for 1 minute. Set aside to cool.

Strain the syrup through a sieve lined with cheesecloth into a clean pitcher, discarding the solids. Stir in the freshly squeezed lemon juice, and season with a pinch of salt. Store in a sealed jar in the fridge until needed.

Dandelion Flower Fritters

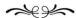

We use blanched dandelion leaves in salads, but the students also love these flower fritters. We cook elderflowers and cowslips in the same way. I suppose everything tastes good tossed in Madagascar vanilla sugar!

Serves 4–5

For the batter
¾ cup all-purpose flour
pinch of salt
1 organic egg
½ cup lukewarm water

sunflower oil, for frying
24–30 fully open dandelion flowers
vanilla sugar, for sprinkling

First make the batter. Sift the flour and salt into a bowl. Make a well in the center, and break in the egg. Using a whisk, bring in the flour gradually from the edges, slowly adding the water at the same time.

Preheat the oil in a deep-fat fryer to 350°F or use a shallow pan with at least 1in of oil.

Shake the flowers just in case there are any insects hidden inside. Holding each flower by its stem, dip them in the batter (add a little more water or milk if the batter is too thick) and fry in the hot oil a couple at a time until puffed up and crisp—approx. 2 minutes. Drain on paper towels. Toss in vanilla sugar and serve immediately.

Blackberry Vodka

We use many different fruits to add flavor to alcohol and have fun experimenting with different combinations. Sloes, damsons, orange rind, wild garlic, rhubarb, peaches, and apricots are all good options.

Makes 2½ cups

1¼lb blackberries
3 cups granulated sugar
2½ cups vodka or gin
3 sweet geranium leaves (optional)

Put all the ingredients into a sterilized 1 quart jar, and set aside in a cool, dark place to mature for a couple of months, shaking the contents every so often to dissolve the sugar.

Strain after 2–3 months, reserving the booze-sodden blackberries, which can be served with yogurt or panna cotta or in a fruit salad. Return the strained vodka or gin to the bottle and store in a cool, dark place for up to a year, but ideally consume within a couple of months as it gradually loses its freshness and appeal.

Marcella Hazan

" When Darina Allen asked us to come to Ballymaloe, her School in Ireland, we accepted the invitation notwithstanding the discouraging descriptions we had heard of Irish food. To our surprise, the ingredients we found were superb. The seafood—I remember the Dublin Bay prawns (known as scampi in Italy), the turbot, the hake, the monkfish—was equal to the best and freshest we had ever had on the Adriatic. The cheeses, breads, and jams were wonderful. To this day, it is Irish butter that I use in my kitchen. We didn't know any of that, however, before going. What we knew is that we loved Darina, and we were grateful that she had forgiven the hard time she had had one day in Bologna when she had been our student.

In Bologna, it had been one of Victor's responsibilities to accompany the class on its field trips and to maintain strict observance of the schedules we had so laboriously worked out. Our longest trip was the one we made to Parma to observe the entire production cycle of Parmigiano Reggiano cheese, an eight-hundred-year-old process. We had arranged with a dairy to hold back, in the morning, a batch of the milk from which they made the cheese, so that the students could watch it being cooked in copper cauldrons of ancient design. They would then have the opportunity to follow the subsequent steps in the cycle, to see the cylindrical mold that shaped the soft mass of the previous day's cheese, a two-day-old cheese being unmolded, a firm month-old round soaking in its brine bath and a year-old 75lb wheel of Parmigiano aging in the cathedral-like space of the maturation vaults. The class had to be on the bus no later than 8 a.m. to leave for the one-hour drive to Parma where the dairy master was waiting. Victor had announced on the previous evening that the bus would pull out at exactly 8 a.m., whether or not every student was on it.

No one had ever been late for that appointment—except for Darina. Diligent, dependable, respectful Darina. She had been in the lobby on time, but then she had returned to her room to look for her camera. Victor didn't know. When she returned, the bus had left. Poor Darina. She found a taxi to take her to the dairy,

but when she got there, the demonstration was over and the class was gone. She continued by taxi to all the other stops on the tour, always arriving too late. Fortunately, she did make it in time to the restaurant by the Po River where a midday banquet in grand Parma style awaited the class and applause awaited her.

Darina and her husband, Tim, met us at Cork Airport and drove us first to her mother-in-law's inn at Ballymaloe, where we would be staying. When we had checked in, she asked, "Would you like to see the School now?" "Certainly," I said. She drove us to a large property in the country. "It was Tim's farm," she said. The stables had been converted into small but charming, rustic rooms for resident students. Chickens scampered over the grounds. A disused truck had been filled with straw and turned into their roost. We passed by row after row of vegetables. "It's where we grow the produce for our classes," Darina said. We walked to the large main building. As I remember it, the first floor had the students' spacious kitchen, with six or more four-burner stoves; the teachers' room; a well-equipped pantry; an auditorium with closed-circuit TV monitors for lectures and demonstrations; and a beautiful dining veranda with many tables facing a flower garden. The second floor held a splendid library, Darina's office, and the administrative offices.

I had never seen a cooking school like it, and I was both awed and made uneasy by its scale. I had said that the classes I would teach would permit full participation by the students.

"How many people are you expecting?" I asked Darina.

"Sixty."

I thought the English language was tripping me up again. I have difficulty discriminating between the sounds of "sixty" and "sixteen." "Did you say sixteen?" I asked.

"No, sixty, six-zero."

"How can that be? I have never done a full-participation class larger than twelve. You must do something. Return the deposits. Get the class down to no more than fifteen, *fifteen*."

Darina smiled. "There is no way I can do that. Many students are already here. Others are on the way. Some are coming from as far as Australia and South Africa. And everyone is so excited by your being here. It will be all right, you'll see."

Victor smiled too. "*Non fasciarti la testa,*" he said, alluding to the family proverb about not bandaging your head before it is broken. "I'll give you a hand."

And he did. I see him still, on the day we made risotto. All the stoves were going, and Victor was flying from pot to pot, making sure that everyone was stirring correctly and that when they ladled in the broth, it was neither too much or too little. We came up with a new cooking statistic: sixty pairs of hands can make wonderful risotto.

My course was the last of the school year at Ballymaloe. When all the students had left, Darina invited me to join her and her staff for a farewell dinner at an unusual restaurant. The chef opened only when he had a minimum of twelve guaranteed reservations. When fewer than those had booked, they were not confirmed until enough other bookings came in to complete the necessary number. The restaurant was on Hare Island, a stony lump breaking the surface of the Atlantic Ocean. Transportation to it was in an open dinghy. It could give us a feeling, Darina said, of what living on the wild west coast of Ireland could be like.

The day started out with a gray sky that soon produced that steady, light drizzle that the Irish affectionately call "soft rain." It may have been soft, but by the time we reached the shore and the dinghy's landing, it was a very wet and cold rain. Out of the trunks of our cars came blankets and towels, into which we snuggled up to our eyes. I felt like a refugee being driven to the sea. We stepped into the open dinghy, the water on its bottom an inch deep. I could see nothing but water: water above, water below, water ahead. By the time we had been rowed to the shore of what looked as inhabitable as a piece of the moon, I was as wet as I could ever be short of dissolving into a puddle. We made land, but our trek wasn't over. We were on a scraggly path, which we followed until we reached the first white stone house, one of two on Hare Island. There still was water above, but at least we had solid land below. When we eventually came to the house, I went in not knowing what I might find or whether there would be any hope of returning to a less liquid state. It was cheerful inside, warm and cozy. We dropped our soaking blankets and, like puppies released from their bath, shook off as much water as we could. Dry towels appeared, and what was even more effective, whiskey and wine. The dinner—I remember a perfect lamb rack—was comfort and salvation. We ate, we drank, we sang, we were happy. On the way back, the sun came out. **"**

Above (left): Marcella and Victor Hazan shelter from the rain under an umbrella on a visit to Hare (also known as Heir) Island.
Above (right): The intrepid group outside the restaurant on Hare Island. Rachel Allen is on Marcella's right and I can be seen to the right of the group wearing a bright blue sweater and my red glasses.

Marcella Hazan's Penne with Cauliflower, Garlic, and Oil

Marcella explains that: "One of the basic mother sauces for pasta is *aglio e olio*, garlic and oil. From it has spawned a multitudinous breed of sauce where we find most varieties of vegetables. An example is this one, featuring cauliflower. In this family of sauces, additional flavorings such as parsley, hot pepper, and anchovies may be used, although not all need to be present. They are almost invariably *sughi in bianco*, 'white' sauces—that is, without tomato. They are supposed to be served without grated cheese, and that is how I prefer them. But one may do as one pleases, and choose to have either Pecorino or Parmesan cheese, depending upon whether one wants the sauce more or less sharp."

Strip the cauliflower of all its leaves, except for a few of the very tender inner ones. Rinse it in cold water, and cut it in half.

Bring 4–5 quarts of water to a boil in a large saucepan, and then add the cauliflower. Cook until tender but compact—approx. 25–30 minutes. Test it with a fork to know when it's done. Drain and set aside.

Put the oil, garlic, and chopped anchovies into a medium sauté pan. Turn the heat to medium and sauté until the garlic becomes golden brown. Stir occasionally with a wooden spoon, mashing the anchovies.

Add the boiled cauliflower and break it up quickly with a fork, crumbling it into pieces no bigger than a peanut. Turn it thoroughly in the oil, mashing part of it to a pulp.

Add the red pepper flakes and a liberal amount of salt. Increase the heat and cook for a few minutes more, stirring frequently. Then remove from the heat.

Bring 4–5 quarts of water to a boil in a large saucepan and add plenty of salt. As soon as the water returns to a boil, add the pasta. When cooked al dente—tender but firm to the bite—drain the pasta well and transfer it to a warm serving bowl.

Very briefly reheat the cauliflower and pour the contents of the pan over the pasta, tossing thoroughly. Add the chopped parsley, toss again, and serve at once.

Serve 4–6

1 head of cauliflower (approx. 1½lb)
8 tablespoons olive oil
2 large garlic cloves, peeled and finely chopped
6 flat anchovy fillets, chopped
¼ teaspoon red pepper flakes
salt
1lb penne or other pasta shape
2 tablespoons freshly chopped flat-leaf parsley

Cauliflower is an underrated vegetable that deserves to be more widely used. Not many people think of serving it with pasta, but this dish is an example of Marcella's brilliance in combining simple ingredients.

Bistecca alla Fiorentina—Grilled T-Bone Steak, Florentine style

"One of Italy's two prized breeds of cattle for meat—Chianina beef—is native to Tuscany. Its only rival in the country is Piedmont's Razza Piemontese. The latter is the more tender of the two and as sweet as cream, whereas the Tuscan is firmer and tastier. A Chianina grows rapidly to a great size so it is butchered when the steer is a grown calf, *vitellone* in Italian. To Italians who love beef, a T-bone grilled in the Florentine style is the ultimate steak. It owes some of its appeal, of course, to the distinctive flavor of the meat, but as much again can be attributed to the Florentine way of preparing it, which can be applied successfully to a fine, well-hung steak anywhere." Marcella Hazan

Serves 2

1 well-hung T-bone beef steak, 1½in thick—
ask your butcher for Black Angus, Hereford, Shorthorn
or one of the traditional crosses
1 garlic clove, peeled and cut in half (optional)
black peppercorns, coarsely ground or crushed with
a mortar and pestle
extra virgin olive oil
sea salt

Light the barbecue in time so the charcoal will be red and glowing with white ash around the outside. Alternatively, preheat a cast-iron grill pan to very hot.

Rub both sides of the steak with a cut garlic clove (if using) and some ground or crushed peppercorns. Score the fat side. Drizzle with a few drops of extra virgin olive oil. Grill the steak to the degree desired. In Tuscany it is eaten very rare, approx. 5 minutes on one side and 3 minutes on the other. After turning, sprinkle salt on the grilled side. When the other side is done, turn it over and sprinkle with salt.

When the steak is cooked to your taste, transfer it to a warm platter and serve at once on a bed of arugula leaves accompanied by cannellini beans or rustic roast potatoes. To serve, cut the meat off the bone with a serrated knife and cut across the grain into thick slices.

Zabaglione Semifreddo

I don't love warm zabaglione, but when it's frozen into a semifreddo it's completely delicious. The praline can be in sheets or more of a crunchy brittle.

Serves 6

For the praline
⅓ cup unskinned whole almonds
¼ cup granulated sugar
sunflower oil, for greasing (optional)

4 organic egg yolks
½ cup superfine sugar
¼ cup dark rum
¼ cup sweet sherry—we use Harvey's Bristol Cream
1¼ cups heavy cream

First make the praline. Put the almonds together with the sugar into a heavy-bottomed saucepan. Set over low heat until the sugar melts and turns a rich caramel color—do not stir. When this stage is reached, and not before, carefully rotate the pan until the nuts are completely covered with the caramel. When the nuts go "pop," pour the mixture onto a lightly oiled Swiss roll pan or marble slab. Set aside to cool and harden. When the praline is cold, break it into chunky pieces—this can be done by crushing it with a rolling pin or by chopping for a few seconds in a food processor if you want it a little finer.

Now for the zabaglione. Choose a medium saucepan, half fill with water, and bring to a boil. Meanwhile, put the egg yolks into a Pyrex bowl that will fit over the pan. Add the sugar and whisk until the mixture is pale and fluffy. Whisk in the rum and sherry. Sit the bowl over the pan of simmering water and continue to whisk until the mixture has at least doubled in volume. Remove from the heat, sit the bowl in iced water and keep whisking until the mixture is cool.

Whip the cream in a separate bowl and fold it into the cold zabaglione, mixing well. Spoon the mixture into a plastic box or lined loaf pan, or divide among six small stemmed glasses. Cover and freeze until firm, approx. 1½ hours. Serve in the glasses or alternatively on pretty, chilled plates, sprinkled with the crunchy praline brittle.

Myrtle Allen

Myrtle Allen's family came from Cork and her father, Henry Hill, was one of a long line of eminent architects. She never cooked as a child and remembers the cook chasing her out of kitchen. She enrolled at The School of Commerce in Cork but failed the cooking exam; she never even went back to get her results, after the liver and bacon she'd made had been spoiled by someone inadvertently turning up the oven and she fled in tears.

She married Ivan Allen in 1943, and they used to joke that they learned lots about each other on their honeymoon. He discovered that she couldn't cook at all, so on their first night at home upon their return, he showed her how to cook scrambled eggs. Ivan was unquestionably a gourmet (rare in those times). He was also a progressive and nationally known farmer. Being surrounded by wonderful local produce, as well as an appreciative husband to enjoy her efforts, encouraged Myrtle to learn more about cooking. She taught herself, sometimes by trial and error, with the help of cookbooks by authors such as Elizabeth David and Philip Harben.

Thanks to Ivan's reputation, they regularly had groups of farmers visit the farm. On one such occasion, Paddy O'Keeffe, of

the *Irish Farmers Journal*, brought a group, and Myrtle cooked lunch for them. Paddy asked her if she might consider writing a cooking column for other farmers' wives. Myrtle mulled over the idea and agreed. She carefully researched for her weekly column, cooking many versions of every recipe until she was happy. These columns eventually led to *The Ballymaloe Cookbook*, which was originally published by the *Irish Farmers Journal* in 1977.

When their six children left home for boarding school, Myrtle began to think about starting a small restaurant, encouraged by the reaction of her friends when they came to dinner. Myrtle and Ivan had bought Ballymaloe House in 1948, so Ivan suggested they set up a restaurant in their home. This was unheard of in Ireland in the early 1960s—there were no country house hotels. They opened in May 1964, and when the children returned home for the school vacation, excited at the prospect of finding "real" restaurant food waiting for them, they were surprised and somewhat disappointed to find her serving exactly the same kind of food she'd always served to her family. Some of the dishes, such as a delicious chicken liver pâté, are still made at Ballymaloe House today.

Myrtle was also keen to expand her culinary repertoire and visited Le Cordon Bleu in London for a week to learn how to make meringues, soufflés, and parfaits. She later attended L'Ecole des Trois Gourmandes in Paris where she had a lesson with Julia Child and Simone Beck, who taught her how to create chicken terrine and rum baba, and she bought savarin molds and genoise pans to bring home with her. Myrtle was no ordinary farmer's wife and was very unusual in 1960s Ireland; she had her finger on the pulse of the international scene.

Ballymaloe House is out in the country far from any centers of population. After a couple of years, people started saying they wanted to stay the night. Myrtle and Ivan discovered that if they opened ten bedrooms to the public, they would automatically get a liquor licence. Getting a licence was very expensive, and they wanted to sell local spirits such as Irish whiskey and Cork gin. And so Ballymaloe House Hotel was born.

Myrtle and Ivan wanted their visitors to feel as though they were guests of the family. Children were always warmly welcomed: there were special children's meals—always beautiful food that they really loved, but homemade. If Myrtle made french fries, she made them from scratch. People came back time and again, and now those who visited as children are bringing their own children back to Ballymaloe. It is not unusual to have visits from families who have been coming here for three generations.

I first met Myrtle when I came to Ballymaloe in 1968. I had heard of the farmer's wife from County Cork who cooked delicious food with local ingredients and wanted to learn more, so I wrote to her and asked if I come and work for her. Unlike many of my friends who were trying to find jobs in the industry and were dealt with rather formally, being shown to the tradesmen's entrance, I received a friendly handwritten letter inviting me to Ballymaloe. Myrtle told me she had children my age and welcomed me warmly into the kitchens at Ballymaloe House Hotel.

She told me almost the opposite of what I'd learned at hotel school. She taught me to focus on the freshest seasonal ingredients and to cook them simply so they taste delicious and are wholesome and nourishing. Myrtle has a brilliant palate and the confidence to do things simply. Her staff worked with her rather than for her, and she was a strong supporter of small local producers. The farmhouse cheesemakers loved her—she included a cheese course in the price of the menu at Ballymaloe House, and, in line with the rest of the food, all the cheeses were Irish.

When I started the School in 1983, Myrtle taught two days of classes while I taught the remaining three. She was inspiring and patient, always able to get the essence of something across. She felt very strongly that the students needed to learn basic things like how to roast a beautiful free-range chicken, how to make stuffing, how delicious green cabbage could be if it was cooked correctly. She even taught students how to cut a loaf of bread properly—to use the knife in a sawing motion without squashing down the bread. People were used to sliced loaves, and cutting bread properly was a simple skill that was getting lost. Myrtle always encouraged people to season with their fingers rather than with a spoon, because she felt that you were removed from the food with a spoon. This is one of her many wisdoms that I pass on to the students.

As well as starting Euro-toques Ireland, Myrtle taught right into her seventies, and now in her late eighties she still gives inspiring talks and continues to encourage people who share her values, just as she encouraged me.

Above (top): Ballymaloe House.
Above (bottom): Myrtle imparting her jam-making wisdom.
Left: Myrtle and me teaching a cooking class together at the School in the mid-1980s.

Hot Buttered Oysters

These wonderfully curvaceous oyster shells tend to topple over maddeningly on the plate so that the delicious juices escape. In the restaurant at Ballymaloe House we solve this problem by piping a little blob of mashed Duchesse potato on the plate to anchor each shell. We sometimes place some Oyster leaves around the edge of the plate, too.

Serves 4

12 Pacific (Gigas) oysters
2 tablespoons butter
½ teaspoon finely chopped flat-leaf parsley

To serve
4 lemon wedges
4 pieces of hot buttered toast (optional)

Open the oysters and detach completely from their shells. Discard the top shell, but keep the deep shell and reserve the liquid. Put the shells into a low oven (225°F) to heat through. Melt half the butter in a pan until it foams. Toss the oysters in the butter until heated through, approx. 1 minute.

Put a hot oyster into each of the warm shells. Pour the reserved oyster liquid into the pan and bring to a boil, whisking in the remaining butter and the parsley. Spoon the hot juices over the oysters and serve immediately on hot plates accompanied by the lemon wedges.

Alternatively, discard the shells and just serve the oysters on the hot buttered toast. The toast will soak up the juice—simply delicious!

Part of Myrtle's genius is to use ingredients as simply as possible. Customers at Ballymaloe House come repeatedly to eat these delicious oysters when they are in season.

Baked Trout with Spinach Butter Sauce

We can sometimes get lovely, fat, pink trout, about 2 years old, which have a wonderful taste—much better than the smaller ones. This is a horrendously rich-sounding sauce but it tastes delicious and the flavor is sublime.

Serves 4

2 x 2lb whole rainbow trout
sea salt and freshly ground black pepper
2–3 tablespoons butter, plus extra for greasing
2 sprigs of fennel

For the Spinach Butter Sauce
2½ cups (3oz) spinach leaves
½ cup heavy cream
5 tablespoons butter

Preheat the oven to 375°F. Gut the trout and wash well, making sure you remove the line of blood from the inside near the back bone. Dry on paper towels, and season inside and out with salt and freshly ground pepper. Put a pat of butter and a sprig of fennel into the center of each trout. Take a large sheet of foil, smear a little butter in the center, put the trout onto the buttered part, and fold over the edges into a papillote shape. Seal well to ensure that none of the juices can escape. Repeat with the other trout.

Put the two foil parcels on a baking sheet, making sure they are not touching, and bake in the preheated oven for approx. 30 minutes.

Meanwhile, make the sauce. Remove the stalks from the spinach, wash and cook in 2 cups salted boiling water. Cook for 4–5 minutes or until just soft and tender, then drain. Press out every last drop of water and chop finely. Put the cream into a saucepan and simmer on low heat until reduced to about 3 tablespoons or until it is in danger of burning. Then, over very low heat, whisk in the butter bit by bit as though you were making a Hollandaise sauce. Stir in the spinach.

When the fish is cooked, open the parcels—there will be lots of delicious juices, so use some of these to thin out the sauce. Put the two parcels onto a hot serving dish and bring to the table. Skin the fish and lift the juicy pink flesh onto hot plates. Spoon the spinach sauce over the fish and serve immediately.

Ballymaloe Chicken Pie

We make this pie from scratch, so it takes a lot of work, but there are few dishes as comforting and satisfying. It is a good recipe to teach the students, as it covers a range of skills.

Preheat the oven to 350°F.

First make the puff pastry. Sift the flour and salt into a bowl and mix to form a dough with 1–1¼ cups of cold water (depending on the flour) and the lemon juice (if using). Cover with waxed paper or plastic wrap and leave to rest for 30 minutes in the fridge. Then roll the dough into a square approx. ½in thick. If the butter is very hard, then beat it (still in the wrapper) with a rolling pin until pliable but not sticky. Unwrap the butter and shape into a slab approx. ¾in thick. Put in the center of the dough and fold over the edges of the butter to make a neat parcel.

Dust your work surface with flour, then flatten the dough with a rolling pin, and continue to roll out into a rectangle approx. 18in long and 6in wide. Fold into three with the sides as accurately aligned as possible. Seal the edges with a rolling pin. Give the dough a one-quarter turn (90°). It should now be on your work surface as though it was a book with the open ends facing north/south. Roll out again, fold in three, and seal the edges with the rolling pin. Cover with plastic wrap or waxed paper and leave to rest in the fridge for 30 minutes. Repeat the rolling process another two times to give the dough six rolls altogether with a 30-minute rest in the fridge between every two turns. Chill for at least 30 minutes before using.

Put 2in water or chicken stock in a heavy casserole and add the vegetables, peppercorns, and bouquet garni. Lay the chicken on top and cover with a tight-fitting lid. Bring to a boil and then transfer to the oven for 1–2 hours, depending on the size of the bird. Watch that it does not boil dry.

Meanwhile, cook the whole or sliced flat mushrooms in half the butter in a hot pan, and season with salt and freshly ground pepper. Sweat the onions in the remaining butter in a small, covered pot until soft. Cut the cooked bacon into cubes.

Once the chicken is cooked, transfer it from the casserole to a large platter and carve the flesh. Degrease the cooking liquid. Arrange the sliced chicken in layers in 1 large or 6–8 individual ovenproof pie dishes, covering each layer with bacon, onions, mushrooms and peas, if using (no need to cook).

To make the sauce, put 2½ cups of the strained and degreased cooking liquid and the dry white wine into a saucepan and bring to a boil. Whisk in the roux. Cook until thick and smooth. Add the cream and bring to a boil again. Taste and correct the seasoning, then set aside to cool.

Serves 6–8

water or chicken stock
2 large carrots, cut into chunks
2 large onions, quartered (don't bother peeling)
2 celery stalks, cut into small chunks
6 black peppercorns
bouquet garni and a sprig of tarragon
1 large (5–6lb) organic chicken
16 mushrooms, sliced if large
2 tablespoons butter
sea salt and freshly ground black pepper
16 pearl onions, peeled but left whole
1lb slab bacon, cooked
¾ cup peas (frozen are fine), optional
½ cup dry white wine
½ cup roux (¼ cup all-purpose flour stirred into
    4 tablespoons butter over low heat)
1 cup heavy cream
18oz puff pastry
eggwash (1 organic egg beaten, plus 1 tablespoon milk), to glaze

For the puff pastry (Makes approx. 2½lb)
3⅔ cups chilled all-purpose flour, plus extra for dusting
pinch of salt
squeeze of lemon juice (optional)
4 sticks (1lb) butter, firm but pliable

To serve
green salad

To assemble the pie(s), pour the cool sauce over the filling and cover with puff pastry. Decorate the top(s) with any leftover puff pastry. Have fun—we sometimes make funny faces, write messages such as "yummy," "scrummy," or "yippee," or put a fine pastry rooster on top if our guests are not too sensitive! Refrigerate until required. (Note: The pie can be prepared ahead up to this point.)

Preheat the oven to 450°F. Just before cooking, brush the top(s) of the pie(s) with eggwash. Bake in the hot oven for 10 minutes, and then reduce the temperature to 400°F and cook for another 15–20 minutes or until golden brown (the individual pies will take approx. 5 minutes less cooking time). Serve with a good green salad.

Ballymaloe Brown Yeast Bread

This bread, a version of the Doris Grant "no-need-to-knead bread" loaf, has been made in Ballymaloe for over 60 years. It's eaten freshly baked on the day it's made, but is also delicious three or four days later and toasts brilliantly. It's a particularly good bread recipe to introduce students to yeast breadmaking, because there's no kneading involved and only one rising. You don't need any special equipment or conditions to make this bread. If your kitchen is warm enough for you, the bread will rise!

When making Ballymaloe Brown Yeast Bread, remember that yeast is a living organism. In order to grow, it requires warmth, moisture, and nourishment. The yeast feeds on the sugar and produces bubbles of carbon dioxide, which cause the bread to rise. Heat of over 120°F will kill yeast. Have the ingredients and equipment at body temperature. White or brown sugar, honey, corn syrup, or molasses may be used. Each will give a slightly different flavor to the bread. The dough rises more rapidly with 1oz yeast than with ¾oz yeast.

We use a stoneground whole-wheat flour. Different flours produce breads of different textures and flavor. The amount of natural moisture in the flour varies depending on atmospheric conditions. The quantity of water should be altered accordingly. The dough should be just too wet to knead—in fact, it does not require kneading. The main ingredients—whole-wheat flour, molasses, and yeast are highly nutritious.

We usually bake this in a standard loaf pan (as seen on page 27), rather than the shallower loaf pan pictured. You can also make three smaller loaves using 3 x 6in pans. These loaves make an ideal present for anyone living alone as they are the perfect size for one person.

Note: Dried yeast may be used instead of baker's yeast. Follow the same method, but only use half the weight given for fresh yeast. Allow longer to rise. Fast-acting yeast may also be used (follow the instructions on the package).

Makes 1 loaf

EITHER 3¾ cups whole-wheat flour OR 3⅓ cups whole-wheat flour
    PLUS ⅓ cup all-purpose flour OR 3⅓ cups whole-wheat flour
    PLUS ½ cup rye flour
1 teaspoon salt
2 cups water at body temperature
1 scant teaspoon molasses
¾–1oz fresh non-GM yeast
sunflower oil, for greasing
sesame seeds (optional)

Preheat the oven to 450°F. The ingredients should all be at room temperature.

Mix the flour with the salt in a large mixing bowl. Measure out ½ cup of the water in a small bowl or Pyrex pitcher, stir in the molasses, and crumble in the yeast. Set aside in a warm place for 5 minutes to allow the yeast to start to work. Meanwhile, grease a 5 x 8in loaf pan with sunflower oil. Check to see if the yeast is rising: it should have a creamy and slightly frothy appearance on top.

Give the yeast a quick stir and pour it over the flour, along with the remaining water. Mix well to form a loose, wet dough; the mixture should be too wet to knead. Put the mixture into the greased pan. Sprinkle the top with sesame seeds, if using. Transfer the pan to a warm place—somewhere close to the oven or near a radiator perhaps—and cover the top with a clean towel to prevent a skin from forming. Set aside for 10–20 minutes, depending on the temperature of your kitchen, or until the bread rises just to the top of the pan. The bread will continue to rise in the oven; this is called "oven spring." Don't allow the bread to rise beyond the top of the pan before it goes into the oven or it will continue to rise and flow over the top.

Bake the bread in the hot oven for 20 minutes, and then turn the temperature down to 400°F and bake for another 40–50 minutes or until it looks nicely browned and sounds hollow when tapped underneath. We usually remove the bread from the pan about 10 minutes before the end of cooking and put it back into the oven to crisp all around, but if you like a softer crust there's no need to do this. Cool on a wire rack.

Versatile Vegetables

My fourth book and TV series, produced in 1994, was called *Simply Delicious Versatile Vegetables*. At that time in Ireland, we had a deeply ingrained meat-eating culture; people didn't feel they were adequately fed unless the meal contained meat or fish. However, we also had a very strange attitude to fish. Owing to Irish Catholic customs, Friday was considered by many a "fast day"; people abstained from eating meat but were allowed to eat fish, if available. Most of the fish was transported inland by bus or by train and so was often at least a week old by the time it reached its final destination. I remember, in my home village of Cullohill, when the fish arrived on the bus from Dublin on Thursday evening. The choice was limited and generally comprised of whiting, occasionally flounder, and a bright, psychedelic-orange smoked haddock. Understandably, eating fish began to be regarded as a penance rather than a pleasure, until thankfully the Vatican lifted this rule in the 1980s, making "fast day" a voluntary choice rather than an obligation.

Potatoes were, of course, essential to every meal and in fact, up until recently, it was not uncommon to be served potatoes in three ways in a country hotel, without anyone thinking it at all unusual. However, vegetables in general were looked down on as second class citizens, and it was against this background that I made my TV series, with the aim to present them in a new light and move them center stage. I wanted to encourage people to be more adventurous, to expand their horizons beyond cabbage, carrots, and parsnips and the odd turnip, and to get them thinking about growing and eating their own. How times have changed! All this is very trendy nowadays, but it certainly wasn't back then as, particularly in rural Ireland, there was the attitude that if you grew vegetables and potatoes "the neighbors would think that you couldn't afford to buy them"!

At home in Cullohill, my family had always had a vegetable garden, so when Tim and I got married, I was longing to start a little vegetable patch of my own. We were young and enthusiatic and decided to clear a bed at the edge of the orchard close to the woods. We grew an extensive range of vegetables, including many

Left: Zucchini blossom, gold rush and coco elle zucchini, sweet Genovese basil, nasturtium flowers, and parsley, freshly picked to make a salad.
Above: A selection of sweet homegrown peppers from the greenhouses at Ballymaloe: Atris, Marconi rossa and Oro.

varieties of beans, brassicas, root vegetables, beets, leeks, and both globe and Jerusalem artichokes, plus more unusual ingredients such as sea kale and cardoons. My confidence grew and, after a year or two, I persuaded Tim to let me take over the old yard where the hay ricks would have been built in earlier years. By then I had traveled quite a bit and was intrigued by the kitchen gardens of the French potagers. I loved the pictures of gardens I'd seen that combined vegetables and flowers and, though a relatively uncommon concept at the time, I decided that the garden ought to be decorative as well as functional.

Frank Walsh, who originally worked with the Strangmans, later with my father-in-law Ivan Allen, and eventually with us at Kinoith for over 60 years, painstakingly laid the paths of old brick in a herringbone pattern for the vegetable garden. Andy Grierson, a school friend of Tim's and a gifted blacksmith, made many of the garden seats and the metal tripods for the sweet peas and runner beans to scramble up.

The vegetable garden is 50 yards long and 22 yards wide. The main design is a diamond bisected by a cross with boxwood parterres at either end. There's a raised summer beech house at

the west end, which was originally made of trellis but the beech hedge we planted has now grown all over the frame to create a little beech house with a garden seat inside. On the north side there's another trellis-covered seat with a golden hop tumbling over the top and sides. This vegetable garden is our gardener Eileen O'Donovan's pride and joy. The beds are crop-rotated every four years in a complex planting system that ensures no two related vegetables are planted in the same place within a four year cycle. Each plant guzzles a particular set of nutrients from the soil and so keeping them in strict rotation provides strong, healthy plants that can resist disease.

The beds are planted to create a pattern of color, texture, and form. Edible flowers, like marigolds, nasturtiums, love-in-a-mist (*Nigella*), and little violas (we call them Johnny-jump-ups), attract beneficial insects into the garden, which help with pollination. Globe artichokes are planted along the south-facing wall and underplanted with catmint (*Nepeta*). This is an old variety of artichoke, which has been passed from one generation of Myrtle's family to another and came from the garden at St Aubyn's in Monkstown to the walled garden at Ballymaloe House, and then onward to us at Kinoith; it's got a fantastic flavor and a wonderful rich purple color, although sadly we don't know the name. Four clipped mophead bays punctuate the four large vegetable beds and give height to the plan.

Even though the vegetable garden is small, less than half an acre, we grow a huge variety of vegetables and herbs. Many, such as globe and jerusalem artichokes, are heirloom varieties and grown primarily for flavor rather than yield. Several types of beans, including French, broad, and scarlet runner; beets; carrots; parsnips; celeriac; a couple of types of chard; zucchini; Florence fennel; and leeks and the onion family—shallots, salad onions, red onions—all feature. We also grow a few varieties of salad potatoes; Pink Fir Apple and Ratte are my favorites. There's a great variety of pumpkins and squash as well as eggplants. We've been delighted with the success of scorzonera and salsify, certainly not easy to find in the shops. We don't grow brassicas or spinach here because the pigeons kept devouring them despite our watchful wicker scarecrows, and it was too labor-intensive and ugly to keep netting them. We also grow a selection of flowers: marigolds, Echinacea, sunflowers, *Nigella*, poppy, catmint, cornflowers—some for cutting, like sweet peas, others for adding to salads, such as the nasturtiums and violas, and others for companion planting, like *Tagetes*. The soil in the vegetable garden is friable and fertile, the result of years

Left: This variety of artichoke has been passed down the generations of Myrtle's family. Sadly, we have never been able to identify it by name.
Above (left): The herringbone paths in the vegetable garden were painstakingly laid over a period of several months by Frank Walsh, who worked with the Allen family for over 60 years and lived in the courtyard at Kinoith. The Ballymaloe Cookery School gardens are open to the public from Easter to the end of October so visitors can enjoy wandering through the gardens, maze, and greenhouse and do a self-guided farm walk. We also offer a guided tour for pre-booked groups.
Above (right): Globe artichoke growing in the vegetable and herb gardens. This variety has less flavor than its rich purple counterpart, so we often let them go to flower in early August when they look particularly stunning.

of enriching the soil with well-rotted farmyard manure, compost, and seaweed.

However, even though the variety is large, we are restricted for space in the kitchen garden and the quantities of each crop are small. Therefore, in 2007, Tim started to prepare a patch in the field close to the greenhouses to plant long rows of both annual and perennial vegetables. There's an asparagus plot and several rows of sea kale, a big patch of Jerusalem artichokes and rhubarb, plus a couple of rows of strawberries. Leeks, rutabagas, carrots, Brussels sprouts, kohlrabi, and others take their turns at either side of the grass path leading from the wildflower meadow to the greenhouses.

We are acutely aware that the maxim "all good food comes from the good earth" sounds a bit hippyish, but then I am, after all, an aged hippy, and we are passionate about caring for and feeding

the soil that feeds us. Unless we have rich, fertile soil, we won't have good food or clean water. To quote Lady Eve Balfour, founder member of the Soil Association: "Agriculture must be looked upon as one of the health services, in fact the primary health service."

This is a fundamental truth that we try to pass on to the 12-week students who pick the vegetables and see them grow. Throughout the seasons, but particularly in summer, the gardeners arrange a plate of freshly picked raw vegetables—crunchy radishes, pea pods, broad beans, florets of Romanesco, beans, baby carrots—on the hall table, with a sign saying "Help Yourself to Food from the Farm," for the students and visitors to munch on; for most people the taste of freshly picked organic vegetables is a total revelation. In the fall, Eileen O'Donovan, our gardener for the past 25 years, piles the squash and pumpkins along the window ledges so the students can learn to identify the different varieties. I love it when I see them all piled up and feel very blessed to live in the middle of a farm.

The huge Irish wooden salad bowl in the Blue Dining Room is legendary; it was hand-turned from Irish beech by Keith Mosse, the most extraordinary and talented woodturner that Ireland has ever produced. Every day, the students fill it with lettuces, salad leaves, both wild and foraged greens, and edible flowers from the garden and greenhouses. At lunchtime it's tossed with a variety of freshly made dressings, but sometimes just with beautiful cold-pressed extra virgin olive oil and a fine wine vinegar. The students love the salad and many tell me they pine for it when they leave.

We use the School as an indoor classroom and the farm, gardens, greenhouses, and seashore as an outdoor classroom. All around the School on the windowsills, in the hall, conservatories, and garden there are edible plants, several varieties of rose geranium, lemongrass, and chile plants, stevia (a powerful sweetener), wasabi, and various citrus including kumquats, lemons, and satsumas.

We've taught a Vegetarian Course at Ballymaloe virtually every year for the past 30 years. In 1996 we started to classify all the recipes at the Cookery School with symbols, including V for vegetarian and VV for vegan. In 1998 we added a vegetarian option to our daily menus and, in 2011, a Salad of the Day made from the seasonal vegetables, fresh herbs, and salad leaves, often paired with beans and grains. In a further effort to highlight the bounty of the seasons, we have a blackboard just inside the door of the Cookery School where we chalk up the produce from the farm and gardens every day. This emphasizes the "farm to table" experience and gives the gardeners a feeling of pride when they see their work being celebrated and acknowledged.

I love the vegetable dishes that I have tasted in Italy, Morocco, and India, and I long for the day when Ireland values vegetables and beans in the same way. In Thailand and Vietnam, the food uses lots of fresh herbs and vegetables and only a little meat. I don't necessarily want to encourage people to become vegetarian but rather to inspire them to eat less but better-quality meat and to enjoy and value vegetables more—after all, they are unquestionably the most important food group.

Research study after research study reminds us what we already know—that our global consumption of meat is unsustainable—and so I'm hopeful that change is afoot. Meat or fish used to be the star on restaurant plates, with a mere nod to vegetables as a pretty garnish, but this is not so much the case any more. In 2011, Hugh Fearnley-Whittingstall produced a TV series and bestselling book called *River Cottage Veg Every Day!*, encouraging people to see vegetables as healthy, cost-effective, and, above all, delicious. In the US, Dan Barber at Blue Hills at Stone Barns has raised the farm-to-table dining experience to a new high, serving what's best from the farm and gardens on the menu every day, exactly as Myrtle Allen has been doing since she opened a restaurant at Ballymaloe House in 1963.

Veganism is also gaining popularity with many high profile fans, including Brad Pitt, Demi Moore, and Venus and Serena Williams embracing a plant-based diet, initially for health concerns, but also for environmental and ethical reasons. Vegans do not eat dairy, eggs, honey, or anything that originates from animals. Some feel that it is part of a more humane and caring lifestyle, particularly if they have concerns about how poultry and animals are handled in mass-production facilities. Vegan diets are low in cholesterol and saturated fats, so it makes it easier for those who may be at risk of heart disease and circulatory problems to follow a recommended diet.

Bill Clinton, who visited Ballymaloe House in 2012 for the Ireland Fund Dinner, had a legendary appetite for fast food—burgers, steak, fried chicken—but now finds himself the poster boy for veganism after shedding 20 pounds. Vegan cookbooks are now outselling vegetarian cookbooks, and one of my favorite food trucks, Cinnamon Snail in Manhattan, serves vegan food. So watch this space—I reckon it's a global trend.

Left: Sharlene Smit, an intern from Durban, South Africa, with a big bowl of freshly picked salad for lunch at the Garden Café. Right: My daughter Lydia writing the Food from the Farm board, which we update daily to highlight the wealth of fresh produce from the surrounding farm and gardens. In the summer and early autumn we often run out of space to list all the available ingredients on the board.

Brussels Sprouts with Avocado and Pecans

Brussels sprouts have a bad reputation in general but roast Brussels sprouts are very trendy in the US right now—they are certainly an acquired taste, which I have grown to love, although there is a fine line between charred and burnt! However, they're also delicious raw, grated into salads, or the fresh outer leaves used to make soup. This recipe uses the outer leaves to make a wonderful salad (it is difficult to give an exact quantity). Roast pumpkin seeds or hazelnuts would also be good here.

Serves 8

For the dressing
finely grated zest of 1 lemon
2 tablespoons freshly squeezed lemon juice
6 tablespoons extra virgin olive oil
1 teaspoon honey
½ teaspoon Dijon mustard
sea salt and freshly ground black pepper

approx. 2lb Brussels sprouts
1–2 blood oranges (depending on size), peeled
2 avocados, sliced
¼–½ cup pecans, toasted
a large handful of small flat-leaf parsley sprigs

In a small jar or bowl, whisk all the ingredients for the salad dressing together.

Peel the outer leaves of the Brussels sprouts (keep the centers for another dish) and put into a bowl. Segment the blood oranges and also add them to the bowl. Drizzle half the dressing over the salad, tossing gently.

Transfer the salad to a wide platter and arrange the avocados haphazardly on top. Sprinkle with the toasted pecans and plenty of flat-leaf parsley, and drizzle on the rest of the dressing.

Vegetable and Red Lentil Broth

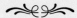

This makes a nice big pot of soup.

Serves 12

1 tablespoon extra virgin olive oil
1lb (4 medium) onions, sliced
3 garlic cloves, peeled and finely chopped
2lb carrots, diced into ½in cubes
1 head of celery (approx. 1lb), diced into ½in cubes (approx 7 cups)
2 tablespoons sweet chile sauce
1 tablespoon Worcestershire sauce
2½ quarts well-flavored vegetable or chicken stock
2½ cups red lentils
sea salt and freshly ground black pepper

Heat the extra virgin olive oil in a large saucepan. Add the onion, garlic, carrot, and celery, and sweat for 10 minutes over low heat.

Add the sweet chile sauce and the Worcestershire sauce and mix well. Cook for another 5 minutes, and then add the vegetable or chicken stock. Bring to a boil and simmer for 10 minutes.

Add the lentils and continue to cook for another 20 minutes or until the vegetables are soft and the lentils have lost their bite. Taste and season. Serve in wide soup bowls.

Pumpkin, Goat Cheese, and Kale Tart

My mother always grew curly kale as a winter vegetable in the kitchen garden behind our house in Cullohill. She would wait for a couple of nights of frost before picking it, as she quite rightly felt that the frost sweetened the taste, turning the starches into sugars as it does for many winter vegetables. She served kale, as many people did at that time, in only a couple of ways—in colcannon or as a green vegetable. We now use it at the School in a huge variety of recipes and dishes from salads, quiches and savory tarts to chips and healthy, energy-boosting drinks.

Serves 8

For the pastry
1½ cups all-purpose, spelt, or whole-wheat flour
pinch of salt
5 tablespoons cold butter
beaten organic egg with a little water, to bind
beaten organic egg white, to glaze

For the filling
1lb pumpkin or butternut squash
1 tablespoon extra virgin olive oil, plus extra for drizzling
sea salt and freshly ground black pepper
2 teaspoons fresh thyme leaves
1½ cups kale, raw and stripped off the stem
 or 3 cups coarsely chopped arugula
¾ cup chopped scallions
2 organic eggs
3 organic egg yolks
1 cup heavy cream
¼ cup grated Parmesan cheese
½ cup grated Gruyère cheese
5oz Ardsallagh goat cheese (or another soft goat
 cheese of your choice)

To serve
green salad

Preheat the oven to 400°F. First make the pastry. Sift the flour and salt into a large bowl. Cut the butter into cubes, toss in the flour, and then rub in with your fingertips. Keep everything as cool as possible; if the fat is allowed to melt, the finished pastry may be tough. When the mixture looks like coarse bread crumbs, stop.

Using a fork to stir, add just enough beaten egg to bring the pastry together. Shape the dough into a ball with your hands—this way, you can judge more accurately if you need a few more drops of egg wash. While rather damp pastry is easier to handle and roll out, the resulting crust can be tough and may well shrink out of shape as the water evaporates in the oven. As a general rule, the drier and more difficult the pastry is to handle, the crisper the crust.

Flatten the pastry into a round, wrap in plastic wrap, and set aside to rest in the fridge for at least 15 minutes. This will make the pastry less elastic and therefore easier to roll.

Meanwhile, peel the pumpkin or squash and cut into 1in chunks. Arrange on a roasting pan and drizzle with extra virgin olive oil. Season with salt and sprinkle over half the thyme leaves. Roast in the preheated oven for approx. 30 minutes or until tender. Set aside to cool.

Bring a large pot of water to a boil, add the kale (if using) and blanch for 2 minutes; drain, and refresh under cold running water. If you are using the arugula, there is no need to blanch it.

Line a 9in tart pan with the pastry and bake blind for about 25 minutes. The base should be almost fully cooked after this time. Remove the parchment paper and beans, brush the base with a little beaten egg white, and return to the oven for another 3–4 minutes. This will seal the base and prevent the "soggy bottom" effect.

Reduce the oven temperature to 350°F. Heat 1 tablespoon oil in a sauté pan, add the scallions, cover with a lid and sweat gently over low heat for approx. 6 minutes or until almost soft.

Meanwhile, whisk the eggs and egg yolks in a medium bowl. Add the cream, Parmesan, Gruyère, remaining thyme leaves, cooled scallions, and kale or arugula. Mix well and season to taste: heat a frying pan, cook a teaspoon of the mixture over low heat for 2–3 minutes until it coagulates, and then taste. Correct the seasoning if necessary.

Add the chunks of cooled roasted pumpkin to the filling and crumble in the goat cheese. Pour the mixture into the pastry shell and bake in the oven for 30–40 minutes or until the center has just set. Serve warm with a freshly tossed green salad.

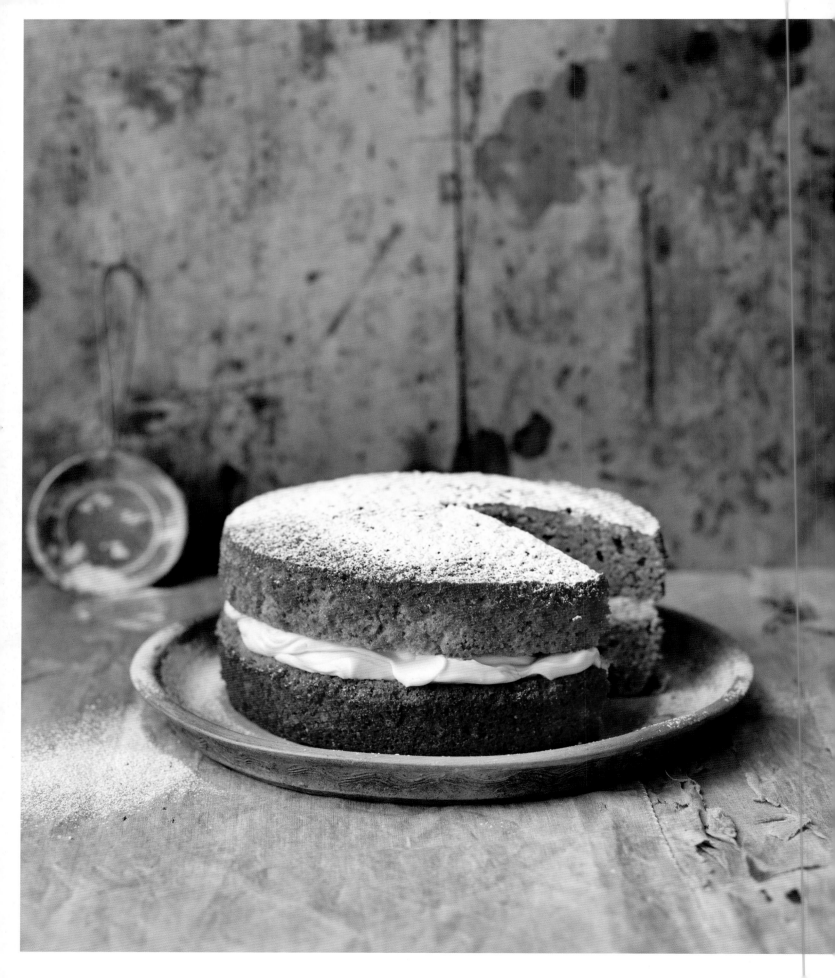

Parsnip and Maple Syrup Cake

Here at the School we subscribe to a variety of food magazines from all over the world. We all love to flick through them—they spark off ideas and occasionally we find a little gem like this recipe for a delicious winter cake, which was inspired by one from *BBC Good Food Magazine*.

Preheat the oven to 350°F. Grease two 8in deep cake pans with a little butter and line the bases with parchment paper.

Melt the butter, sugar, and maple syrup in a pan over low heat. Set aside to cool slightly, and then whisk in the eggs. Sift the flour, baking powder, and pumpkin pie spice into a large mixing bowl. Stir in the butter and sugar mixture and mix carefully. Next add the grated parsnip, apple, pecans or hazelnuts, orange zest, and juice, and combine thoroughly.

Divide the mixture between the two pans and bake in the preheated oven for 35–40 minutes or until the cakes are just starting to shrink from the sides of the tins. Cool on a wire rack.

Just before serving, beat the mascarpone and maple syrup together. Spread over the base of one cake and top with the other. Dust with confectioners' sugar just before serving.

Serves 8

12 tablespoons butter, plus extra for greasing
¾ cup brown sugar
½ cup maple syrup
3 large organic eggs
2 cups self-rising flour
2 teaspoons baking powder
2 teaspoons pumpkin pie spice
2 medium parsnips, peeled and grated
1 medium eating apple, peeled, cored, and grated
½ cup pecans or hazelnuts, roughly chopped
zest and juice of 1 small orange
confectioners' sugar, for dusting

For the filling
1 cup mascarpone
3–4 tablespoons maple syrup

I often wonder which thrifty housewife started using zucchini, beets, celeriac, and other root vegetables in cakes, but it is a more unusual way of cooking vegetables and a useful way to use up a glut, while adding nourishment to something sweet.

Keeping Pigs

In the mid-eighties, when we could no longer buy the sweet, juicy pork I remembered as a child, I decided to get our own pigs. I met a farmer in West Cork while I was filming one of my *Simply Delicious* series and I bought two weanlings from him. They settled in happily but I needed an unrelated boar. Then, as luck would have it, I was walking in the Knockmealdown Mountains in County Tipperary with a few locals and we chatted on and off, as one does on a long walk. I told them about my pigs and one man told me that he also kept a few but was having difficulty selling them in the market because they were black-and-tan Tamworths and so considered "queer looking." I couldn't believe my ears. He had a black Berkshire boar for sale and this was exactly what I needed. We made a deal, shaking hands as we crossed a stream on stepping-stones, and that spot has been known as the Ford of the Black Pig ever since.

We have kept traditional breeds—Saddlebacks, Red Duroc, and Gloucestershire Old Spot for many years and the pork that they produce is completely delicious, sweet, and succulent. Our happy, lazy pigs are born in the fields and live freely all their lives—rooting in the ground and eating organic meal and surplus greens from the gardens and greenhouses. After about 5–6 months they make a short trip to Frank Murphy, our local butcher in Midleton, where they are humanely slaughtered. Frank prepares and splits the carcass and saves everything, from nose to tail, at our request. Many of the students on the 12-week course are delighted to have the opportunity to learn how to butcher (break up) a pig. Being free-range, the pigs have had quite a lot of exercise and developed a fair amount of muscle, so we hang them in a cold-room for a week to 10 days.

We use every single scrap of the animals: the blood is made into puddings, the head into head cheese, in which the ears are sometimes included, or the ears are prepared as crispy pigs' ears. We make lots of sausages, salami, chorizo, and a variety of cured meats, from bacon and hams to dry-cured jamon—a never-ending journey that continues to thrill both us and many of the students.

In 2006, we introduced a course called How to Cure a Pig in a Day and use every single scrap as part of our Forgotten Skills series, and we've noticed how the interest in keeping a few pigs at home has grown phenomenally since then. In general, people are incredibly eager to relearn the skills needed to rear and grow one's own food—the US is witnessing a considerable homestead revival, while in the UK, there's a waiting list for urban gardens in virtually every city and town. Thankfully, there is at least one upside to the downturn in the economy, encouraging us to discover a degree of self-sufficiency and recognize its importance.

In 2008, one of our past students, Ted Berner, started Wild Side Catering and became one of the very first people to bring back the traditional method of roasting pigs and other meat on a spit. It proved to be a great hit, and he is in huge demand for weddings, parties, and music festivals all around Ireland.

Since 2005, visitors to the School and gardens, which have been open to the public since the late 1980s, can enjoy a self-guided farm walk. We've included explanatory signs in strategic places around the farm and gardens to provide information about the animals and plants, breeds, and varieties. There is also a treasure hunt sheet so children can have a treasure hunt around the farm.

Left: A Gloucestershire Old Spot sow with her litter of piglets, which are called "bonhams" in Ireland, snuffling around the muddy fields. Above: A newborn piglet on the farm at Ballymaloe. We have two litters every year, ranging in size from 10–15 piglets.

Above: Our current sow, a cross between the Gloucestershire Old Spot and Saddleback breeds. During the outbreak of hoof-and-mouth disease in 2001, when there was a ban on the movement of animals, our Saddleback boar died. We were looking for another boar to replace him, but were advised to try a cross of Gloucestershire Old Spot and Saddleback, which was believed to produce even better quality meat with a little less fat, so we thought we would try it out and we've been enjoying the results ever since.

Cooking with the Clergy

When I was a child, every parish in Ireland had a priest and every priest had a live-in housekeeper, a woman of "good repute," usually a spinster or widow, who cooked and cleaned and washed and kept house. By the early 1990s, education, women's liberation, and increased opportunities meant that fewer women were prepared to do the housekeeping, so the supply dwindled and many clergy found that when their old housekeeper retired it was impossible to find a replacement. Most priests could scarcely boil water or make toast, so they were unable to fend for themselves and were virtually helpless. After two separate people mentioned that their "brother the priest" was desperate to learn a little bit of simple cooking and that I'd be doing a great service if I offered a course specifically for priests, I did.

In July 1996, we scheduled a two-and-a-half-day hands-on course called A Cookery Course for Clergy and we had eager students enrolling from all over the country. The course itself caused quite a stir and we were inundated with press requests, including those from the *Daily Express* and *Irish Catholic*. There were articles in *Esquire* and the *Guardian*, while several TV channels, including the BBC, wanted to film it. I was very protective of the privacy of my class, however, and it was a special few days for all of us as we taught the priests the basics and helped them to hone their culinary skills.

The first day consisted of two long demonstrations, covering everything from breakfast to dinner, from pinhead oatmeal and scrambled eggs to grilled chicken breast with arugula and tomato salad; simple nutritious whole-wheat bread; purée of onion soup; lamb stew with bacon, onions, and garden herbs; mushrooms à la crème, which they could eat on toast or slather over a steak, and crêpes with orange butter. On the morning of the second day we gave the clergymen the chance to practice what we had preached to them, and then followed this up with further demonstrations. On day three, the fathers honed their new skills. It was all very intensive, with an emphasis on the practical application of the lessons. The underlying idea was to teach some basic dishes and then to show how they may be given infinite variety by changing certain ingredients—how the grilled chicken breast can lose its arugula and tomato salad in favor of mushrooms à la crème, which in turn can be used as a pasta sauce. Father Michael said he had learned a lot from the course—"I didn't know you could cook vegetables in three minutes. I'd say there'll be fewer tins in the garbage can beside the cooker." Others, like Father Patrick, were

happy that they now felt able to cook for friends who would come around after Mass on a Sunday.

By the end of the course everyone knew a mornay from a roux and how to make meals using each. They could use a chopper, skin a fish, and even defrost homemade stock in plastic cartons by putting it in the dishwasher. Some left compiling and comparing lists of cooking equipment they wanted to buy on the way home, while one loaded a starter pack for a fresh herb garden into the trunk of his Volkswagen Golf.

Left: The front of the Cookery School—this welcoming seat and some of our fancy fowl, including a Frizzle Bantam pecking around in the gravel are often the first sights to greet students on arrival.
Above: Matthew Fort's article in the Guardian *about the Cooking with the Clergy course—one of the many pieces of press coverage that the class received.*

The Shell House

Perhaps it was because I was born about as far away from the coast as it's possible to be in Ireland that I have always had a fascination for seashells. As children, an expedition to the beach in Tramore, County Waterford, was the highlight of our summer and I always brought home a little collection of shells in my sand bucket. I'd lay them out on the porch outside our kitchen and long for the sea.

When I moved to Cork in 1968, within sight and sound of the sea, I continued to collect shells on the nearby beaches and dreamed of making a shell grotto, reminiscent of those I'd seen in *Country Living* magazine. As luck would have it, when I was flicking through a copy of *House & Garden* magazine in early summer 1994 I came across an enchanting article about Blott Kerr-Wilson, a shell artist from Wales who was so crazy about shells that she used them to cover the bathroom in the housing project in Peckham in London where she lived at the time. She had won a "design a room" competition in *The World of Interiors* magazine so her phone number was at the end of the article. I telephoned and left a message on her phone asking if she ever came to Ireland and explaining that I'd been collecting shells for years and would love to chat with her about a shell house. I then thought better of my rambling message and finished by saying that if a man answered when she returned the call to hang up!

Blott was obviously intrigued by my long, convoluted message and fortunately I picked up the phone when she returned the call. I asked if she ever came to Ireland. She said she didn't have any plans to but was between jobs and would be delighted to if there were a reason for the visit. I suggested that she try to find a cheap flight and she called back within hours to say she could come the following week. "Wonderful," I thought, "I must tell Tim." However, somehow the right moment didn't present itself and the morning of Blott's arrival, I had to teach so I never had the chance to explain to Tim before he left for the airport. On the way back to Ballymaloe, Blott blurted out all my grandiose plans, much to Tim's astonishment, and yet in such a charming way that Tim was delighted with the idea by the time they returned to the School!

Tim and I had decided to build an octagonal folly at the end of the herbaceous borders. Designed by our friend, the renowned gardener Jim Reynolds, it was to incorporate the gothic windows I'd bought from Edward Byrne's architectural salvage yard in County Carlow and also the thousands of shells I had collected, many from local beaches, others brought home from vacations abroad or sent by friends who knew I loved them. David Hugh-Jones of Rossmore Oysters provided mussel, whelk, and oyster shells. Still more mussel and scallop shells were collected by the chefs at Ballymaloe House and Aherne's Townhouse Seafood Restaurant in Youghal, who kindly saved them after their guests had enjoyed the contents. Blott also sourced lots of exotic shells from Marine Arts in Penzance in Cornwall. On June 1, 1995, our contractor, Will Kenneally, constructed scaffolding inside the octagonal folly and, like Michaelangelo in the Sistine Chapel, Blott started her work, beginning in the apex of the roof.

I tried to communicate to Blott what I had in mind but neither of us can draw and so Blott decided she would just get started and I could decide if I liked her work. If I didn't, we had four hours to change our minds before the tile cement set. However, once Blott started to work, I realized she was so much more creative than I could ever be. The result was completely magical and every panel and window reveal is different. The work took five months and 20,000 shells to complete. Benjamin Krebs, then Blott's boyfriend, now her husband, also helped out and graded and sorted all the pebbles for the floor under a leaky plastic cover—she was surprised he stuck around, because it was such a horrid job! Perdi Fenn then joined Blott to pebble the floor for a few weeks before the end. A stream of water circulates from a little pool in the center and around the outside of the floor on a continual basis.

The initials of my four children—I for Isaac, T for Toby, L for Lydia, and E for Emily—are incorporated into the shell or pebble pattern, as well as 1995, the year of Tim's and my 25th wedding anniversary.

The Shell House was officially opened on October 27, 1995, the date of our 25th wedding anniversary, and it is considered to be a monument to Tim's patience with all my crazy ideas. However, he also loves the Shell House and thinks it is one of the most exciting things that we've created at Kinoith. In 2006, Blott returned to make and install a "shelldolier" as a celebration of our daughter Lydia's wedding in the garden.

The Shell House was my way of recycling shells. To this day, I can't bear to waste shells; after we eat our "Plate of Irish Shellfish" lunch, I encourage the students to keep the shells and use them to decorate picture frames or mirrors or to plan their own shell grotto.

Above: A view to the octagonal Shell House from the herbaceous border, which leads up to it. The roof slates are rounded to resemble fish scales. We also fly a colored pennant from the top for all celebrations and events.
Right: A window in the Shell House.
Far right: A detail of the Shell House with whelks, cockles, periwinkles, and oyster and abalone shells.

Strawberry, Raspberry, Blackberry or Apple Granola

❧

This fruit granola is served for breakfast throughout the year at Ballymaloe and is a dish we've made from the beginning of the School; the fruit varies with the season. It is a recipe that we teach at the start of the 12-week course to encourage students to eat breakfast and we felt it was useful for the clergy to learn, too. It can be made in a matter of minutes and is high GI (glycemic index), which means that it releases energy slowly to help keep you going throughout the day.

Serves 4

3 heaping tablespoons rolled oatmeal (Quaker Oats)
6 tablespoons water
1 cup fresh strawberries, raspberries, blackberries, or
grated sweet apple (such as Orange Pippin, Gala, or Pink Lady)
1 teaspoon honey

Soak the oatmeal in the water for 10–15 minutes. Meanwhile, mash the strawberries roughly with a fork. Stir the fruit into the oatmeal and sweeten to taste with honey—a teaspoon is usually enough, but it depends on how sweet the fruit is.
    Serve with cream and brown sugar.

When buying pork it is important to look for organically reared heritage breeds, such as Gloucestershire Old Spot, Tamworth, Berkshire, Red Waffle, Mulefoot, Duroc...

Pork Belly with Green and Black Olive Tapenade

❧

This recipe is inspired by a dish I ate at Amisfield Winery near Queenstown on the South Island of New Zealand. They sourced high-quality pork from a heritage breed for this dish and, as ever, the resulting texture and flavor was much superior to that of intensively produced pork. There is usually a higher proportion of fat on these old breeds, since they needed it to protect them outside in winter, which results in juicier and more succulent meat.

Serves 6–8

5lb pork belly with skin
Maldon sea salt and freshly ground black pepper
arugula leaves

For the tapenade
¾ cup pitted green olives
¾ cup pitted black olives
2 large garlic cloves, peeled and finely chopped
2 anchovies (preferably Ortiz), mashed
¼ cup extra virgin olive oil, plus extra to serve

Score the pork skin at ¼in intervals. Sprinkle both the rind and the flesh side with salt and set aside for 2–3 hours. Wash and dry well.
    Preheat the oven to 350°F. Put the pork skin-side up on a cutting board and season again with salt and black pepper. Pour ½in water into a roasting pan, put the pork on a wire rack inside the pan, and roast for 25–28 minutes per 1lb. Baste with the rendered pork fat every now and then.
    Meanwhile, make the tapenade. Roughly chop the olives and combine them with the finely chopped garlic, mashed anchovies, and extra virgin olive oil. Mix and taste.
    To serve, cut the pork into 2in squares—allow three pieces per person. Drizzle a little of the chunky tapenade over and around the pork and serve with a sprinkle of sea salt and a drizzle of extra virgin olive oil.

Mother's Sweet White Scones

These scones are my mother's recipe, which I introduced to a wider audience in my first *Simply Delicious* TV series. I thought this would be a useful recipe to teach the clergy in the special course I ran for them, since it is simple and quick, but also makes a large amount, so they could freeze leftovers and reheat them quickly in the oven for visiting parishioners.

When my mother made these for us as children, they were always tender and delicious—but adding a few golden raisins was as adventurous as we got. These days, we teach numerous twists on the original (see right).

Makes 18–20 scones

7¼ cups all-purpose flour
pinch of salt
¼ cup granulated sugar
3 heaping teaspoons baking powder
12 tablespoons butter
3 organic eggs
2 cups milk

To glaze
eggwash, made by whisking 1 organic egg with a pinch of salt
granulated sugar, for the topping

Preheat the oven to 475°F. Sift all the dry ingredients into a large, wide bowl. Cut the butter into cubes, toss in the flour, and rub in with your fingertips until the mixture resembles very coarse bread crumbs—surprisingly, this results in lighter scones. Make a well in the center. Whisk the eggs with the milk in a pitcher. Add to the dry ingredients and mix to a soft dough. Turn onto a floured board. Don't knead but shape just enough to make a round. Roll out to 1in thick and cut or stamp into scones. Stamp out the scones with as little waste as possible; the first scones will be lighter than the second rolling. If you cut them into squares or triangles with a knife or pastry cutter, as my mother did, there is no need to roll again.

Transfer the scones to a baking sheet—there is no need to grease it. Brush the tops with the eggwash and dip each one in granulated sugar. Bake in the hot oven for 10–12 minutes, until golden brown on top. Transfer to a wire rack to cool.

Serve split in half with homemade jam and a dollop of whipped cream, or with just butter and jam.

Variations

Golden Raisin Scones
Add ¾ cup plump golden raisins to the basic mixture after the butter has been rubbed in.

Muscatel Raisin and Rosemary Scones
Add ¾ cup Muscatel raisins and 1 tablespoon of chopped rosemary to the basic mixture after the butter has been rubbed in.

Cherry Scones
Add 1 cup quartered candied or dried cherries to the basic mixture after the butter has been rubbed in.

Crystallized Ginger Scones
Add ½ cup chopped crystallized ginger (or drained and chopped stem ginger) to the basic mixture after the butter has been rubbed in.

Candied Citrus Peel Scones
Add ¾ cup candied orange and lemon peel to the basic mixture after the butter has been rubbed in. Coat the citrus peel well in the flour before adding the liquid to stop it from sticking together.

Sugar and Spice Scones
Add 4 teaspoons of ground cinnamon to the basic mixture with the flour. Instead of dipping the glazed scones in granulated sugar, use 1 teaspoon of ground cinnamon mixed with ¼ cup sugar.

Poppy Seed Scones
Add ¼ cup poppy seeds to the dry ingredients.
Serve with freshly crushed strawberries and whipped cream.

Chocolate Chip Scones
Chop 4oz best-quality chocolate and add to the basic mixture after the butter has been rubbed in.

Strawberry, Raspberry, or Blueberry Scones
Add 1 cup chopped fresh strawberries (or whole raspberries or blueberries) to the basic mixture after the butter has been rubbed in. Increase the sugar by 2 tablespoons.

White Chocolate and Raspberry Scones
Add ¾ cup fresh raspberries and 3oz chopped white chocolate to the basic mixture after the sugar has been rubbed in.

Slow Food

On September 7, 1996, I accepted the SEI (Società Edictrice Nationale) prize for food and wine culture from the Premio Langhe Ceretto in Italy for my book *Irish Traditional Cooking*, and I gave a spirited speech about the effect of EU regulations on our food culture. Ireland became a member of the EU in 1973. By 1996, we were really beginning to experience the effects of the changing food hygiene regulations—suddenly there were new and more stringent regulations in many areas of food production. The cost of complying with these, e.g., upgrading butcher's shops and slaughterhouses, was much more than the producers could afford. This was endangering, and in some cases eliminating, food businesses, such as family butchers, bakeries, cheesemakers, and home bakers. There were many local home bakers who had cooked a few scones, a couple of loaves of soda bread, and maybe an apple tart for the local shops, who found the environmental health officers knocking on their doors asking if they had a license to do so. Of course they didn't, it had never been required before. Most were scared off and stopped. The effect was to eliminate an integral part of our food culture, preventing local people from taking pride and satisfaction in their produce, plus the extra "mad money" they earned from their baking that in virtually every case went back into the local economy, or perhaps bought a new pair of shoes or music lessons for a child.

In my speech, I warned the Italians, who still have such a diverse food culture, to be on their guard lest they allow the tidal wave of new food regulations to eliminate their artisan producers. Italy has only been a united country since 1861, prior to which it was made up of a patchwork of principalities, each with its unique traditions and jealously guarded recipes, so the Italians have hugely important regional specialties that it is vitally important to safeguard.

After my speech—delivered through an interpreter—received a standing ovation, a gentleman literally ran up to me from the audience and asked, "Have you ever heard of Slow Food?" I hadn't, and he said, "You have just been giving a speech that encapsulates the philosophy of Slow Food—you must start Slow Food Ireland."

He was one of the founders of Slow Food International. This organization, which was officially launched in 1986, could be described as the Greenpeace of gastronomy—the antidote to the fast food culture that threatens to engulf us. Slow Food defends biodiversity, encourages and supports artisan food production, and safeguards foods and food cultures in danger of extinction. The movement started as a result of Carlo Petrini's outrage when he encountered the smell of mass-produced French fries wafting from the first McDonald's in Piazza di Spagna in Rome. What started as a single group of disenchanted Italians who were passionate about saving endangered foods, farmhouse cheeses, salamis, and old seed varieties has developed into a vibrant international movement.

After my return to Ireland, Slow Food Italy wrote asking me to set up Slow Food Ireland, but Tim was adamant that I was already overcommitted and must not take on another project. So Giana Ferguson of Gubbeen Cheese launched Slow Food Ireland in the summer of 1998 at a wonderful gathering in Gubbeen, which included the former Irish Taoiseach Garret FitzGerald and legendary artisans such as Bill Hogan, maker of the wonderful Gabriel farmhouse cheese, Sally Barnes who smokes fish, Adele O'Connor from her bakery in Schull, and Toby Simmonds of The Real Olive Company. Renato Sardo from the Slow Food office in Italy came over to meet us all and to explain what was involved in setting up a Slow Food Convivium, which is a local chapter or branch of the organization. Local convivia work autonomously to defend their cultural heritage and support a more sustainable food future. There are more than 1,500 convivia worldwide, and they are the backbone of Slow Food.

The Slow Food philosophy of "good, clean, and fair" has been a major influence in my life and an affirmation of the value of the innate philosophy of Ballymaloe. The vision of "a world in which all people can access and enjoy food that is good for them, good for those who grow it, and good for the planet," is one that I can readily identify with.

I eventually set up the East Cork Slow Food Convivium at the Ballymaloe Cookery School in 1999, and we have had regular Slow Food events ever since, some based at the school, others on nearby farms or in local restaurants where the menu celebrates the food of the area. We now have over 100 members in East Cork. In 2005, we launched the East Cork Slow Food Educational Project with four local schools—the list has now expanded to nine. The children visit Ballymaloe several times a year and are split into two groups. The first group heads out on to the farm and learns about livestock and growing, while the second group has a cooking lesson and prepares a delicious lunch for everyone to share.

On Palm Sunday, April 16, 2000, the West Cork Convivium held its second Slow Food Celebration of Taste at the West Cork Natural Cheese Farm. The weather forecast was appalling, yet

Above: The launch of Slow Food Ireland, Gubbeen House, Schull, in August 1998. Pictured are, left to right: Annie Barry, chef at Ballydehob; Sally Barnes, of Woodcock Smokehouse, Skibbereen; Bill Hogan, of West Cork Natural Cheese in Schull; Giana Ferguson, of Gubbeen Farm; Myrtle Allen; former Irish Taoiseach (Prime Minister) Garret FitzGerald; and me.

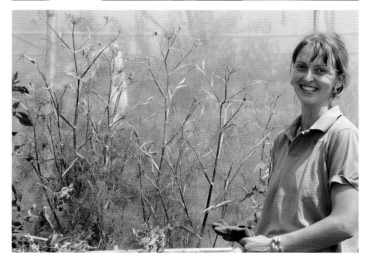

about 100 like-minded people made their way up the winding lane to Bill Hogan's farm where the legendary Gabriel and Desmond farmhouse cheeses are made. The sun shone all afternoon on the merry band of food producers and bon viveurs. The gathering was like a who's who of the artisanal food scene. The party took place indoors, outdoors, upstairs, and downstairs. Bill just threw his gates and doors open and delightedly welcomed the eager foodies. Out in the yard, Fingal Ferguson, son of cheesemakers Tom and Giana, who make the much-loved Gubbeen cheese, had set up a beautiful stall and was busy frying slices of his delicious home-cured smoked bacon. Like many of the artisans, he has gone from strength to strength in the intervening period.

During Carlo Petrini's week-long visit to Ireland in 2004, he met with Minister for Agriculture and Food, Joe Walsh, Bord Bia, UCC, food historians, farmers and fishermen, artisan food producers, chefs, fish smokers, butchers, teachers, and Slow Food members. His primary purpose in coming to Ireland on this occasion was to announce details of the University of Gastronomic Sciences in Pollenzo and Colorno in Italy. This project, the first in the world, was to help to create a new type of professional: an expert who is able to lead and elevate the quality of production, to teach others how to taste, to guide the market, and to communicate about and promote foods and beverages. The stated goal was that: "The University will provide those with an interest in understanding food with a humanistic, sensory approach, knowledge of traditional and industrial processes, and an appreciation of cooking and gastronomic tourism. In a world where 'specialities' and 'typical local products' are increasingly important and are raising the standards of the market, gastronomes will be able to communicate a wealth of knowledge, in advising new businesses, designing distribution outlets, and advising the restaurant trade. Though undervalued in the past, this profession is destined to become a true interpreter of food culture." At a dinner at Ballymaloe House, Rory O'Connell's menu reflected an abundance of wonderful Irish produce and the local foods of the area. Among the many delicious dishes served were Carpaccio of Beef with Horseradish Mayonnaise, Ballymaloe Potted Crab, Nora Aherne's Traditional Duck with Sage and Onion Stuffing, all finished off with Carrageen Moss Pudding with new season's Rhubarb Compote.

Many students become Slow Food members after we explain the philosophy and they often attend a couple of events while they are here. I would hope that they continue their membership when they leave the school, possibly join a convivium elsewhere, or go out there and make a difference.

In 2012, Slow Food offered a special Slow Food youth membership for students under 35, which boosted the numbers. Membership is growing worldwide, with now over 100,000 members in 150 countries around the globe. The events are always lots of fun and have a strong educational element—it could be a tasting of local honey combined with a talk on how to keep hens; a visit to a local butcher's shop or slaughterhouse combined with a talk on how to recognize and cook lesser known cuts of meat; or a discussion about the risks and benefits of raw milk with chief scientists from Moorepark Dairy Research Station.

A terrifying number of varieties of vegetables and plants have already been lost or are in danger of extinction. Old varieties of fruit and vegetables, traditional and rare breeds of animal, not considered to be of commercial value, are also under threat. According to Edward Wilson's estimate in *The Diversity of Life* (1992), in one century over 250,000 varieties of plant have become extinct—and plants will continue to vanish at the rate of three species every hour, or 27,000 a year. Also, according to Food and Agriculture Organization of the United Nations (FAO) estimates, 75 percent of agricultural crop varieties have disappeared and three-quarters of the world's food comes from only 12 plant and five animal species. In the US, for instance, 7,000 apple varieties and 2,500 pear varieties were once grown, but today just two pear varieties account for 96 percent of the entire market. Another example is potatoes: It is estimated that at one time over 5,000 varieties existed around the world, while today just four varieties are primarily grown for commercial purposes.

This loss has direct consequences on the food we eat. Out of around 30,000 edible natural species, just 30 crops provide 95 percent of the world's nutritional requirements. Of these 30, wheat, rice, and corn provide more than 60 percent of the calories consumed worldwide (FAO, 1999). Domestic animal species are in a similar situation. According to the latest report on the status of animal genetic resources in the food and agricultural sector—published by FAO in 2007—20 percent of the races surveyed in the 169 countries involved in the study are at risk of extinction. About 60 percent of these are mammals; the remaining 40 percent are poultry.

Slow Food has done much to highlight the problem of conservation and the importance of action on a national and international scale through its various projects: Presidia, Arc of Taste, Slow Food Awards, Salone del Gusto, and Terra Madre. At Salone del Gusto in Turin, the biggest artisan food fair in the world,

Left (top): Bill Casey, our neighbor from the village, cures and smokes salmon in the smokehouse on our farm in Shanagarry and explains the process to the 12-week students. He has been smoking for 20 years and occasionally smokes wild salmon from the Blackwater River especially for us to use at Ballymaloe House and the School.
Left (middle): A glimpse into the dairy and packing area at Gubbeen Farm outside Schull in West Cork, where two generations of the Ferguson family are involved in artisan production. Perhaps most famed for their washed rind cheeses, their son Fingal is also acclaimed for his range of charcuterie and cured meats and daughter Clovisse has created a wonderful organic garden, where she grows a wide range of vegetables and salad leaves to supply local restaurants and farmers' markets. This kind of enterprise is an example of the type of artisan producers that Slow Food encourages and supports.
Left (bottom): Clovisse Ferguson.
Above (top): Fingal Ferguson, one of the new generation of young artisan producers who have blazed a trail, inspired others, and won multiple awards. In addition to producing his own charcuterie, Fingal also makes beautiful, collectible kitchen knives in his workshop on the farm.
Above (bottom): Giana Ferguson in her dairy at Gubbeen.

Above (top): Igor harvesting red and white onions on the farm to dry for use over the winter.

Above (middle): James Cullinane and Chris O'Brien hanging bunches of onions from the rafters of the greenhouses—the perfect airy and dry environment for curing. You can also see our crop of garlic drying on lower wires. The garlic cloves are sown around the shortest day of the year and harvested around the longest day.

Above (bottom): A bunch of garlic ready to hang in the greenhouses.

hundreds of producers sell their products to a public increasingly craving forgotten flavors. Terra Madre, meaning Mother Earth, is an international meeting of food communities held biannually in Turin. Slow Food brings 5,000 farmers and food producers from all over the world together there so that they can meet and share concerns and solutions for a sustainable future and thereby build a global network of food "communities." Held over four days in the enormous Palazza del Lavoro, the participants represent about 1,000 food communities from 150 countries. Terra Madre provides a meeting place and a forum for people from around the world—for farmers, artisans, food producers, seed-savers, fishermen, distributors, cooks, cheesemakers, fish smokers, cured meat producers, bakers, and merchants to come together to exchange ideas, share diverse experiences, and to try to find solutions to similar problems.

Some shared goals include protecting the rights of the small farmer and promoting sustainable agriculture, as well as uniting against the growing domination of the multinationals and large corporations. Participants often come with amazing stories to tell, some clutching precious seeds, others with grains, all with a deep knowledge of their own food culture. Many dress in their colorful traditional clothes and distinctive headdress—from Indian feathers to cowboy hats, sombreros, and headscarves. Masai peasants meet Afghan raisin farmers, American maple syrup producers meet yak herders and cheesemakers from Kyrgyzstan, and Irish wild-salmon smokers meet Ghanaian fishermen. Speakers stress the need for biodiversity, speak out against transgenic crops, illustrate how globalization is causing the erosion of rural communities and how the indiscriminate use of pesticides and antibiotics is destroying the land and how the World Trade Organization (WTO) accords affect farmers and food producers. Slow Food, since its inception in 1986, has already battled and successfully saved a growing number of foods and drinks threatened with extinction. It defends our right as consumers to free choice. Prince Charles, an organic farmer himself, addressed the closing session of Terra Madre in 2004. In his speech to the conference, the Prince highlighted the huge social and environmental costs of cheap "fast food." His Royal Highness said: "Any analysis of the real costs would have to look at such things as the rise in food-borne illnesses, the advent of new pathogens such as E.Coli 0157, antibiotic resistance from the overuse of drugs in animal feed, extensive water pollution from intensive agricultural systems, and many other factors. These costs are not reflected in the price of fast food, but that doesn't mean that our society isn't paying them."

I have attended every Salone del Gusto and Terra Madre conference and come back on a high, totally inspired. We bring a delegation of 70–80 people from Ireland and Bord Bia, our National Food Board, and always have a stand at Salone del Gusto to promote and highlight the Irish food products that we are so proud of. Slow Food has granted a *presidia* (a protection) around our Irish raw milk cheeses, so they always have a stand at Terra Madre as well. Members of The Irish Farmhouse Cheesemakers Association (CÁIS) man the stall themselves and charm the Italians and the delegates from all over the world.

During this challenging economic time in Ireland, Slow Food membership is falling, but even though membership is considered by many to be a barometer of success, I am not so depressed. I understand that for many today, it's about survival and even though they may not be able to renew their membership, many are still living their lives by the principles of Slow Food—good, clean, and fair. This philosophy underpins everything we do at Ballymaloe and the students who spend 12 weeks with us seem to feel deeply committed to spreading the Slow Food philosophy.

Above (top): Watering the many plants in the Ballymaloe greenhouses.
Above (bottom): At the start of every 12-week course I emphasize to the students the importance of good, clean, fertile soil.

A Plate of Irish Charcuterie and Cured Meats

One of my favorite easy entertaining tricks is to serve a selection of Irish artisan charcuterie from inspired producers like Fingal Ferguson and Frank Krawczyk from Schull, West Cork, and James McGeough from Oughterard, County Galway. More recently, Martin and Noreen Conroy's son Matthew, from Woodside Farm, is making outstanding salami, chorizo, and air-dried meats from their own Saddleback pigs, having spent a considerable period of time apprenticed to Massimo Spigaroli in the Emilia-Romagna region of Italy. The quality of these cured meats is so wonderful that I'm always bursting with pride as I serve them.

a selection of cured meats, such as air-dried smoked
Connemara lamb, smoked venison, prosciutto, Gubeen salami,
chorizo, and chistora, Pat Mulcahy's Ballinwillin House wild boar
and venison salami, Derreenatra salami, West Cork Kassler,
pork rillettes, head cheese, etc.
a selection of crusty country breads, such as sourdough, yeast,
and soda bread
tiny gherkins or cornichons
fresh radishes, trimmed but with some green leaf attached
good green salad of garden lettuce and salad leaves

Arrange the meats on a large platter, open a good bottle of red, and tuck in! Accompany with bread, gherkins, radishes, and salad.

Smoked Wild Irish Salmon with Horseradish Cream, Arjard, and Pickled Red Onions

Wild Irish salmon is a now a rare treat, but for the last couple of years we have managed to get a small number from fishermen on the Blackwater River. We treasure each one and eat some fresh, cure and smoke some ourselves, or give them to Bill Casey, our local smoker, to smoke for us. We hot- and cold-smoke the salmon and teach the students both methods of preserving. For this recipe we use cold-smoked salmon, but flakes of the hot-smoked variety would also be delicious.

Serves 4

6–8oz cold-smoked wild Irish salmon,
cut into ½in cubes

For the Pickled Red Onions
1 cup white wine vinegar
½ cup granulated sugar
pinch of salt
3 whole cloves
1 cinnamon stick, broken
1 dried red chile
1lb red onions, peeled and thinly sliced on a mandolin

For the Arjard (cucumber salad)
2 shallots, peeled and thinly sliced lengthwise
1 red chile, seeded and sliced into rings
1 green chile, seeded and sliced into rings
¼ cup sugar
6 tablespoons water
6 tablespoons malt vinegar
½ teaspoon salt
1 cucumber, quartered lengthwise and thinly sliced

To serve
chervil sprigs and wild garlic or chive blossom in season
freshly ground black pepper

To make the pickled onions, put the vinegar, sugar, salt, and spices in a heavy-bottomed pan and bring to a boil. Put in one-third of the sliced onions and simmer for 2–3 minutes, or until they turn pink and wilt. Lift out the cooked onions with a slotted spoon and transfer them to a 1 pint sterilized jam jar with a nonreactive lid. Repeat with the rest of the onions, cooking them in two batches. Top off the jar with the hot vinegar, put on the lid, and set aside to cool overnight. Once cold, store in the fridge.

To make the Arjard, put all the ingredients except the cucumber in a heavy-bottomed saucepan. Bring to a boil and simmer for 3–5 minutes. Set aside to cool. Once cold, pour the marinade over the slices of cucumber and set aside to marinate in the fridge for at least 30 minutes.

To serve, arrange the cubes of salmon on a plate, add some Arjard and pickled red onion and scatter a few sprigs of chervil, wild garlic, or chive flowers over the top. Finish with some freshly ground black pepper.

Ardsallagh Goat Cheese and Thyme Leaf Soufflé

We have several farmhouse goat-cheesemakers in Ireland.
We use Ardsallagh goat cheese, St. Tola from Inagh in
County Clare is also heaven, as is Gortnamona from
Cooleeney farm in County Tipperary and Corleggy from
County Cavan.

We bake this soufflé until golden and puffy in a shallow
oval dish instead of the traditional soufflé bowl. It makes a
perfect lunch or supper dish. Little individual bowls also make
wonderful appetizers. Reduce the cooking time accordingly.

Preheat the oven to 450°F. Brush the bottom and sides of a 12in
shallow oval dish (not a soufflé dish) or six individual wide, rimmed
soup bowls with melted butter.

Put the cream and milk into a saucepan, add the carrot, onion,
peppercorns, and fresh herbs. Bring slowly to a boil, and then set
aside to infuse for 10 minutes. Strain, discarding the flavorings
(we rinse them off and throw them into the stockpot if there is
one on the go).

Melt the butter, add the flour, and cook for a minute or two.
Whisk in the strained cream and milk, bring to a boil and whisk
until the sauce thickens. Cool slightly. Add the egg yolks, goat
cheese, Gruyère, and most of the Coolea or Parmesan (reserving
some for the topping). Season with salt, cayenne, freshly ground
pepper, and nutmeg. Taste and correct the seasoning.

Whisk the egg whites stiffly and fold them gently into the mixture
to make a loose consistency. Spoon into the prepared dish, scatter
the thyme leaves over the top, and sprinkle with the reserved Coolea
or Parmesan.

Bake in the preheated oven for 12–15 minutes (9–11 minutes for
the individual soufflés), or until the sides and top are nicely puffed up
and golden—the center should still be creamy. Garnish with thyme
flowers. Serve immediately with a good green salad.

Serves 6

5 tablespoons butter, plus extra for greasing
1 cup heavy cream
1 cup milk
a few slices of carrot
1 small onion, quartered
4–5 black peppercorns
a sprig of thyme, a few flat-leaf parsley stalks, and a
   little scrap of bay leaf
½ cup all-purpose flour
5 large organic eggs, separated
4oz goat cheese (we use Ardsallagh), crumbled
¾ cup Gruyère cheese, finely grated
½ cup mature Coolea or Parmesan cheese, finely grated
generous pinch of salt, cayenne, freshly ground black pepper,
   and nutmeg
2 teaspoons fresh thyme leaves

To serve
lots of thyme flowers, if available
green salad

The Maze

Ever since I visited Hampton Court in the 1970s, I have been intrigued by labyrinths and mazes and wondered how I could possibly justify planting a maze at Ballymaloe. For me, 1991 was "The Year of the Maze," so I had a flash of inspiration: I'd give Tim a present of a maze for his 50th birthday—a stroke of genius! As luck would have it, Peter Lamb, a scholarly friend of ours, had designed a beautiful Celtic maze, inspired by an illustration from the *Book of Kells*, but didn't have a site so was delighted to share his design if there was a possibility of the drawing becoming a reality. Friends who had planted a new maze at Dunbrody in County Wexford invited me along to see the site and explained that a maze must have a proper puzzle. A good drawing doesn't necessarily work; if not well designed, people can get hopelessly lost in the maze. They introduced me to Lesley Beck, a UK maze designer, who explained that a maze must have a main entrance and a short exit. She worked her magic on Peter's plan and instructed Will Kenneally, our contractor, who is happy to tackle anything, on how to mark out the complicated pattern.

We chose a site where the old orchard had been and decided to edge the paths with lumber. Kinoith gardens already had several handsome beech hedges so we choose yew, traditionally used in mazes, calculated the number (several thousand) and ordered them from Bill Montgomery in Northern Ireland. We brought electricity and water into the center of the maze so we could have a fountain, which never materialized, but for years we had fun with a pedal, which, when curious visitors pressed it, shot a jet of water 30ft (9m) into the air and drenched them. Initially the plants were only about 18in tall. We had hoped they would shoot up when they settled in but instead many looked sickly and eventually died. We replanted, but these plants died, too. Everyone was baffled, and various theories were put forward: residues of weed killer in the soil, compaction… we still don't know the reason, but I suspect that it was waterlogging, since that field had a particularly thin topsoil and heavy clay subsoil. Eventually, in 2003, we decided to try beech and hornbeam because the latter

just loves it in Shanagarry. Now, 20 years later, we have a fantastic Celtic maze.

From time to time Tim and I would talk about creating a folly in the center of the maze to tantalize and encourage people. The Petal Folly is the fantasy of architect and friend Jeremy Williams, made from fiberglass in a workshop in Dublin in 2011 and installed in the yard in 2012. We had many chats about the color; Jeremy favored wild fuchsia, purple, and cherry red, which we thought would be wonderful when the leaves were green in summer, but we weren't so sure would work with the rusty fall colors. After much deliberation, Jeremy suggested an Irish muralist named Michael Dillon, and the result was perfect. The exterior, which is clearly visible over the maze, resembles an Indian tent, while the interior is rich red and gold, embellished with exotic birds and flowers. On more than one occasion we've had to rescue people who have gotten hopelessly lost, including a batch of exuberant students on a moonlit night in midsummer 2012. The occasional empty wine bottle tells tales of partying, too!

Above: The Petal Folly, in the center of the Celtic maze.

The Memory Arboretum

When news reached us in 1997 of the tragic death of one of our past students, Karen Harte (12-week course, January 1985), who drowned in an accident in the Caribbean, we were all deeply shocked and saddened. Tim and I decided to start a memory garden, close to the avenue, so we planted an apple tree in Karen's memory and have continued to add to the garden ever since.

We also planted an apple tree for Robert Lett, a copper beech for Thomas Fitzgerald, Lord Earl of Offaly, and a liquid ambar tree for Anna Fitzgerald, who was lost in the tsunami in Thailand in 2004. A crab apple was planted for Philippa Corbin, a sweet chestnut for Geoffrey Harrison, and a Japanese walnut for Martin Maher. There are now seven trees with a plaque under each to commemorate the past student and a garden so that visitors can rest and reflect. There are other trees planted in the garden and two rosemary bushes in tubs—rosemary for remembrance. Parents and family of the students occasionally come to visit the memory arboretum and are very moved to see the tree planted in remembrance of their loved one.

Watercress, Sorrel, and Wild Leek Broth

My brother Rory O'Connell, author of *Master It* and cofounder of the Ballymaloe Cookery School, introduced us to these light broths. We ring the changes throughout the year, depending on what delicate greens are in season.

Melt the butter in a large, heavy-bottomed saucepan and allow to foam. Add the potatoes, onions, leek, and garlic. Coat in the butter and season with salt and pepper. Cover the pan with wax paper and a tight-fitting lid. Cook over very low heat to allow the vegetables to sweat gently until barely tender—about 10 minutes. Don't overcook; the diced potato must not collapse.

Add the stock and bring to a simmer, stirring gently. Cook for 10 minutes; the broth should be barely bubbling. If it cooks too fast at this stage, the delicate flavor of the chicken stock will be lost. Do not replace the lid on the saucepan. Taste and correct the seasoning. (This is the soup base; if necessary, you can set it aside at this stage to finish later.)

To finish the soup, bring the base back to a simmer. Add the wild garlic leaves, watercress, and sorrel and allow them to wilt—this will only take a few minutes. Taste and correct the seasoning. Finally, sprinkle the wild garlic flowers over the top and serve immediately.

Serves 4–6

4 tablespoons butter
6oz potatoes, peeled and cut into ½in dice
¾ cup onions, finely chopped
½ cup wild leeks (*Allium babingtonii*), thinly sliced
2 garlic cloves, peeled and finely chopped
4 cups chicken stock
5 cups wild garlic leaves, finely chopped
sea salt and freshly ground black pepper
1¼ cups watercress, finely chopped
1½ cups sorrel, finely chopped

To serve
wild garlic flowers (from either *Allium ursinum* or *Allium triquetrum*, as illustrated opposite), if available

Cabbage, kale, Swiss chard, and scallions also work well in this soup if wild garlic and leek are not in season.

Boiled Leg of Mutton with Wild Garlic Sauce

It is very difficult to get hold of mutton these days, unless you ask a farmer to rear it specially for you. George Gossip, a game teacher at the School, organized for a farmer he knew in County Galway to keep four sheep for us for over two years, when they become classified as mutton. They had a rich gamey flavor and we hope to have more again this year. Kay Harte occasionally serves corned mutton at her Farm Gate restaurant in the English Market in Cork City.

Trim the knuckle from the shanks and end. Remove the aitch bones as you would with roast lamb. Put the leg of mutton into a deep saucepan. Cover with cold water, add the salt, and bring slowly to a boil. Simmer for 5 minutes and then skim thoroughly. Tuck the vegetables around the edge and add the thyme. Continue to simmer, covered, for 1½– 2 hours, depending on the size—as a rough guide, allow 15 minutes per 1lb plus an extra 15 minutes. Once the meat is cooked, you should be able to pierce it easily with a skewer.

To make the Wild Garlic Sauce, pour the milk into a pan and bring to "shivering" point. Melt the butter in a heavy-bottomed pan, stir in the flour and cook, stirring, for 1 minute. Remove the pan from the heat and whisk in the hot milk. Return to the heat and stir continuously with a wooden spoon until the sauce thickens. Simmer for 2–3 minutes to cook out the flour, and season with salt and pepper. Finally, stir in the chopped capers and wild garlic. Taste and correct the seasoning.

To serve, transfer the lamb to a hot serving dish and surround it with the vegetables. Serve the Wild Garlic sauce separately, sprinkled with wild garlic flowers if you have them.

Variation—Corned Mutton with Caper and Wild Garlic Sauce
Corned mutton cooked in the same way is, if anything, even more delicious. In a bowl, mix all the brining ingredients to dissolve the salt and sugar. Put the leg of lamb or mutton into a clean stainless steel saucepan, cover with the cold brine and the lid or a clean dish towel and allow to brine for 3–7 days, depending on your taste. Cook in unsalted water.

Serves approx. 8–10

1 leg of lamb, weighing approx. 6½lb
4 quarts water
1 tablespoon salt
4 carrots, peeled and halved (or quartered, if large)
2 white turnips, peeled and halved or quartered
3–4 celery stalks, cut into 2–3 pieces
a sprig of thyme

For the Wild Garlic Sauce
2 cups whole milk
1 tablespoon butter
1 tablespoon all-purpose flour
2 tablespoons chopped capers
3 tablespoons freshly chopped wild garlic
salt and freshly ground black pepper

To serve
wild garlic flowers (optional)

For the brine (see Variation)
5¼ quarts cold water
1¾lb sea or pure rock salt
a couple of sprigs of thyme
2 teaspoons juniper berries
2 teaspoons crushed peppercorns

Honey Mousse with Lavender Jelly

J. R. Ryall, the pastry chef at Ballymaloe House, loves to make this dessert in June using the lavender from the walled garden at Ballymaloe, just before the flowers open. Using only the best quality local honey will make this feather-light mousse truly unforgettable.

Serves 6

1½ cups heavy cream
1 teaspoon powdered gelatin
1½ tablespoons cold water
½ cup best-quality local honey
1 tablespoon Grand Marnier, to taste
1 large organic egg

For the Lavender Jelly
½ cup granulated sugar
1 cup water
12 fresh lavender heads
1½ teaspoons powdered gelatin
2½ tablespoons cold water

First, make the honey mousse. Whip the cream to soft peaks and set aside in the fridge. Sprinkle the gelatin over the cold water in a small heatproof bowl and allow to "sponge." Once fully rehydrated, melt the gelatin by placing the bowl over a saucepan of hot but not boiling water. Add the honey and Grand Marnier and stir until the mixture is an even consistency. Set aside to return to room temperature.

Next, using an electric mixer, beat the egg to a pale mousse, then gently fold into the whipped cream. Fold the cream mixture into the honey and gelatin in three stages. Pour the mousse into a 1-quart serving dish and chill in the fridge until set.

To make the Lavender Jelly, put the sugar and 1 cup water in a heavy-bottomed saucepan and bring slowly to a boil. Once the syrup has boiled, remove the saucepan from the heat and drop in six lavender heads. Set aside to cool to room temperature.

Meanwhile, sprinkle the gelatin over the 2½ tablespoons of cold water in a small heatproof bowl and allow to "sponge." Once fully rehydrated, melt the gelatin by placing the bowl over hot but not boiling water.

Strain the cooled syrup through a strainer, add to the melted gelatin and mix well. Arrange six lavender heads on top of the set honey mousse and carefully spoon over enough liquid jelly to cover the lavender. Chill until the jelly is set—about 1 hour—then serve.

The Wood-burning Oven

Above: Philip Dennhardt making Saturday Pizzas in the Garden Café at Ballymaloe.
Right: Pizzas cooking in the wood-burning oven.

My first encounter with a wood-burning oven was in Italy in the 1980s and later at Alice Waters' Chez Panisse restaurant in Berkeley, California, where the most irresistible food was emerging from it. I had loved the flavor of the food since tasting Wolfgang Puck's bubbly thin crust pizza in Los Angeles a few years previously and so when we opened the Garden Café at the School in the summer of 1998, I decided I wanted a wood-fired oven of my own. So I went to California on a research trip.

My journey took me to Mendocino County, where, behind the community center in a small town called Elk, we found a clay adobe oven large enough to roast a pig. I soon discovered that the man behind many of the great ovens that I saw was an oven-builder from New Zealand named Alan Scott, who had since returned home to his native country. When I arrived at Chez Panisse, Alice told me all about the vagaries of their wood-burning oven, since there had been some teething problems, and she suggested I forget about trying to have one built, romantic as that was; better to go to the Italians, who have been making wood-burning ovens for centuries, and buy a kit. She found me the name of a brilliantly efficient Italian company called Refrattari Reggello and, much to my amazement, I had the oven within six weeks. The company gave fantastic instructions for installation in English and I also took my contractor over to see the River Café's oven in Hammersmith, London, to observe it in operation. Ruth Rogers and the late Rose Gray had said it was instrumental in their cooking and they used it every day—it was therefore a good place to visit to see how this type of oven could work.

Cooking with a wood-burning oven is very different from using a standard oven. There's no temperature gauge for a start, so one needs to be much more observant and learn to judge the heat of the oven by the intensity of the fire and the color of the ash. The oven has to be heated gradually at first, because if the oven is cold a sudden large fire can crack the base and permanently damage the oven. The management of the wood is a whole skill in and of itself, as is knowing which woods to use, since some generate much more heat than others. It is important not to use any wood that might have traces of preservatives or residues of paint—these can give off toxic fumes, which of course taint the food. Dry wood produces more heat than damp wood, which smolders and is therefore inefficient. If the oven is not hot enough, pizzas take longer to cook and don't have the crisp base and bubbly edges that we all love so much.

In 1998, we found a young chef, Stevie O'Brien Gleeson, who had been working with a wood oven in Tosca, a pizzeria in Suffolk Street in Dublin. Stevie spent the summer season with us in the Garden Café and taught us how to work with fire. People came from far and wide for the pizza—the café was open seven days a week and the students loved it, too. That year, Stevie concentrated on pizza, but the following year my son Isaac became more adventurous—he made a delicious roast tomato soup and we also used the oven to roast fish, meat, and vegetables.

In May 2008, 10 years after we installed the oven, our son-in-law, Philip Dennhardt, decided to do a "pop-up" pizzeria for just four hours from 12:30–4p.m. every Saturday in the Garden Café (the School is usually closed on Saturdays so the dining room is open to the public). The pizaa toppings reflect the ingredients in season on the farm and in the gardens and make use of local farmhouse cheeses and occasionally shrimp, squid, or fresh crab from the nearby fishing village of Ballycotton. There is always a Pizza Margherita, a Pepperoni and a Marinara, and just two others, a vegetarian and a nonvegetarian option. It has proved so popular that Saturday Pizzas are now an institution—there's cool music and a fun atmosphere, plus the 12-week students get the opportunity to learn how it all works and how to cook with fire—the half-day pizza, calzone, panzarotti, piadina, and sfinciuni demonstration is an integral part of the course.

Wood-burning ovens are now quite widespread—popular in many restaurants and not just pizzerias. You'll often see mobile ones at farmers' markets and festivals and many people build small versions in their yards. Philip Dennhardt gives a Pizza Workshop using the wood-burning oven at the Ballymaloe Cookery School several times a year and Simon Mould, who now runs the Volcano Pizza stand at Midleton Farmers' Market, is an old student of his. The regulators, who were wary of this trend at the outset, presumably regarding concerns about health and safety, have become more accepting of it and realize that cooking in wood-burning ovens is a time-honored tradition that adds immeasurably to the flavor of the food.

Pizza with Roast Peppers, Olives, and Gremolata

At Saturday Pizzas the toppings change every week, depending on the season. We love to make this one with homegrown bell peppers in the summer, but the misshapen Spanish and Italian peppers are also fleshy and flavorful. We use Kalamata, Niçoise, or green Picholine olives.

First, make the dough. Put the water into the bowl of a food processor. Add the mother to the water, if using. Crumble the yeast into the flour and add to the water, along with the salt. Mix for 5 minutes at medium speed. Pinch the dough between your thumb and index finger—it should feel stretchy. Let the dough rest for 5 minutes, then mix for another 20 minutes. The dough should be smooth and stick to the side of the mixing bowl. (If you don't have a dough hook on your food processor, you can knead the dough by hand.)

Transfer the dough to an airtight container that is four times bigger than the size of the dough, to allow for expansion. Transfer the container to the fridge for at least 6 hours, preferably overnight.

Remove the dough from the fridge and sprinkle a work surface with a little flour. Transfer the dough to the work surface, then divide into eight 5oz pieces using a small knife. Knead the dough into round balls roughly the size of tennis balls. Put the dough balls onto a baking sheet, sprinkle with flour, and transfer to the fridge to rest for 6 hours. Remove the dough from the fridge 1 hour before you cook the pizza.

Preheat the oven 400°F. To make the tomato sauce, arrange the tomatoes cut-side up in a roasting pan in a single layer. Scatter the garlic cloves over the top and season with salt, pepper, and sugar. Drizzle the balsamic vinegar and olive oil over the tomatoes. Roast in the preheated oven for 15–20 minutes, until the tomatoes are completely soft and the garlic is squishy.

Meanwhile, put the peppers for the pizza on a separate baking sheet, drizzle them with olive oil and roast in the oven for 30–35 minutes, until they start to blacken. Remove from the oven, peel, seed, and cut into strips. Set aside.

Grate the mozzarella into a small bowl and drizzle with a little extra virgin olive oil. Set aside.

To finish the tomato sauce, remove the tomatoes and garlic from the oven and push them through a strainer, discarding the skins and seeds. Taste and correct the seasoning.

Increase the oven temperature to 475°F. Roll out the pizza dough into a 10in circle. Sprinkle a little semolina over the surface of a pizza paddle and put the pizza base on top.

Makes 1

5oz pizza dough
½ red bell pepper
½ yellow bell pepper
extra virgin olive oil, for drizzling
4oz mozzarella
semolina, for dusting
¾ cup black olives (you can remove the pits if you prefer)
sea salt and freshly ground black pepper

For the pizza dough (Makes 8 x 5oz dough)
2½ cups cold tap water
2oz mother—leftover dough from the previous batch (optional)
¾oz fresh yeast
7¼ cups strong Italian flour, such as Tipo 00 or strong baker's flour, plus extra for dusting
1 tablespoon dairy salt

For Isaac's Roasted Tomato Pizza Sauce
1lb very ripe tomatoes, halved
6 garlic cloves, unpeeled
sugar
1 tablespoon balsamic vinegar
2 tablespoons olive oil

For the Gremolata
2½ tablespoons freshly chopped flat-leaf parsley
1 teaspoon grated or finely chopped lemon zest
2 garlic cloves, peeled and finely chopped

Spread ¼ cup of tomato sauce over the base of the pizza (leftover sauce can be stored in a sealed container in the fridge). Arrange the roasted bell pepper slices and olives over the tomato sauce. Season with a little sea salt and freshly ground black pepper. Sprinkle the mozzarella over the top of the pizza.

Bake in a wood-burning oven or a fully preheated oven for 10–12 minutes, or until the pizza base is crisp and the top is bubbly and golden.

Meanwhile, make the Gremolata by combining all of the ingredients in a bowl. To serve, sprinkle the gremolata over the top of the pizza.

Fava Bean, Blue Cheese, Parsley, and Lemon Pizza

When the first of the fava beans and fennel are in season, Philip Dennhardt makes this pizza. Crozier Blue is a gentle blue cheese made by Henry Clifton Brown in County Tipperary from his herd of milking sheep. This fennel sauce is also delicious as a base for a seaweed pizza, or any pizza with fresh greens, like kale, spinach, or broccoli. It also freezes perfectly so make the full amount and use as required.

First, make the pizza dough according to the instructions on page 168.

Meanwhile, make the fennel sauce. Heat the oil in a pan, add the onions and garlic, and sweat until soft but not colored. Add the fennel slices and water, season with salt and pepper, and simmer for about 25 minutes, or until soft. Blend until smooth. Taste and correct the seasoning, if necessary.

Preheat the oven to 475°F. Blanch the fava beans in boiling water for 2 minutes. Drain, refresh under cold running water, and set aside.

Roll out the pizza dough to form a 10in circle. Sprinkle a little semolina all over the surface of a pizza paddle and put the pizza base on top. Drizzle the olive oil over the base of the pizza and sprinkle with a pinch of sea salt. Spread about ½ cup of the fennel sauce over the pizza base (any leftover sauce can be frozen until required). Scatter the fava beans and blue cheese on top and sprinkle with the mozzarella.

Bake in a wood-burning oven or a fully preheated oven for 10–12 minutes, or until the base is crisp and the top is bubbly and golden. Sprinkle the chopped parsley over the pizza and serve immediately, accompanied with the lemon wedges.

Makes 1

5oz pizza dough
20 fava beans
1 teaspoon extra virgin olive oil
pinch of Maldon sea salt
8 cubes of blue cheese, ½in each
a large handful of grated mozzarella

For the pizza dough (Makes 8 x 5oz dough)
2½ cups cold tap water
2oz mother—leftover dough from the previous batch (optional)
¾oz fresh yeast
7¼ cups strong Italian flour, such as Tipo 00 or strong baker's flour, plus extra for dusting
1 tablespoon dairy salt

For the fennel sauce
1 tablespoon extra virgin olive oil
2 onions, thinly sliced
3 garlic cloves, peeled and crushed
5 bulbs of fennel, thinly sliced
2 cups water
sea salt and freshly ground black pepper

To serve
1 teaspoon finely chopped fresh flat-leaf parsley
lemon wedges

Ballymaloe White Sourdough Bread

Once you have established or acquired a starter, making sourdough bread is a three-day process, and one which, once you get started, will soon become a routine part of your day. Every loaf will be slightly different, depending on the activity of the wild yeast starter.

This is the only recipe in the book without US measurements, because bakers operate using the metric system—you'll find it very convenient, too.

STAGE 1 Ballymaloe Sourdough Starter—Levain
Some starter recipes suggest mixing the full amount of flour with water and leaving it for six days. We have found, however, that we get a much more active starter when we feed it (i.e., add more water and flour) every day. You will need to allow at least six days for your sourdough starter to develop fully; in fact, sometimes, when your starter is new, it is recommended to throw out approximately 300g and feed it again with 150g of water and 150g of strong baker's flour, and leave it for another 24 hours. This helps to make a stronger active yeast; however, if you don't want to waste your starter, go ahead and make some loaves. They will be a bit flat in the beginning, but persevere.

You will need:
2-liter (2-quart) airtight jar, such as a Mason jar
300g pure spring water
300g strong white flour (preferably organic)

Day 1: Choose a large airtight jar that will hold at least 2 liters—a Mason jar is fine. Put 50g of barely tepid (not hot) pure spring water and 50g of strong white flour into the jar. Mix well, close the jar, and set aside at room temperature for 24 hours.
Day 2: You should begin to see some bubbles at this stage. Add 50g of water and 50g of flour. Mix well, close the jar, and set aside for another 24 hours at room temperature.
Day 3: Add 50g of water and 50g of flour. Mix well, close the jar and set aside for another 24 hours at room temperature.
Day 4: Add 50g of water and 50g of flour. Mix well, close the jar, and set aside for another 24 hours at room temperature.
Day 5: Add 50g of water and 50g of flour. Mix well, close the jar, and set aside for another 24 hours at room temperature.
Day 6: Add 50g of water and 50g of flour. Mix well, close the jar, and set aside for another 24 hours at room temperature.

Your sourdough starter is now ready for use. You should have at least 600g of lively, bubbly starter, enough to make the following sourdough recipe.

Note: It's good to use your starter immediately. However, it can be stored in an airtight jar in the fridge. (It will need to be fed to reactivate it before use.) The more you use your starter the stronger it will get—in fact, the first few loaves may be disappointing, but do persevere; the thrill of taking a beautiful loaf of sourdough out of the oven is worth the effort.

Once you've established the sourdough starter, making a loaf of sourdough bread from start to finish will take anywhere from 24 to 36 hours, depending on how lively the starter is.

Starter Tips
• Your starter should smell distinctly beery, slightly yeasty, and fermented, and it should be really bubbly. It may develop a layer of gray liquid on top, but that's fine—just stir the mixture.
• Your starter must not be allowed to get too warm.
• Starters grow best at comfortable room temperature.

STAGE 2—Making the Sponge

You will need:
230g sourdough starter (see left)
240g barely tepid water
240g strong white flour (preferably organic)

Day 1: Put 230g of sourdough starter into a bowl. Add 120g of barely tepid water and 120g of strong white flour. Beat well, cover with plastic wrap, and set aside at room temperature overnight.
Day 2: Next morning, add 120g of barely tepid water and 120g of strong white flour. Beat well, cover with plastic wrap, and set aside at room temperature for 6–7 hours.
By now the "sponge" should be active and bubbling. To check that it is ready, perform the Float Test: Fill a measuring cup with cold water, add 1 teaspoon of starter, and see if it floats. If it sinks, set it aside to ferment for a little longer.

STAGE 3—Making the Bread

You will need
340g "sponge" (see left)
200g pure water at body termperature
20g rye flour
300g strong white flour (preferably organic), plus extra for dusting
10g salt (2 percent)

You will need a 9in bread basket (Banneton), lined with
  a well-floured napkin

Put 340g of the "sponge" into the bowl of a stand mixer and put the remainder back into the starter jar—you have now fed your starter, ready for the next loaf of sourdough. Add the water to the "sponge." Beat well with a wooden spoon. Add the rye flour, white flour, and the salt.

Transfer the bowl to the mixer. Insert the dough hook and mix for a few minutes, until the dough comes together. Then rest the dough for 25–40 minutes—this will make it easier to knead.

The dough will seem far too wet, but continue to mix it with the dough hook until the texture of the dough is smooth and it comes away from the sides of the bowl—about 8 minutes. Increase the speed for another 5–8 minutes, or until you can lift the dough hook clean out of the bowl. If the dough hook cuts through the dough, put it back in the bowl and mix the dough a little longer, about 3–4 minutes.

Remove the dough from the mixer and transfer to a clean work surface (no flour needed). Allow the dough to rest for 1 hour, folding it like a square package (to trap air) every 20 minutes. At first you will notice the dough spreading, but as you fold it, it will slowly start to rise, holding its shape.

It is important to rest the dough after each folding. After the last folding, dust the work surface with flour. Shape the dough into a round ball and put it in the floured and lined bread basket. Slide the filled basket into a large plastic bag and refrigerate overnight.

The following morning, remove the basket from the fridge and take it out of the plastic bag. Set aside and allow to rest at room temperature for 1–2 hours, or until doubled in size.

Preheat the oven to 475°F and dust a baking sheet with flour.

Turn the bread gently onto the floured baking sheet and slash the top with a sharp knife or razor blade. Slide the baking sheet into the oven, spray the inside of the oven with a water mister—the moisture will help the bread develop a nice crust—and close the oven door.

Mist the bread at regular intervals and bake for 35–40 minutes, or until the bread is crusty and it sounds hollow when tapped underneath.

Remove from the oven and set aside to cool on a wire rack.

Going Organic

Above: Tim inspecting the flat pod French bean crop growing in the greenhouse. We've been growing these for several years and, in general, find them far superior to the round variety.
Right: A fine crop of beautiful tomatoes grown on seaweed- and compost-fed soil.

At Ballymaloe House and the Cookery School, we have always been passionate about sourcing beautiful fresh produce; it's the essence of what we do and we've always understood that unless we put substantial effort into finding the freshest seasonal produce from artisan producers, local farmers and fishermen, we simply can't get the "wow factor." Experience has taught me that the simpler the food, the more vital it becomes to have pristine, fresh ingredients, pure and natural, and this is one of the most important things I emphasize to students. The reality is that unless you start off with beautiful raw ingredients you need to be a wizard to transform them into something truly delicious, and often that's where all the "cheffy" bells and whistles, fluffs and foams are needed to compensate for the fact that the flavor isn't there in the first place.

When we opened the School in 1983, the surrounding 100-acre farm was not organic. In the 1970s, the land was farmed conventionally by my brother-in-law, Rory Allen, in a rotation of potatoes, sugarbeets, and barley. As the years passed, however, I became aware of a growing body of research that warned of the dangers of pesticide and herbicide residues in our food and I grew increasingly uneasy.

One food crisis followed another: in 1987, the story of BSE (Bovine spongiform encephalopathy) broke about a mysterious and incurable brain disease killing dairy cows that had taken hold in Britain the previous year. Worse still, the meat had entered the food chain and crossed over to humans, and so Variant Creutzfeldt-Jakob disease (vCJD) became an ugly reality. Furthermore, this was just a mere taste of the macabre revelations to come. In 2001, an outbreak of hoof-and-mouth disease occurred, both in the UK and Ireland, with the consequent slaughtering of huge numbers of cattle. In December 2008, there was the Dioxin scandal, when it was found that some of the national pork production was contaminated with dioxins, highly toxic compounds that are the by-product of various industrial processes. On and on it goes, with the most recent being the horsemeat scandal, when horsemeat of doubtful origin was found in hamburgers in many countries across Europe. All these examples

Above: A wheelbarrow full of sweet Genovese basil destined for the compost heap. We pick off the flowers to encourage the plants to sprout and become bushy rather than going to seed.

Right: A crop of peas growing in the greenhouse. We use them at every stage—the pea shoots, flowers and tendrils, or wizard's whiskers, the pods, and eventually the peas themselves. Tim is vigilant that we don't pick off too many pea flowers, since this can endanger the eventual pea crop, which, after all, is the object of the exercise!

Far right: An apple ripening on one of our many apple trees.

are the consequence of pushing animals and plants beyond their natural limits to produce the maximum amount of food at minimum cost in order to fulfill our endless quest for cheap food.

In the early 1980s, a brilliant grower named Jill Gairdner worked with us on the farm and in the greenhouses. She told us about an inspirational organic farmer named Rod Alston in County Leitrim, who had gradually turned a patch of wet bog land into fertile soil that produced a wide variety of organic vegetables, herbs, salad leaves, and fruit. When I was filming *Simply Delicious Versatile Vegetables*, I took a television crew there and was mightily impressed by what had been achieved. In 1994, Rod contacted me about his vision to establish an organic center and research station in Ireland and asked if I would be a patron. I agreed and The Organic Center was established in 1995 on 19 acres of land near Rossinver and has, despite the challenges, gradually established itself and offers a wide range of excellent courses on organic horticulture, green building, seed sowing, planting potatoes, growing in polytunnels, and even working with horses. Rod detached himself from the center in 2000, but he was one of the founding fathers of the organic food movement in Ireland, and my involvement in the center increased my interest in organic produce.

My own "eureka moment" came one day in 1996, in the middle of a cooking class when I was telling the students yet again about the importance of beautiful, nourishing produce. Out of the corner of my eye, I saw a tractor with a boom spraying goodness knows what onto the field behind the Cookery School. I couldn't bear it; I felt like a complete hypocrite and so resolved at that moment to do whatever it took to go organic. That evening I said to Tim that I knew it was a "big ask" but we had to farm the land ourselves again. It was a huge request, because previously we had nearly lost the roof over our heads through farming, and Tim was rightly scared that the farm would be a big black hole to absorb the Cookery School's hard-earned profits. We struck a deal, however. I agreed to his condition, that the farm had to at least break even, and he agreed to mine, that I would join the Rural Environmental Protection Scheme (REPS), which gave an increased payment to organic farms during the transition period. A reasonable request you might think, but we have never been fans of the grant system, preferring instead to borrow minimally, work like mad, and pay back what's owed. Tim agreed, however, that this might tide us over during the conversion period.

We applied to the Organic Trust, and they inspected the farm and explained the criteria. After we registered, we entered a two-year conversion period, during which the use of any chemicals or sprays was forbidden, but after this time we were awarded full Organic Trust certification. It was a steep learning curve. At that time, the perception of organic farming was far from positive. People imagined weed-infested fields, cosmetically challenged produce, low yields, and sick animals that couldn't be treated with antibiotics. Our hugely skilled farm staff, none of whom had any training in organic growing, was quite resistant to the idea at first, convinced I would still want beautiful produce. However, with the acre of greenhouses that we have at Ballymaloe (a relic of our commercial horticulture enterprise), which we use to grow as many as 50 crops a year, albeit in small quantities, we realized that no one in the British Isles was attempting to grow this kind of variety organically, and quickly our farm and garden team rose to the challenge.

Good advice was very hard to come by, and we were told it would take 20 years to rebuild the fertility of the land. Fortunately, I had heard about the Soil Association, a membership charity based in the UK that campaigns for healthy, humane, and sustainable food and farming use. We joined in 1998 and attended our first Soil Association conference in Circencester in 1999, which proved another turning point. The Soil Association is a wonderful networking organization with a palpable generosity of spirit. We heard some truly brilliant and visionary speakers—Patrick Holden, Helen Browning, Professor Jules Pretty, Professor Nic Lampkin, Jonathon Porritt, and Richard Young—and met so many kindred spirits and received generous advice and support. The conference was totally inspirational and we all returned on a high.

In 2000, we began to see the fruits of our labors when the quality of the crops and the health of the animals stunned all the intial sceptics. The local vet once quipped that "he would be broke if he were depending on us" because he was called so seldom. It was such a joy to have our own organic produce, not only for the family and Ballymaloe House, but also for the students who now come from all over the world to participate in a truly organic farm to fork experience.

The organic farm has continued to develop over the years. We have a few pigs—traditional breeds, including Saddlebacks, Red Duroc, and Gloucestershire Old Spot. We also have three, soon to be five, Jersey cows, which we milk every day and, including these, we currently have 20 beef animals—cows and their offspring. A growing body of research reinforces the argument about the benefits of raw milk from a small organic, grass-fed herd and we offer this to the students, many of whom are tasting it for the first time. (It goes without saying that the herd must be healthy and disease-free.)

In 2007, we converted the farm building below the school into a milking parlor and installed the smallest milking system in Ireland. When *Ear to the Ground* came to film, the presenter Daragh McCullough was greatly amused by this and said that it was the only one in Ireland that had a cluster for every cow. In our system, the cows are milked once a day, in the morning. The calf stays with the cow during the day, but we separate them at night, so there's lots of milk for the morning's milking. This system works really well and there's ample milk for us and for the calf.

When we increased our herd from two to three Jersey cows, we occasionally had surplus milk. We couldn't bear to waste a drop so Tim and Eileen O'Donovan (our gardener and herself a farmer's daughter), experimented with making yogurt using only live yogurt as a starter and our own rich Jersey milk. The resulting yogurt is utterly beautiful, thick and unctuous, with a layer of Jersey cream on top—no milk powder or aspartamane, no flavoring or coloring— just beautiful milk and live culture. It's a revelation to the students who love to make it, and many past students have now gone on to make their own homemade yogurt and turn it into a small business.

In 2009, Tim bought a 50-liter stainless steel vat from a German company called Asta and started to experiment with cheesemaking; he quickly became completely fascinated. The students were also intrigued and now every batch of 12-week students has the option to learn how to milk a cow, separate the organic milk from the cream, and learn how to make many dairy products, including cheese. As each student's cheese matures, they look after it lovingly and as they leave they pack it into their suitcases to share with their family and friends all over the world.

Left (above): *We grow a couple of varieties of grapes in the greenhouses: Muscat d'Alexandrie and Black Hamburg. We have also been trying some varieties of wine grape for Colm McCan, consultant sommelier at Ballymaloe House. So far, the results have not been promising, and it doesn't look like we are going to be producing Grand Cru wines any time soon.*

Left (below): *A zucchini blossom ready for stuffing or to add to a salad or fritters.*

Above (left): *Eileen O'Donovan, a woman of many talents—gardener extraordinaire, who also milks the cows and makes butter, cheese, and yogurt from their rich milk.*

Above (right): *Susan Turner, consultant Head Gardener at the School. She also teaches organic gardening to the 12-week students who have a particular interest in the subject, as well as a whole series of day courses on gardening, compost-making, seed-saving, and garden design for the general public.*

The pigs and cows are also part of the self-guided Educational Farm walk, which my son Toby and his wife, Penny, initiated in 2009, due to popular demand. The trail takes visitors through the farm and gardens and into the greenhouses and provides interesting information about all their diverse features and activities—the various animals, plant varieties, breeds of poultry, composting, milking parlor, dairy, photovoltaic system, and student vegetable beds. We also sometimes lead guided tours of the farm and garden for special interest and team-building groups.

Attitudes to organic food are changing, albeit slowly, particularly during these challenging economic times. Interestingly, 80 percent of sales of baby food in the UK are organic and several of the biggest baby food manufacturers are reported to be considering discontinuation of conventional baby food. The hope is that this bulge of concern about how food is produced will continue to gather momentum through the generations. Virtually all supermarkets now sell a range, sometimes limited, of organic produce, but local farmers' markets sell an extensive range of local and imported organic produce, which was unheard of 15 years ago.

According to Patrick Holden, formerly of the Soil Association and now of the Sustainable Food Trust, the Departments of Health and Agriculture and the farming organizations are ignoring at their peril the detrimental consequences of intensively produced food—a public health time bomb that needs to be addressed. Even though I didn't get politically involved in the organic movement in Ireland, preferring to lead by example, 14 years later the range of organic produce we grow is arguably the most diverse in the country, in excess of 80 crops. We employ 50–56 people on our 100-acre organic farm throughout the year, depending on the season, which may just be a record in the "developed world"!

Since 2001, two French horticultural colleges have been sending interns to work in the organic gardens and greenhouses. We were amazed when their lecturers told us that they don't know of anywhere in the whole of Europe where there is such bio-diversity and a wide range of experience for their students, with the extra bonus of good food. Even though the greenhouses are not heated, we grow year round and have planted peaches, nectarines, apricots, figs, kiwis, grapes, loquats, and citrus fruit around the perimeter and over the central path. This year's big excitement is our pomegranate tree, which has produced fruit for the very first time. Students and visitors to the garden are intrigued to see these fruits flourishing happily in Shanagarry.

Since about 2008 we have put a farm stand outside the Ballymaloe Cookery School Shop, so local people and visitors can buy fresh organic produce from the farm and gardens, and pick up free recipes and cooking suggestions. We also sell our handmade organic Jersey butter, yogurt, and raw milk. The shop, managed by Toby and Penny, also sells a range of craft, kitchen, and household items, as well as jam and preserves.

Above (top): My sister Elizabeth O'Connell, who worked in the gardens for many years.
Above (bottom): Haulie Walsh, our farm manager, who has been working with us since his teens.
Right: A crop of peppers flourishing in the greenhouse.

Patrick Holden

" It would be hard to overstate the significance of the contribution that Darina Allen and her extended family at the Ballymaloe Cookery School have made toward the development of a new food culture fit for the 21st century.

In my book, Darina is nothing short of an Irish national treasure. Over the last 30 years she and her husband, Tim, have created at Ballymaloe what I believe should be seen as one of the templates upon which our future food systems are designed. Ballymaloe is a truly inspirational example of a project that combines training and education in culinary skills, local production and sourcing, and the integration of the cultural and social dimension, and it is upon this fusion that I believe the long-term success of all truly sustainable food production systems will depend.

I first met Darina around 20 years ago, in the late 1990s, at a time when the Soil Association ran an annual conference on sustainable and organic food production at the Royal College of Agriculture, Cirencester. It was typical of Darina, who was already a well-known food celebrity in Irish circles, with her own hugely popular television show, that she came year after year as a delegate and participant, thus greatly contributing to the extraordinary conviviality and energy that characterized the Cirencester conferences at that time.

After capitulating to her irresistible offer of a visit to Ballymaloe, I was immediately intoxicated and inspired by the atmosphere of the Cookery School, the openness and generosity of Darina and Tim, and the unique and unforgettable Irish hospitality, which has become a hallmark of all the ventures of the Allen family and the Ballymaloe community.

As Darina showed us around the Cookery School, I could only marvel at the story of its genesis, as she related how, when she and Tim took on the 100-acre family farm, situated close to the already famous Ballymaloe House hotel, they not only had the vision to imagine the piggery converted into a cooking school, but also the courage to press ahead and convert the building, despite the polite refusal of the local bank manager to give them a loan!

Since those early beginnings, they have developed the Cookery School to the point where it now has an international reputation and is widely regarded as the best institution of its kind in the world. It is a remarkable testament to Darina's extraordinary qualities—her tenacity, warmth, and enthusiasm, but above all her talent for communicating what she has learned and understood to others.

I deeply admire Darina's lifelong dedication to what could perhaps be described as the fusion of science, art, and alchemy required for the successful preparation and transformation of high-quality ingredients into delicious, nourishing food, eaten in the company of friends and loved ones. For me, this is surely the ultimate physical and cultural expression of quality of life in all civilized societies.

I've always known that high-quality raw ingredients grown sustainably should form an essential element of food culture, but without people like Darina, the sustainable food movement always risked failing to break into the mainstream and remaining confined to a ghetto of well-meaning but worthy practitioners.

By way of a "case study," my daughter Alice was lucky enough to have more than a taste of the Ballymaloe experience after Darina, at virtually no notice, generously allowed her to join one of her legendary 12-week courses. The experience was to prove a turning point in Alice's career development, not only providing her with the foundation of culinary skills, which have been of inestimable value to her ever since, but of equal significance, through some sort of osmosis, she returned intoxicated with the spirit of Irish magic that pervades Ballymaloe. This has shaped not only her subsequent thinking, but also her career pathway as a grower and champion of the emergent food culture. This has been especially gratifying for me, since it is becoming clear that her generation is now taking over the baton from their aging parents!

One of the key reasons that this has happened is because in addition to being a cooking school, Ballymaloe has also become a center for culture and the arts, a magnet for young people who would otherwise have probably migrated to Dublin or equivalent cities, but for whom the combination of the atmosphere and social attractions of a community built on sustainable food foundations with added career opportunities in education and culture, in the end proves to be a more a seductive option.

The entire Ballymaloe project has become one of the beacons of inspiration, which will hopefully inform the evolution of a new 21st-century food culture, and should be regarded as a place of pilgrimage for all those who decide to travel along this path. **"**

Left and Above: Beautiful organic produce from the farm and greenhouses at Ballymaloe.

Garden Peas with Fresh Mint

~❧❧~

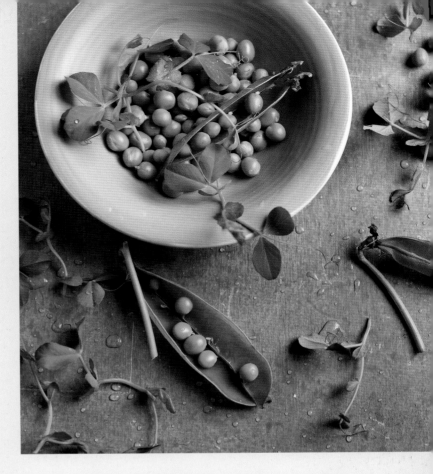

We eat most of our pea crop raw and fresh off the plant. During the pea season, we serve them to our guests in the drawing room at Ballymaloe House so they can nibble the freshly picked peas directly from the pods, either with their drinks or as a first course.

Serves 8
¾ cup water
1 teaspoon salt
1 teaspoon sugar
a sprig of mint
1lb garden peas, freshly shelled
2 tablespoons salted butter
1–2 teaspoons freshly chopped mint

Bring the water to a boil in a medium saucepan. Add the salt, sugar, mint, and peas and bring back to a boil over high heat, simmering until the peas are cooked, about 4–5 minutes. Strain, reserving the water for soup or gravy.

To serve, pour the peas into a serving bowl, add the butter, and sprinkle some freshly chopped mint over the top. Add a little extra seasoning, if necessary. Serve immediately.

Variation
Frozen peas can be extraordinarily good; the cheaper brands tend to lack flavor, so buy the best you can afford. A mixture of fresh peas and fava beans, tossed in a little good butter and some freshly chopped mint is also splendid.

Peas in the Pod

freshly picked peas

Pick the peas and put them in individual bowls for each person. Serve as a first course. Everyone will love it—both the peas and the experience.

Corn with Butter and Sea Salt

~❧❧~

Unless you actually grow your own, or are fortunate enough to have a close neighbor who grows corn, you'll never be able to taste it at its most exquisite. For perfection, it should be cooked within minutes of being picked.

Serves 4
4 ears of corn, ideally just picked
5–7 tablespoons salted butter
sea salt

Bring a large saucepan of water to a fast rolling boil and add lots of salt (3 teaspoons of salt for every quart of water). Peel the husks and silks off the corn and trim the ends. Put the corn into boiling water, bring back to a boil, and cook for 3 minutes. Drain. Serve immediately with butter and sea salt.

Beet Purée with Toasted Cumin Seeds and Buffalo Curd on Poppadoms

A delicious combination inspired by a canapé I tasted at The Dutch House in Galle, Sri Lanka, made by Eloise Schwerdt.

Trim the beets, leaving the whole root and 2in of leaf stalks on top. Hold them under a running faucet and wash off the mud with the palms of your hands so that you don't damage the skin (otherwise the beets will bleed during cooking). Put in a saucepan, cover with cold water, and add a little salt and sugar. Cover and bring to a boil, then simmer for 1–2 hours, depending on the size of beets. You can tell beets are cooked if they dent when pressed with a finger. If in doubt, test with a skewer or the tip of a knife.

Drain, peel off the skins, and chop coarsely. Put the beet flesh into a blender with half of the buffalo curd (or goat cheese) and a drizzle of olive oil. Pulse to a smooth purée and season to taste with salt, pepper, and a drop of balsamic vinegar (if using). Taste and add a squeeze of lime juice, if necessary.

Preheat the sunflower oil to 350°F in a deep-fat fryer or use a shallow pan with at least 1in of oil. Cut each poppadom into eight triangles and deep-fry in the hot oil until crisp.

To serve, put a dollop of beet purée on each poppadom triangle, crumble a little of the remaining buffalo curd (or goat cheese) over the top. Finish with a little pinch of toasted cumin seeds and cilantro.

Makes 30–32

8oz beets
sea salt
sugar
5oz Buffalo curd or soft goat cheese
extra virgin olive oil
freshly ground black pepper
balsamic vinegar (optional)
1 lime (optional)
sunflower oil, for deep-frying
4 poppadoms (or pitas, if you can't find poppadoms)

To serve
1 tablespoon toasted cumin seeds, lightly crushed
cilantro

Asparagus with Romesco and Crème Fraîche

The asparagus season was in full swing during the Ballymaloe Literary Festival of Food and Wine in May 2013, so Skye Gyngell chose to cook this recipe to celebrate.

Preheat the oven to 350°F.

Put the nuts on a baking sheet and toast on the middle rack of the oven for 3 minutes to color them slightly. Remove from the oven, then roughly pound to a paste using a mortar and pestle.

Pulse the bread in a food processor until you have crumbs, scatter them on a baking sheet, and bake until golden—about 6–8 minutes.

Put the tomatoes on a baking sheet and drizzle with a dash of olive oil. Add the whole chile and roast with the tomatoes for 10 minutes. Remove from the oven and add to the hazelnuts in the mortar and pestle. Pound to a coarse paste. Add the garlic, sherry vinegar, and paprika, and mix together. Add the toasted bread crumbs and pour in the remaining olive oil and season to taste. Stir well to combine.

Bring a large saucepan of water to a boil and season liberally with salt. While the water is coming to a boil, prepare the asparagus by snapping off their woody ends. Plunge the asparagus into the water and cook until just tender when pierced with a knife. The cooking time will largely depend on the size and thickness of the spears, but as a general rule of thumb, it should take about 1 minute. Drain and dress with the extra virgin olive oil, lemon juice, and a little sea salt and pepper.

Divide the asparagus between four plates, or place on one large plate if you prefer. Split the crème fraîche between the plates and sprinkle the Romesco sauce over the top. Serve immediately.

Serves 4

20 asparagus spears
good pinch of sea salt
1 tablespoon extra virgin olive oil
a few drops of lemon juice
sea salt and freshly ground black pepper

For the Romesco
12 blanched almonds
12 hazelnuts
1 thick slice of chewy, peasant-style bread, such as ciabatta
2 ripe tomatoes, peeled
½ cup extra virgin olive oil, plus extra for drizzling
1 whole red chile (the ancho variety, if you can get hold of one)
2 garlic cloves, crushed to a paste
1 tablespoon good-quality sherry vinegar
1 teaspoon sweet-smoked paprika (I prefer Spanish to Hungarian)

To serve
2 tablespoons crème fraîche

Top (left): My daughter Lydia manning the Ballymaloe Cookery School stand at Midleton Farmers' Market.

Top (right): Myrtle Allen giving a speech at the opening of Midleton Farmers' Market.

Middle (left): We like to make handwritten and illustrated labels for the produce we sell at the stall.

Middle (right): Local artisan fish smoker Frank Hederman's smoked mackerel from his Belvelly smokehouse, near Cobh.

Bottom (left): Mozzarella and a selection of olives at Toby Simmonds' olive stall.

Bottom (right): The range of produce on offer at the Ballymaloe Cookery School stand includes everything from meringues, cakes, and granola to homemade jams.

Farmers' Markets

In 1995, I went to San Francisco to visit my friend Mary Risley, who owns the Tante Marie Cooking School. I arrived late in the evening pretty exhausted, but Mary announced that we must be up early the next day to go to see the new farmers' market in a parking lot on the Embarcadero near Green Street. I'd seen tons of great markets in France, Italy, and Spain—Boulevard Raspail in Paris, the Rialto Market in Venice, and La Boqueria in Barcelona— and wasn't at all eager to be dragged out of bed at dawn to see a collection of stalls, but Mary is even bossier than me, so I was rousted out of bed at 7:30 a.m.

This was like no market I'd ever seen before; stallholders were a mixed bunch of urban farmers and professionals who had chucked in their careers in favor of a more agreeable self-sufficient lifestyle in Mendocino or Marin county. Stalls were piled high with their homegrown organic vegetables, orchard and stone fruit and berries, dried peaches, artisan breads, free-range chickens and eggs, garden flowers, homemade cookies and cakes, and one stall sold nothing but bunches of beautiful sweet peas in recycled silver tin cans. Several local restaurants and cafés had decamped to the market because that's where all the action was on a Saturday morning; it was absolutely the coolest place to see and be seen.

Suddenly I had a lightbulb moment: During the mid-1990s, the supermarkets in Ireland had gone over to a central distribution system, which meant that their stores were discouraged from buying more than a couple of percent of their stock locally; in some cases they were actually penalized for buying local. This had a devastating effect on local producers who were too small to be in the system and who relied on local stores for their livelihood. So on one side there were local people who were desperate to buy local food, and on the other were producers desperate to sell, but there was no way they could meet unless customers went directly to the farms, which simply wasn't feasible for the majority of the population. It was suddenly blindingly obvious: local markets were the answer. If we could reestablish the markets then local farmers could sell their produce directly to local people. Bingo!

"Country Markets" were established by the Irish Countrywomen's Association in 1946 for the sale of home-produced food and handcrafts. When first set up, it gave women working in the home an opportunity to sell their produce: jams, cakes, bread, hand-knitting, flowers, and plants. The markets are still held weekly indoors in many country towns and are well worth visiting, but we thought we could take this idea further with a proper farmers' market selling produce on a larger scale.

My mother-in-law, Myrtle Allen, loved the idea, so in June 1996, we started the first new-age farmers' market in Ireland on the Coal Quay in Cork City, where there has been a market for over 400 years under the auspices of the Cork Free Choice Consumer Group, of which Myrtle was president. The Cork Free Choice Consumer Group was formed in 1989 by the customers of two highly skilled French cheesemakers, Martin Guillemot and Anne-Marie Jaumaud, living in West Cork, whose business was threatened by a raft of new food hygiene regulations. They were unable to save the cheesemakers but continued to find, support, and promote producers of high-quality food in Cork city and county, especially small specialists and traditional producers, and to put them in touch with interested consumers. They still meet monthly in the Crawford Art Gallery and have a speaker on a food-related topic. Sometimes small food producers come along and give a presentation and tasting, on other occasions it might be a talk on GM, water quality, where to find a decent chicken or good heritage pork, additives in food, how to cook inexpensive cuts of meat, a healthy diet, fun food for children, or making the most of your polytunnel growing winter vegetables.

My *Simply Delicious* series was on television at the time so it was a source of great amusement to all and sundry when I turned up with my stall, two iron trestle tables with a couple of teak boards on top and a blue gingham cloth. I wish I could remember what I brought with me. It was a May weekend, so only the first of the early vegetables were ready to harvest, a few lettuces, bunches of our neighbor Patty Walsh's rhubarb, homemade granola, some jam,

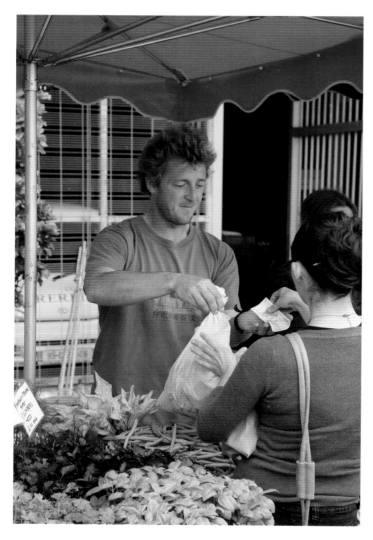

Above: A customer buying delicious fresh produce at the Ballymaloe Cookery School market stall. Every weekend, unless I am away, I am on the stall at Midleton Farmers' Market with my shawl. I love the camaraderie between the stallholders and the banter with the customers is, as Frank Hederman once said, "like pure therapy."

a few chutneys, local honey, and some home baking. We printed little flyers and left them in local restaurants and gradually people heard about the market.

The difficulties encountered by small producers of good products was investigated at meetings. A delegation went to Dublin to ask the health and safety officials to reconsider the ban on the sale of goods from home kitchens. A committee was set up to study the risks, and later the Artisan Food Forum was set up in January 2004 to liaise with the Food Safety Authority about the challenges faced by the artisan sector. Considerable progress has been made.

The Midleton Farmers' Market was launched in 2000 on Saturday, June 10—Pentecost weekend, a "moveable feast"—with 12 stalls. After initial discussions about the location with the local community, it was set up behind the Court House with the full support of the Chamber of Commerce and the Urban Council. From an initial 12 stalls, the market has blossomed and gone from strength to strength. Among the original stallholders were: Frank Hederman with his smoked fish; Ardsallagh goat cheese; Kate O'Donovan with her salad dressings; Willie Scannell selling floury Ballycotton potatoes; Ted Murphy with vegetable and flowering plants and hanging baskets; Dan Aherne with beef from his farm, which was in the process of converting to organic production at that time; Toby Simmonds' olive stall; Caroline Robinson, who grows the most beautiful chemical-free vegetables on her farm near Bandon in West Cork; Jill Bell, now from Well and Good Health Food Shop in Midleton; and several different bread and cake stalls. Mrs. Burns, who has been a vegetable trader for over 40 years, was also one of the founding members, selling a variety of local vegetables, bundles of fresh carrots and turnips, all in season. Before long, there was a waiting list for spaces for stalls.

Ballymaloe Organic Farm and Gardens also had a stall from the beginning. The stall sells homegrown organic vegetables, lots of free-range eggs, brown bread, jams and chutneys, and over the years has branched out into offering little bunches of sweet peas, Nora Aherne's ducks, fresh herbs, salad dressings, elderflower cordial, and occasionally organic free-range pork from our own Saddleback pigs. Today, Julija Makejeva cooks all week for the Midleton Farmers' Market and Farm Shop beside the Cookery School.

Some of the students at the Cookery School are interested in the farmers' market as a career option, so they love to come to the Midleton Farmers' Market weekly to learn how to set up and operate a farmers' market. They also love to help Julija and Igor, who man the stall. We do a detailed evening lecture on every

12-week course for students who are particularly interested in trading in or setting up a farmers' market.

Clodagh McKenna was one of my first students to get involved; she sold homemade chicken liver pâté from the corner of the Ballymaloe Cookery School stall until she got a stall of her own, where she sold delicious homemade fresh pasta, parsley pesto, tomato fondue, toffee apples, brown soda bread, and seasonal soups and dressings. (Later, she went on to write a book and do a TV series on farmers' markets, which has led to a very successful career in food.)

Many stallholders who started selling in a small way at farmers' markets, testing their products and getting the reaction of the public, have gone on to establish successful food businesses, including Deirdre Hilliard of Just Foods. Deirdre started in 2004 with a stall selling her homemade soups using organic and, where possible, local ingredients. She now has a commercial kitchen in Cobh and supplies supermarkets and restaurants. Paddy O'Connell made granola and accessed the market in the same way with the help of his mother, Una, who initially roasted baking sheet after baking sheet of grains in their home kitchen. His granola is now very successful nationally. His friend Ross Staunton also started in the farmers' market in Dublin, then spent some time in Australia and, on his return, opened a gourmet food store and café called The Foodgame in Stoneybatter, Dublin, selling lots of Irish artisan produce.

Farmers' markets are set up with the express intention of providing an outlet for farmers and small food producers to sell local seasonal produce to the consumers who are desperately seeking this kind of food. Farmers' markets are quite different from some of the established markets. Aside from a few rare exceptions like Skibbereen in West Cork, they do not sell clothes, CDs, tools, or bric-a-brac, but simply sell local food to local people; the producers themselves or an appropriate representative must man the stall. The markets enable farmers and food producers to sell their goods locally, which benefits them and the local community. They keep the money circulating within the local area and attract people to adjacent retail businesses. Farmers' markets also help the environment by encouraging sustainable agriculture and small-scale, less intensive production. They reduce the effects of long-distance transportation of food and the need for excess packaging. The variety of produce they offer is amazing and, of course, most abundant during the growing season. For example, as you enter the Midleton Farmers' Market area, you might see Kate O'Donovan, who sells her delicious homemade marinades, dressings, and dips,

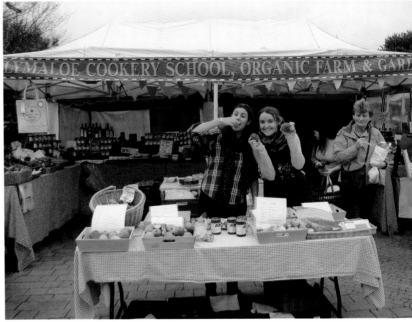

Above (top): A busy stand at Midleton Farmers' Market.
(bottom): Students enjoying their time working on the Ballymaloe Cookery School stand. They come weekly on a rotating basis to learn how to set up and operate a successful farmers' market. Students also have the opportunity to attend a detailed lecture on the subject as part of the 12-week course.

or Mrs. Burns, with her selection of local vegetables. Artisan baker Declan Ryan sells his Arbutus, soda, yeast, and sourdough breads. Local farmer Dan Aherne and his wife, Anne, invested in a refrigerated truck and now sell their organic beef. He responded to the numerous requests for free-range organic chickens and now can scarcely fulfill the demand. Oren Little of the Little Apple Co. drives down from Kilkenny every Saturday to sell apples and delicious apple juice, as well as daffodils in the spring.

As you enter Midleton Farmers' Market, which moved to a new site in the Circus Field in 2009, you see Willie Scannell selling his Ballycotton potatoes. He, like so many others, was a victim of the supermarkets' central distribution policy, but now that the Midleton Farmers' Market gives him the opportunity to sell his potatoes directly to the consumer his future is secure, and he's branched out into selling a selection of vegetables including lettuces, cabbages, white turnips, radishes, and onions.

There are now 26 stalls selling a wide variety of produce, from freshly caught fish, which the O'Driscoll brothers from West Cork will fillet as you wait, to O'Connell's handmade chocolates, Woodfield free-range pork and charcuterie, gluten-free produce, Ballyhora wild and cultivated mushrooms, Green Saffron spices, crepes, and lots of organic produce.

From the beginning, the market has been enthusiastically supported, not only by the local community, but also by the local shops that report an increase in business on market day. From a base of one farmers' market in 1996, there are now in excess of 160 around Ireland—some are small, others, such as Mahon Point, Midleton, and Douglas, are large and vibrant. It has helped change the way many people shop and provides another option for those who want to engage with the people who produce their food.

From these humble beginnings, farmers' markets have spread all over Ireland and continue to gather momentum. Despite the challenging economic climate of recent years, farmers' markets have held their own, and have meant the difference between survival or closure for many farmers, fishermen, and food producers.

Of all the projects I've been involved with over the years, I think it's true to say that the reestablishment of the farmers' market is the one of which I am most proud—several people are on record that they feel they would not still be farming were it not for the fact that they get the full fair price for their product directly into their hands at the farmers' market. How wonderful is that?

Left: The range of delicious, fresh, organic produce on offer at the Ballymaloe Cookery School stand.
Right (top): Organic peppers grown at Ballymaloe.
Right (bottom): Willie Scannell, one of the founding members of the Midleton Farmers' Market, whose floury Ballycotton potatoes draw customers from far and wide.

Heirloom Tomato Salad with Wasabi Mascarpone

We've been growing heirloom tomatoes ever since I first tasted them in San Francisco in 1999. I arrived home with packets of heirloom seeds and our gardener, Susan Turner, also sourced a great selection from the Heritage Seed Library in London. One year we grew over 50 varieties: The flavor, texture, and appearance are completely different; some are tiny, others huge, but all are delicious. This salad is inspired by one eaten at Yotam Ottolenghi's NOPI restaurant.

Serves 4

18oz heirloom tomatoes, such as Tibet Apple, Oxheart, Cherokee Purple, Black Prince, Yellow Brandywine, German Pink, and Big Red
3 tablespoons extra virgin olive oil
1 tablespoon Chardonnay vinegar
pinch of sugar (optional)
a handful of micro greens and purple basil leaves

For the Wasabi Mascarpone Dressing
½ cup mascarpone
2–3 tablespoons milk
2–3 teaspoons wasabi
1 tablespoon pine nuts, lightly roasted
1 teaspoon finely chopped tarragon
2 teaspoons finely sliced scallions
sea salt and freshly ground black pepper

To serve
crusty bread

First, make the dressing. Loosen the mascarpone with a little milk. Stir in the wasabi, pine nuts, chopped tarragon, and scallions. Season with sea salt and freshly ground black pepper and set aside to mature for 15–30 minutes.

Slice the heirloom tomatoes in half or into quarters, depending on size, and put them in a bowl. Season with sea salt and freshly ground black pepper. Whisk the oil and vinegar together and drizzle over the tomatoes. Taste, adding a pinch of sugar, if necessary. Put a generous tablespoon of wasabi mascarpone in the center of a white plate or in a small bowl. Pile the heirloom tomatoes onto the plate and scatter the micro greens and basil leaves over the top. Serve immediately with lots of crusty bread.

Roast Jerusalem Artichoke Slices

What would we do without kale and Jerusalem artichokes in the winter? For us, they are must-have winter vegetables, so versatile and fantastically nutritious. Jerusalem artichokes have the highest inulin content of any vegetable (a prebiotic that helps to develop and preserve a healthy intestinal flora).

Try to grow them yourself—if you plant one you'll have at least a dozen or more the next year because they spread like wildfire. They have tall green foliage and yellow flowers in early fall. When they are freshly dug, you hardly need to peel them—a definite advantage. They also make tasty gratins, soups, and purées, and are delicious raw. You'll need to put them into acidulated water if you are not using or cooking immediately, because they discolor as they oxidize.

Serves 4–6

1lb Jerusalem artichokes, well scrubbed
2 tablespoons extra virgin olive oil
sea salt
a few thyme or rosemary sprigs (optional)
freshly ground black pepper

Preheat the oven to 400°F and line a roasting pan with baking parchment.

Slice the artichokes into rounds $^1\!/_3$in thick. Toss them in extra virgin olive oil and season well with salt. Arrange in a single layer on the prepared roasting pan. Roast in the hot oven for 10 minutes, until golden on one side, then flip them over and cook them on the other side until golden. Test with the tip of a knife—they should be tender. Sprinkle with thyme or rosemary (if using), season with black pepper, and serve.

Sweet Chile Sauce

The students adore this Sweet Chile Sauce. We also make and sell this both at Midleton Farmers' Market and in the Farm Shop beside the School; people love it. We often joke that we need to set up a helpline because it's so popular. Serve with everything!

Makes 12–13 x ½ pint bottles

60 red chiles (we use medium hot Serrano chiles or Dutch chiles)
30 garlic cloves, peeled
3 quarts white wine vinegar
9 cups granulated sugar
7½ tablespoons salt

Pulse the chiles and garlic in a food processor. Put the vinegar and sugar into a heavy-bottomed saucepan and stir over medium heat to dissolve the sugar. Add the puréed chile and garlic mixture to the pan, along with the salt. Bring to a boil, then simmer over medium heat until the sauce has reduced by half—at least 1 hour. Pour into 12–13 x ½ pint sterilized bottles, put on the lids, and set aside to cool. Store in a cool, dark place for up to 12 months.

Madhur Jaffrey

Above (top) and (bottom): Madhur Jaffrey and me in the original Cookery School in 1988.

When the Ballymaloe Cookery School was launched I realized that I had the opportunity to invite my food heroes from all over the world to teach at the School. The fact that they were not only happy, but also excited, to come to Ireland to teach at a little cooking school in the middle of a farm was the most thrilling revelation to me.

Madhur Jaffrey was high on my list of culinary icons. Her Indian cooking series was on television—I couldn't wait to buy the book and was enchanted, though somewhat intimidated, by some of the recipes, which included long lists of exotic-sounding ingredients and spices. I yearned to learn more. I can't quite remember how I managed to find Madhur's contact details, possibly through Zanne Stewart, then food editor of *Gourmet* magazine. It was one of the first transatlantic phone calls I had ever made, and I was overawed by the reality of being able to talk to someone on the other side of the world, so I really had to psych myself up. I distinctly remember listening to the ring tone and wondering whether Madhur would pick up. She did, and I then had to summon up all my courage to ask whether she would come and teach at a little cooking school in Ireland. She graciously said yes to my invitation. I now know that she had read about the Ballymaloe Cookery School in *Gourmet* magazine's cover story in March 1986 and was intrigued. I was totally thrilled and remember getting off the phone, punching the air, and rushing off to tell Timmy, my PA, Rosalie, and my parents-in-law the good news.

Madhur arrived, dressed in one of her many exquisite saris, with her lovely husband, Sanford, in July 1986. Even then, Madhur had a global following. The course was totally overbooked, and people flew in from London to attend. Madhur cooked delicious food with a little apron over her saris.

Madhur sent the menu and list of recipes well ahead of time. The challenge for us in July 1986 was to source all of the ingredients. Many were completely unfamiliar, not only to me, but to many of my suppliers. Even some names were different, so Sanford sweetly offered to go to Cork with Tim to choose the correct dals. I knew about orange lentils (from lentil soup at boarding school), but what on earth was chana dal, rajma dal, urad dal, toor dal (also known as split or yellow pigeon peas) and moong dal…? Then there was amchoor (mango powder made from dried unripe green mangoes), asafoetida, tamarind, gram flour, ajwain (or ajowan) seeds, kalonji, Oriental sesame oil, poha, mooli radish, and lima beans.

Fresh ginger and spices were easy enough to source from the English Market in Cork, where Mr. Bell's stall was a rich source of ethnic ingredients, but some, like fenugreek and black cardamom, I had never used before. Chiles were also a minefield. We managed to find some dried ones similar to those Madhur needed.

Even rice created a challenge; Tim was intrigued as Sanford showed him how to judge really fine basmati rice by its smell and appearance. The rice shouldn't be dusty in texture or have lots of broken grains. He urged us to buy loose rice rather than prepackaged so we could examine it for quality. Cilantro also had to be imported from London and so, sadly, was not at its best when it arrived.

So much has changed—all these ingredients are now readily and widely available. Cilantro is a must-have herb, and we grow it year-round, in the greenhouses in winter and outdoors in the herb garden in summer. We've also learned to use everything from the leaves to the stems, roots, flowers, and seeds in the dishes we cook and teach the students.

On Madhur's last visit she was particularly impressed by the quality of the spices that our past student Arun Kapil, of Green Saffron, imports directly from his relatives' spice gardens in India. Madhur whetted our appetite for India to such an extent that we now make annual visits and each year come back with more recipes, food memories, and images to share with our students at the School.

Madhur's classes are not just cooking classes, but lessons in the history, culture, and customs of her beloved India. She taught four more classes at the School in July 1988, July 1991, July 1996, and July 2001, and returned in 2013 for the inaugural Ballymaloe Literary Festival of Food and Wine, giving both a cooking demonstration and a talk on her latest book, *Curry Nation*.

Right (top): Me, Dervilla Flynn, Suzanne Walsh, Madhur, Breda Murphy, Claire Cullinane, and Rachel Allen.
Right (middle): Me and Madhur enjoying afternoon tea in the sunroom.
Right (bottom): Madhur Jaffrey giving a cooking demonstration at the Ballymaloe Literary Festival of Food and Wine, May 2013.

Shrimp Curry

The spicing in Sri Lankan curries is subtle but pretty perky. They are usually served as part of a selection of curries, such as Cashew Curry, Pineapple Curry, and Garlic Curry, with lots of raitas and side dishes—truly a feast. (Pictured bottom right on page 203.)

Serves 8

2¼lb jumbo shrimp in their shells
2 tablespoons vegetable oil
a sprig of fresh curry leaves
1–2oz red onion, finely chopped
4–6 garlic cloves, peeled and finely chopped
3–4 green chiles, finely sliced
1 cinnamon stick
2 teaspoons chile powder
pinch of ground turmeric
½ teaspoon ground fenugreek
1¼ teaspoons salt
½ cup coconut milk

Peel, devein, and wash the shrimp, reserving the heads and shells. Set aside.

Put the shrimp heads and shells in a food processor with a splash of water and grind to a smooth paste. Set aside.

Heat the oil in a medium saucepan and, once it is very hot, add the curry leaves. Add the onion, garlic, chile, spices, salt, and shrimp and stir well over high heat for about 5 minutes. Scoop in the ground extract of shrimp, pour in the coconut milk, and simmer gently for 7–10 minutes.

Serve as part of a selection of curries or with rice, a green salad, and fruit raita.

Pumpkin Curry

Fresh curry leaves are more readily available these days, and you can usually buy them from Asian suppliers. They may also have pandanus leaves, which also make a terrific ice cream and custard. (Pictured top right on page 203.)

Serves 8

2¼lb pumpkin, peeled and cut into 1in chunks
4 green chiles, finely sliced
2 tablespoons finely chopped Bombay (or red) onion
2 garlic cloves, peeled and finely chopped
a sprig of fresh curry leaves
1 teaspoon salt
1 teaspoon ground fenugreek
1 teaspoon mustard powder
pinch of ground turmeric
½ cup coconut milk

Put all the ingredients in a medium saucepan and bring to a boil. Simmer until the pumpkin is cooked—for 10–20 minutes, depending on the type of pumpkin.

Serve with a selection of curries or on its own, accompanied by rice.

Cashew Curry

The Dutch House in Galle is one of my favorite places on earth to stay. This delicious Sri Lankan curry recipe, plus the others on the previous page, were given to me by Chef Shanti at The Sun House and Dutch House in Galle.

Put the cashews in a saucepan, cover them with boiling water, and set aside to soak for at least 3–4 hours, preferably overnight. Drain under cold running water. Return the cashews to the pan, cover with fresh water and cook until tender but not soft—for about 10 minutes. Drain well.

Preheat the oil in a medium saucepan, add the curry leaves, onions, and garlic and fry over medium heat until the onions are golden—about 3 minutes. Add the cashews along with the powdered spices and salt and cook for 5–10 minutes, stirring occasionally.

Pour in the coconut milk, bring to a boil, and simmer for 8 minutes. Scatter the cilantro over the top and serve with poppadoms or boiled rice.

Serves 8

18oz dried unsalted cashews
vegetable oil, for frying
a sprig of curry leaves
2 onions, finely chopped
5 garlic cloves, peeled and finely chopped
1 teaspoon ground fenugreek
3–4 teaspoons chile powder
1 teaspoon ground cinnamon
2 teaspoons curry powder
¼ teaspoon ground turmeric
1¼ teaspoons salt
½ cup coconut milk

To serve
cilantro
poppadoms or boiled rice

Food Allergies

Like many people of my generation, I never even realized that food allergies or intolerances existed until the mid-1980s. In fact, I vividly remember the moment at dinner in a very famous restaurant called Spago in Los Angeles while I was over for an IACP Conference in 1986. The waiter seemed to be taking ages to take the order around the table and I overheard several of the American guests saying things like "I can't do pork," "I don't eat dairy," "I'm allergic to chicken," "No gluten, please—I have a wheat intolerance." I had just about heard of celiac disease before, but the others? What was that all about?

It was my first trip to the US; I was wide-eyed with wonder. No one else at the table seemed to think it in the least unusual so I decided that they were all neurotic over there! I just absorbed it all and when I came home I remember telling everyone about this episode and several others and dismissing it as people's imagination. Little did I know that within a few years many people in these islands would be displaying signs of not one, but, in some cases, multiple food allergies.

This was not a subject we needed to address in any detail in the early years of the School, when we had only an occasional celiac or diabetic student, but in more recent years the number of students with food allergies and intolerances has increased dramatically. The main foods that people are allergic to are wheat, dairy, pork, chicken, oranges, mushrooms, and now even celery and pine nuts.

From the mid-1980s, we began to get requests at the Cookery School for a course on food with no dairy products, and an increasing number of requests for gluten-free food. In June 1991, we offered a No Butter, Cream, or Booze course—ideal for anyone allergic to dairy. In 2000, we taught Delicious Food for Celiacs, which was run as a longer course in 2002 and morphed into a course in Healthy Gluten-free Eating by 2006. This course, taught by one of our former students and teachers, Rosemary Kearney, is a huge success. Rosemary has been a celiac all her life and is a beautiful cook. Teaching these courses is especially touching. The participants are a mixture of those with celiac disease, some newly diagnosed and still in the process of adjusting. Others have been lifelong sufferers and are desperately trying to find good food, convinced that they will never be able to taste a delicious slice of cake or a dessert. Others are parents or partners of people with celiac disease who are trying to cook for them. They are blown away by the food and so grateful for simple recipes that work—one woman actually burst into tears when she tasted Rosemary's muffins. We run three Healthy Gluten-free Eating courses a year and the numbers continue to rise. All our 12-week students attend this course as well, because knowledge of cooking for food allergies is now an essential part of a chef's repertoire, since those with celiac disease and other allergy sufferers have increased in numbers. Direction on how to cope with, and cater for, people with food allergies and intolerances is an integral part of the course. The course also presents an opportunity for students to provide delicious food for those with celiac disease and to service the growing demand for "free-from" food.

The most common allergies and intolerances seem to be connected to wheat, dairy, and eggs, although many students discover that they can eat our organic free-range eggs without any ill-effect. We have also had students who have been diagnosed as dairy intolerant but who find that they can eat our organic yogurt and drink our raw milk. This leads to questions and debate over whether it is the raw product that's the problem or what's done to it in processing that is resulting in the increase in the number of food allergy sufferers—it would be fascinating to have more research on this subject.

Recently the Food Safety Authority of Ireland (FSAI) issued a list of 14 foods that restaurant guests may be allergic to: nuts, gluten (including cereals containing gluten), milk, shellfish, eggs, celery, fish, milk, crustaceans, almonds, cashews, peanuts, oats, and wheat. Since the late 1990s, we have asked our incoming students to make us aware of any food issues. The figures seem to be growing each term, and those suffering from food allergies can now be in excess of 25 percent of a class.

Approximately 1 percent of the Irish population is affected by celiac disease. In the United States, the prevalence among healthy individuals is 1 in 133, according to the University of Chicago Celiac Disease Center. It is a complex issue, but there is unquestionably a genetic element to the disease. For this book, I tried hard to get definite answers to the allergy queries, but it is difficult to get definitive data. Some contend that the numbers are significantly greater today because diagnosis is better, which is unquestionably the case. Certainly there is a greater awareness of the problem, but self-diagnosis can skew the figures.

Several major studies are underway, including an EU-funded multidisciplinary project involving 17 European member-states on the "Prevalence, cost, and basis of food allergy across Europe." Some of the data is already available at www.europrevall.org. The next big body of work being carried out is by the European Food Safety Authority (EFSA), as a result of a request by FSAI. They are due to publish a draft report in 2013, then put it out for consultation and publish a final opinion in 2014. The questions asked by FSAI, which the report will tackle are: the prevalence of each allergy in the European Union; recommendations for threshold concentrations of each allergen in food that would provide an acceptable level of protection for at-risk consumers; the suitability, or otherwise, of qualitative and quantitative DNA-based tests for the detection and quantification of food allergens in comparison with immunological or other methods.

The jury is definitely out, but in my observations over 30 years, the amount of people who say they have some type of food allergy or intolerance has increased dramatically. We have had to remove peanut oil from the School altogether, having had several students with a nut allergy who carry an epinephrine injection in case they suffer an extreme allergic reaction. Our staff, teachers, and fellow students are briefed on how to deal with a crisis situation if we have a student with a severe allergy.

The whole issue has made people more aware of and concerned about what goes into our food, and I feel deeply saddened that we are increasingly in a situation where people are becoming uneasy, and in some cases paranoid, about their food, sadly with some justification. This was absolutely not the case when I was a child; in fact, it is a growing phenomenon of the last 20 years.

Dairy-free is easier in many ways—for those who must eliminate all dairy products from the diet, vegetable or extra virgin olive oil can be substituted in many cases, and there are many excellent recipes for olive oil cakes, cookies, and ice creams.

Today, few people eat the food of their local area. At Ballymaloe, we've been not only advocating, but living the "support local" message for well over 60 years, long before the Cookery School was started in 1983. Locally produced food, particularly local honey, milk, free-range eggs, and vegetables, are said to carry the antibodies of the area, so it's really important to incorporate as much local produce into our diets as possible. We're fortunate to live in the center of an organic farm, but many people whose only option is to buy food in the usual retail channels, tell me they feel very vulnerable and helpless. Most of the food we consume comes from all over the world, containing bacteria and enzymes that we are unfamiliar with and that our ancestors were never subjected to. Could this be a factor in the extraordinary growth in food allergies and intolerances? Hay fever sufferers often find relief if they consume really local honey made from the pollens of the plants in the area where they live, and the same could potentially be true of other allergies. We would love to have more research done in this area.

Left: A student on a short course deep in concentration during a hands-on cooking session. Students on the short courses wear civvies, while those on the 12-week courses wear full chef's whites. In the early days, they used to wear a variety of traditional chef's hats, which have now been replaced with bandanas and baseball caps.
Above: The ever cheerful Gary Masterson, one of the tutors at the School. Here he is in the pantry preparing for the afternoon cooking demonstration.

Debbie Shaw's Red Quinoa Tabbouleh with Roasted Pine Nuts and Pomegranate

Debbie Shaw, a teacher at the Ballymaloe Cookery School, is our in-house nutritionist. This is Debbie's version of the classic Middle Eastern salad tabbouleh. She uses quinoa instead of bulgar wheat. Quinoa is an ancient Incan grain and a nutritional powerhouse, with all the amino acids (proteins) the body needs and more calcium than milk. It is a great alternative source of calcium for anyone on a dairy-free diet. It is also wheat- and gluten-free, easy to digest, and very satisfying—everyone loves this salad.

Rinse the quinoa in a strainer under cold running water for 2–3 minutes to remove the natural bitter outer coating. Put the quinoa and salt in a saucepan with a tight-fitting lid and cover with the carefully measured cold water. Bring to a boil, reduce the heat to very low, and cook for 12 minutes, covered, or until the grain is tender. Remove the pan from the heat, keeping the lid on the pan, and set aside to steam for another 10 minutes to fluff up the quinoa.

To make the dressing, mix the olive oil, lemon juice, and honey together in a jar and season to taste.

To serve, add the remaining ingredients to the warm quinoa and pour the dressing over the top. Mix well, then season with freshly ground black pepper, and a little more salt, if necessary. Serve with grilled fish or chicken, or add some cooked chickpeas for a vegetarian option.

Serves 8

1⅓ cups red quinoa
½ teaspoon salt
1½ cups cold water
½ cup freshly chopped flat-leaf parsley, stems removed
½ cup freshly chopped mint, stems removed
seeds of 1 pomegranate
¾ cup chopped scallion, white and green parts
½ cup pine nuts, roasted in a dry frying pan with no oil over medium heat until lightly browned—keep them moving or they will burn!
⅓ cup dried cranberries
2 medium carrots, peeled and coarsely grated
1½ teaspoons ground cinnamon
1 teaspoon ground allspice

For the dressing
¼ cup fruity extra virgin olive oil
juice of 1 lemon
1 teaspoon honey
sea salt and freshly ground black pepper

Carrot and Sweet Potato Soup with Cilantro and Cashew Pesto

For me, soup is comfort food. This is a quick and easy, low fat, dairy-free, and seriously tasty soup. It is also a winter immune super-booster. The carrots and sweet potatoes are high in beta-carotene, which is converted to vitamin A in the body, essential for fighting infection and maintaining strong immunity. The ginger and garlic offer potent antibacterial and antiviral protection.

Heat the olive oil in a large saucepan. Add the carrots, sweet potatoes, onion, chile (if using), garlic, and ginger and season with a generous pinch of salt and pepper. Sweat the vegetables over low heat, until tender but not colored. Add the stock and bring to a boil. Continue to cook until the vegetables are completely tender.

Meanwhile, make the pesto. Put all of the ingredients into a food processor and blend together.

To serve, blend the soup with the cilantro and pour into soup bowls. Drizzle each one with a teaspoon of the Cilantro and Cashew Pesto before serving. (Any leftover pesto can be stored in a glass jam jar in the fridge, covered with a little olive oil, for 2–3 months.)

Serves 4–6

2 tablespoons olive oil
6 carrots, peeled and diced
2 medium sweet potatoes (orange, not white), peeled and diced
1 large onion, diced
1 red chile, seeded and finely chopped (optional)
3 large, juicy garlic cloves, peeled and finely chopped
1in piece of fresh ginger, peeled and finely grated
sea salt and freshly ground black pepper
3–4 cups homemade chicken or vegetable stock
2 tablespoons freshly chopped cilantro

For the Cilantro and Cashew Pesto
3 cups cilantro (leaves and soft stems)
½ cup flat-leaf parsley (leaves only)
¼ red chile, seeded and finely chopped
1 stick of lemongrass, tough outer stem removed, very finely chopped
1 large garlic clove, peeled and finely chopped
1 tablespoon chopped cashews
juice of ½ lime
½ cup extra virgin olive oil
pinch of sea salt and freshly ground black pepper

Spiced Pear, Pecan, and Ginger Crumble

This is a low-fat, dairy-free, and truly tasty dessert. We use coconut oil (which, in spite of its name, is solid, not liquid) instead of butter in this humble crumble. Because of their grainy texture and high pectin content, pears are a natural diuretic and help detoxify the body. Ginger is a super immune booster with potent expectorant and antiseptic properties. In addition, its active compound, gingerol, improves circulation and soothes an upset stomach.

Serves 6–8

8 large ripe pears, peeled and cored and cut into
1in slices lengthwise
1 tablespoon dark-brown muscovado sugar
1 tablespoon finely grated fresh ginger
juice and finely grated zest of ½ lemon

For the crumble
½ cup white spelt flour
4 tablespoons solid coconut oil (not extra virgin),
broken into 1in pieces
1½ tablespoons dark-brown sugar
1 teaspoon ground cinnamon
⅓ cup oats
1 tablespoon maple syrup
2 tablespoons coarsely chopped pecans

Preheat the oven to 350°F.

First, make the crumble topping. Put the flour in a bowl and mix in the coconut oil pieces using a fork until it resembles large bread crumbs. Add the sugar, cinnamon, oats, maple syrup, and chopped pecans. Mix, then chill in the fridge while you prepare the pears.

Toss the pears with the brown sugar, grated ginger, lemon zest, and lemon juice and put them into an ovenproof dish. Sprinkle the chilled crumble topping loosely over the top. Bake the crumble for 20–25 minutes, or until the topping is toasted and the pears are tender. Serve warm.

Gluten-free Raspberry Muffins

A deliciously light muffin—good at any time of the day! Teeny-weeny raspberry muffins baked in mini baking cups are adorable to serve with coffee, and they have the bonus of being gluten-free.

Makes 16 regular muffins (or 24 mini muffins)

12 tablespoons salted butter
1 cup almond flour
1½ tablespoons grated lemon zest
1¼ cups gluten-free confectioner's sugar, sifted
2 tablespoons fine cornmeal, sifted
3 tablespoons cornstarch, sifted
5 organic egg whites
1½ cups raspberries

Preheat the oven to 400°F and line 1–2 large muffin pans or 2 mini muffin pans with baking cups.

Melt the butter in a saucepan and cook until it turns pale golden in color.

Mix together the almond flour, lemon zest, confectioner's sugar, cornmeal, and cornstarch in a large bowl and pour in the melted butter. Gently mix together.

In a separate bowl, lightly beat the egg whites until they are slightly frothy. Fold the egg whites into the almond and butter mixture. Divide the mixture between the baking cups and dot with the raspberries.

Bake the large muffins for 20–30 minutes or the smaller muffins for 15–20 minutes, or until golden and springy to touch. Set aside to cool on a wire rack.

Dust with gluten-free confectioner's sugar just before serving.

Rory O'Connell

" Ink is what springs to mind when I think back to the early days when Darina and I founded Ballymaloe Cookery School. Not squid ink, but printing ink from the old machine we used for copying recipes for our students. How I hated that manually operated and monstrous piece of equipment that now would look positively antique. How I celebrated the arrival of our first photocopier, where all of the ink was carefully sealed in a cartridge and that allowed me to print an entire week's work of recipes without looking like I had come off second best after an entanglement with the world's largest cephalopod. Spanking clean sheets of printed paper and stapled together, too—life-changing stuff.

It was not all glamorous photoshoots and filming sessions in those days, but a constant cycle of shopping, teaching, learning, growing, running, printing, testing, digging, cleaning, washing, clearing up, chair moving, and endlessly reacting to the needs of a new and quickly growing business.

There were surprises, and the biggest one for me was that I not only could, but also really loved to teach. This was not the sort of teaching that prepared students for an exam in several months' time, but for a deadline with ingredients the following day. I knew pretty quickly if my words and actions had achieved the desired effect—it was there on the plates the very next day. It was fun though, great fun, and our teaching and the joy of sharing our love of food and where it comes from always seemed to be wrapped up in a large parcel of laughter.

There have been many standout memories of course—the pleasure of hearing news of the successes of past students with their own businesses, cookbooks, television programs, or just becoming really good happy cooks for the nourishment and pleasure of themselves and their loved ones.

I was also learning myself and had the great honor of standing alongside and assisting visiting chefs and culinary icons such as Jane Grigson, Claudia Roden, and Madhur Jaffrey. To be on their right or left with a view into their saucepans and bowls, to be within a whisper of their words, to see their hands bringing their writing to life was as thrilling, inspirational, and educational for me as I suspect it was for the students in the audience.

Watching the gardens and farm progress has also been a joy. To see students growing and harvesting the food that they are about to cook or slipping their hands into silky cheese curds gained from milk from the farm's cows or churning butter from the same cow's cream has lifted what we do to an altogether different level. We are now getting to the heart of the matter. We are not just a cooking school that teaches recipes; we are a place of learning that truly focuses on the essence of the matter at hand. In our case, that essence is food. "

Left: Rachel Allen and Rory O'Connell, who have been a mainstay of the School with me for many years.

Above (top): Rory, me, and Rachel in the Garden Café.
Bottom (left): Rory and me teaching in matching aprons in the early days of the Cookery School.

Middle: Rory and me teaching together after we had expanded the School in 1989.
Bottom (right): Rory teaching a class watched by an avid group of students.

Rory's Moroccan Harira Soup

"Moroccan food can be wonderful. It is one of the great cuisines of the world and in the hands of the skilled and knowledgeable cook strikes a beautiful balance of sweetness, saltiness, sourness, and heady aromatic flavors.

In Morocco this soup is traditionally served to break the fast during the holy month of Ramadan. There are thousands of different recipes, with each household adding its own particular twist to suit tastes and preferences. Chickpeas, lentils, and sometimes beans, meat—either beef or lamb—vegetables, herbs, and spices are the basic ingredients. The smell of this soup cooking in the kitchen transports me back to exotic and mysterious Tangier. I prefer to use lamb rather than beef and find a more balanced flavor is achieved. This is a purely personal preference and I don't think there is a right or a wrong combination of ingredients. You may find the addition of the rice at the end of cooking to be unusual, but it gives a velvety finish to the soup. Sometimes the rice is replaced with tiny bits of pasta, like orzo. Claudia Roden, in her wonderful book, *Arabesque*, mentions how in some cases a sourdough batter is added to give the velvety consistency or just a simple mixture of flour and water. In any event, this addition of starch needs to be very close to the time of eating or the rice or pasta can become soft and flabby.

This soup is substantial, as you can imagine it would need to be after fasting from sunrise to sundown. I like to serve it with lots of freshly chopped cilantro and a lemon wedge on the side. The warmer the weather, the more inclined I am to squeeze a little lemon juice into the soup."

Rory O'Connell

Serves 8

⅔ cup dried chickpeas, soaked in cold water overnight
⅔ cup puy lentils
1lb boneless lamb, trimmed of all fat and cut into
   ½in cubes
1 large onion, finely chopped
1 teaspoon ground turmeric
½ teaspoon ground cinnamon
¼ teaspoon each of ground ginger, saffron strands and paprika
sea salt, freshly ground black pepper and sugar
3½ tablespoons butter
½ cup long grain rice
4 large ripe tomatoes, skinned, seeded, and chopped
2 tablespoons freshly chopped cilantro
¼ cup freshly chopped flat-leaf parsley

To serve
lemon wedges

Drain the chickpeas, discarding the soaking water. Put in a large saucepan with the lentils. Add the diced lamb, onion, turmeric, cinnamon, ginger, saffron, and paprika. Cover with 5 cups of water and stir gently to mix. Season lightly with salt and pepper. Bring to a boil and skim off any froth that rises to the surface. Add half the butter.

Reduce the heat, cover with a lid and simmer for 1–1½ hours, or until the chickpeas are tender. Keep an eye on the level of liquid in the pan and add a little more water, if necessary.

Toward the end of the cooking time, prepare the rice. Bring 3 cups of water to a boil in a saucepan. Add the rice, stir gently, and cook until tender. Drain the rice, reserving the cooking liquid.

Cook the chopped tomatoes in 3 tablespoons of the reserved cooking liquor until they collapse. Season with salt, pepper, and a pinch of sugar.

Add the cooked tomatoes to the soup along with the cooked rice and the remaining butter. Bring to a boil, stirring, and simmer for 5 minutes. Taste and correct the seasoning. If necessary, add some of the reserved rice cooking liquid to thin out the soup a little. Add the chopped cilantro and parsley, ladle into bowls, and serve with the lemon wedges on the side.

Slow Roast Shoulder of Lamb with Aioli and Salsa Verde

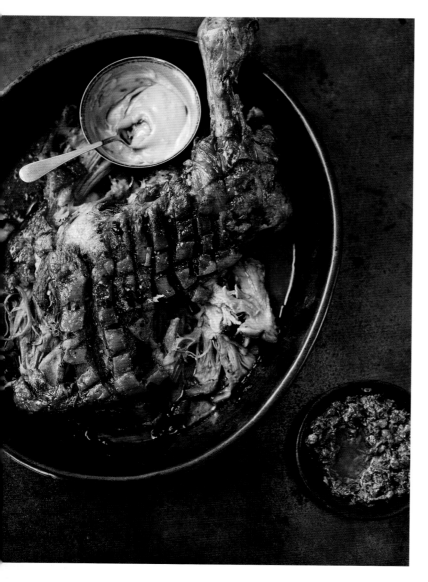

Rory is a thoughtful cook who makes beautiful food; he is also immensely creative, so his dishes always look tantalizing and irresistible. He often cooks this lamb for the student farewell dinner in early summer.

Rory says of this recipe: "A few years ago, butchers had some difficulty selling the shoulder of lamb because it was considered inferior to the leg and loin. Now all that has changed, and the cooking world realizes that the shoulder is every bit as good as the more "prime" cuts and in some ways actually better. The hardworking and muscular shoulder has marvelous flavor but needs long and slow cooking to gently tenderize it so that the flesh becomes sweetly succulent. The cooked lamb in this dish should be soft and melting and will be gently pulled apart for serving rather than carved. This recipe requires time. You can't rush the cooking of a shoulder of lamb, but once it is in the oven, there is plenty of time to prepare sauces and vegetables to accompany it.

I suggest two sauces here: the first a garlicky mayonnaise that is thinned with some of the lamb cooking juices, and the second a fresh-tasting and piquant herb salsa. The two combine really well with the soft flavorsome meat.

Shoulder of lamb is readily available and here the shoulder is cooked whole with just a sprinkle of sea salt and freshly ground black pepper. If the shoulder is excessively fatty, as may be the case later on in the lamb season, trim some of it off, or ask your butcher to do it for you.

The aioli to serve with the lamb is based on mayonnaise. I urge you to make your own mayonnaise either by hand or in a food processor. Good mayonnaise is one of the cornerstones in any good cook's repertoire.

Salsa verde has become something of a cliché in the last few years and as a result the quality has suffered. That doesn't mean that when made with fresh herbs and good ingredients, it can't be as exciting as the first time any of us tasted it. It is a wonderful, refreshing foil for the sweet lamb and rich aioli. Search for the best quality anchovies and capers for the salsa; they vary enormously in quality, so what seems like a bargain when you are buying them may disappoint at a later stage.

Preheat the oven to 350°F. Put the lamb shoulder in a wide roasting pan, skin-side up. Score the skin several times to encourage the fat to run out during the cooking and to crisp up the skin. Season with salt and pepper. Roast in the oven for 30 minutes, then reduce the temperature to 325°F and continue to cook for another 3½ hours, or until the meat is falling off the bone.

While the lamb is cooking, make the salsa verde. Remove the stems from the arugula and herbs and discard. Chop the leaves to a texture halfway between coarse and fine, so that the individual flavors of the herbs stand out in the finished sauce. Put the chopped herbs in a small bowl and stir in the remaining ingredients for the salsa. It is unlikely that the salsa will need salt, because the anchovies are already quite salty, but very occasionally a pinch might be needed. Taste and correct the seasoning, if necessary, adding a little lemon juice if you want to sharpen up the salsa. Chill until ready to serve.

The crushed garlic can be mixed into the mayonnaise for the aioli, however, this sauce cannot be finished until you have the juices from the cooked lamb.

To test if the lamb is cooked to a melting tenderness, pull the shank bone: if it is ready, some of the meat should come away easily from the bone. When the lamb is cooked, remove it from the oven and transfer it to a serving plate, covered with foil, to keep warm in a low oven (250°F). There will be plenty of fatty cooking juices in the roasting pan. Strain these through a strainer into a glass bowl or measuring cup and set aside for a few minutes, until the fat has risen to the surface. Skim off the fat carefully and thoroughly with a large spoon.

To finish the aioli, add 4–6 tablespoons of the degreased cooking juices to the garlicky mayonnaise and stir well to achieve a consistency similar to softly whipped cream—the mayonnaise should now just lightly coat the back of a spoon. Taste and correct the seasoning, if necessary.

Pour the remaining degreased cooking juices into a small pan, bring to a boil, and season to taste.

To serve the lamb, remove the meat from the bone in largish pieces using a pair of tongs or a serving fork. Divide the meat between hot serving plates, drizzle some of the hot cooking juices over the top, and accompany with the salsa verde and aioli.

Serves 8–10

1 whole shoulder of lamb on the bone, weighing
   about 8lb
Maldon sea salt and freshly ground black pepper

For the Aioli
6 large tablespoons homemade mayonnaise (see page 72)
2 garlic cloves, peeled and crushed to a paste

For the Salsa Verde
1 bunch of arugula, about 3½oz
1 bunch of flat-leaf parsley, about 3½oz
6 large sprigs of mint
6 sprigs of tarragon
1 tablespoon capers, coarsely chopped
2 garlic cloves, peeled and crushed to a smooth paste
8 anchovies, very finely chopped
1 tablespoon Dijon mustard
1 cup olive oil
finely grated zest of 1 lemon and a little juice

Chocolate and Caramel Mousse with Dark Caramel Sauce

This rich and concentrated mousse is another of Rory's recipes. He likes the combination of the chocolate and the burned sugar caramel and serves this with caramel sauce and heavy cream. He advises that it is important to use chocolate with 62 percent or 70 percent cocoa solids here to give the depth of chocolatey flavor needed to counteract the sugar in the caramel.

Put the chocolate and butter in a heatproof bowl. Put the bowl over a saucepan of cold water, making sure the water is not touching the bottom of the bowl, and put over medium heat. Bring the water to simmer and immediately remove from the heat, allowing the butter and chocolate to melt gently in the bowl over the saucepan.

Separate the eggs, putting the whites into a spotlessly clean bowl for beating later. Beat the yolks to a pale mousse in a separate bowl.

To make the caramel, put the sugar and ½ cup of the water into a heavy-bottomed saucepan and put over low heat. Stir occasionally to encourage the sugar to dissolve before the liquid comes to a boil. Once it boils and has become a syrup, remove the spoon and do not stir again. Continue to cook the syrup until it darkens to a deep chestnut-colored caramel. If it is coloring unevenly in the saucepan, tilt the pan gently to and fro to get it to even out by running the dark caramel into the paler syrup. Keep going until the caramel is a deep chestnut color and almost burned. (For safety, I usually put the saucepan in the dry sink before adding that ½ cup of water—this way, the spluttering caramel just splashes on to the sides of the sink rather than the work surface.) Then immediately and quickly add the remaining ½ cup of water, hot, if possible, to reduce spluttering. Do not be tempted to stir. If you put a cold spoon into the caramel, it will "block" and become solid.

Now the caramel will look a bit odd, but once you return the saucepan to the heat it will cook out to a single consistency again. Cook the caramel until it thickens again. When you dip a spoon into the caramel and allow it to drop off the spoon, it should fall in a thickish thread. Slowly and carefully pour the hot caramel onto the beaten egg yolks, beating all the time. A food processor with the whisk attachment or a handheld electric mixer will do this job perfectly. The mixture will beat to a mousse in a matter of minutes.

Stir the melted chocolate and vanilla extract into the mousse. You may need to be a little vigorous with the stirring.

Serves 6

8oz dark chocolate (about 62 percent cocoa solids), chopped into ½in pieces
3½ tablespoons salted butter, diced
4 organic eggs
1 cup, plus 2 tablespoons granulated or superfine sugar
1 cup water
1 teaspoon pure vanilla extract

For the Dark Caramel Sauce
1 cup, plus 2 tablespoons granulated sugar
⅓ cup cold water
1 cup hot water

To serve
heavy cream
raspberries (optional)

Beat the egg whites until stiff peaks form, but do not allow them to overwhip and become grainy. Stir a quarter of the egg white into the mousse to soften the mixture, and then fold in the rest of the egg whites lightly yet thoroughly.

Pour the mixture into a shallow serving dish or six individual serving dishes. There will not be a lot of mousse, but it is rich so the servings should be small. Transfer to the fridge to chill for 4 hours.

To make the Dark Caramel Sauce, dissolve the sugar in the cold water over very low heat. Stir until the sugar has dissolved, then remove the spoon and simmer until the syrup caramelizes to a chestnut color. If sugar crystals form during cooking, brush down the sides of the pan with a wet brush, but do not stir. Remove the pan from the heat, pour in the hot water, and continue to cook until the caramel dissolves and the sauce is smooth. Let cool.

Serve the mousse with the dark caramel sauce and heavy cream. Perfectly ripe raspberries, particularly the fall varieties, are delicious served with this mousse.

Cooking with Spices

When Rory and I started the School in 1983, virtually our whole repertoire consisted of much-loved recipes from Ballymaloe House and from the few short courses I had taught with Myrtle. But quite quickly we began to expand our collection by testing recipes. Sometimes it was a delicious dish adapted from a meal I ate in a restaurant, others were recipes inspired by reading cookbooks or magazines or recipes I came across in my travels.

Guest chefs brought new recipes, techniques, and ingredients, including a variety of spices and Asian flavors. Claudia Roden brought Moroccan and Mediterranean specialties, Sri Owen introduced us to Indonesian and Malaysian food, Deh-ta Hsiung to Chinese favorites, Madhur Jaffrey to Indian and later Thai, Vietnamese, and other Far Eastern dishes. We became more and more adventurous.

In the early days of the School, even garlic still seemed exotic to many. Students would ask to omit it from a recipe because it didn't "agree with them." The same was true for many fresh herbs, because other than parsley, thyme, and chives, they were seen as peculiar and strange—rosemary, for example, and tarragon, marjoram, and chervil even more so. Myrtle grew all of these and used them in her cooking, but for most people these herbs were unavailable and unfamiliar. So in the mid-1980s, we added a 2½-day course called Cooking with Fresh Herbs to the School schedule. We also grew a huge variety of fresh herbs in pots and gave advice on herb combinations and on how to start your own herb garden.

Except for the basics like thyme, parsley, and chives, fresh herbs were not sold in supermarkets at that time. Basil was virtually unavailable, even the seed was difficult to come by, but I had developed a craving for basil after attending Marcella Hazan's course in Italy. We grew several different varieties in the greenhouses and made lots of pesto and Genovese basil oil for the winter.

Fresh chiles, too, were almost impossible to buy, except from specialty shops, until the late eighties, so once again we grew our own. One year, we had 15 varieties, including Scotch Bonnets and habanero, which were so hot we could scarcely handle them.

Left: In the early years of the School even garlic was exotic to many students.
Above: Dried red chiles.

At first, I would explain the basics to students: the smaller the chile, the more wary you need to be; the seeds and pith are the hottest part, so you should remove and discard those if you don't want too much heat. Red chiles are often hotter than green, since they are riper. I teach students to be careful not to rub their eyes or any other sensitive part of the body when handling chiles.

At first students were concerned about heat, but gradually they began to distinguish the different flavors of various types of chile and started to use them accordingly, e.g., jalapeño and serrano chiles for Mexican dishes and Thai chiles for Asian food. Chiles are widely available in supermarkets now, but the variety is still very limited. Most common are the red and green Dutch chiles (known as Holland finger) and the thin Thai chile and tiny chiles, sometimes called rat droppings. The latter pack a punch, and we refer to them as scud missiles. They are so tiny you can scarcely see them in a Thai beef salad, but if you eat one unexpectedly it's like being paralyzed—you turn bright red, are rendered speechless, and your eyes bulge.

Spices have had a similar evolution over the past 30 years of the School. In the early 1980s, we knew about a handful of spices: cloves for apple tart and hot whisky, caraway seeds for seed cake, dried ginger for rhubarb jam, ground ginger for gingerbread. There was pepper, of course, but ground white pepper was still used in most homes and pepper mills were considered posh, and whole black peppercorns had to be ordered specially.

Madhur Jaffrey, Sri Owen, and Claudia Roden introduced us to the magic of a whole range of Indian and Asian spices and showed us how to tease up to five different flavors out of each spice, depending on how one used it and when it was added to a dish.

At first, it was quite difficult to source a wide variety of fresh spices, but as Irish people have gradually become exposed to spicy food, both here in Ireland and on their travels, they cannot get enough of it. In 2004, we started to put on a range of Cooking with Spices courses. We choose 8–10 spices and use many of our favorite recipes to illustrate how to cook with them. Everyone loves the food and leaves with the skills and confidence to experiment with them at home.

In 2006, Anglo-Indian past student Arun Kapil started to import spices from his family's spice garden in South India. We were thrilled to be able to get superb quality, and really fresh spices. Today, spices, chile, and fresh herbs are a central component of much of our food, and our students get ever more adventurous.

Above: Jars of a huge number of spices line the shelves at the Cookery School as we try to introduce students to a diverse range of flavors from a variety of international cuisines.
Right: Over the past 30 years of the School the number of spices that students are familiar with has greatly increased, partly due to the food and spice markets, such as this one, that they encounter on their travels.

Sri Owen's Beef Rendang

Sri Owen was one of our earliest guest chefs in July 1989. Sri was born in West Sumatra and lived in Indonesia until moving to England in 1964. She introduced us to many gems, including this rendang, a wonderful slow-cooked dish from Malaysia, Indonesia, and Sumatra that is usually served for feasts and celebrations. It should be chunky and dry, yet succulent.

Serves 8

3¼lb beef brisket or good stewing steak
5 shallots, chopped
4 garlic cloves, peeled and chopped
1¼in piece of fresh ginger, roughly chopped
4 red chiles, seeded and roughly chopped (or 2 teaspoons chile powder)
1 bay leaf
1 stick of lemongrass, bruised
1 teaspoon ground turmeric
sea salt
6 cups coconut milk

To serve
a handful of fresh mint leaves (optional)
lime wedges

Cut the meat into 1½in cubes. Purée the shallots, garlic, ginger, and chiles (or chile powder) in a food processor. Scoop the purée into a wide sauté pan or wok, add the bay leaf, lemongrass, turmeric, salt, and meat and pour in coconut milk. Bring to a boil, stirring, over medium heat. Reduce the heat and bubble away gently for 3 hours, stirring occasionally. After this time, the sauce should be fairly thick.

Continue to cook, stirring frequently, until the coconut milk starts to become oily and then keep stirring until all of the oil has been absorbed by the meat. Taste and add more salt, if necessary.

Serve hot, with a bowl of fluffy rice. Sri likes to serve fresh mint leaves and segments of lime with the rendang.

Note: Rendang keeps well in the fridge and reheats perfectly.

Spiced Cauliflower and Tomato with Parsley

This recipe comes from Chhatra Sagar in Rajasthan, where we have eaten some of the most delicious food in India.

Serves 6–8

1 tablespoon extra virgin olive oil
1 bay leaf
2 cloves
2in cinnamon stick
2 black cardamom pods
¾ cup chopped onion
2–3 teaspoons finely grated fresh ginger
1 large garlic clove, peeled and crushed
2 fresh chiles, chopped
2 teaspoons ground cumin
2 teaspoons ground coriander
2lb very ripe tomatoes, or 2 x 14oz cans of chopped tomatoes
sea salt, freshly ground black pepper, and sugar
2 tablespoons freshly chopped cilantro
2lb cauliflower florets
4oz green beans

To serve
2 tablespoons flat-leaf parsley

Heat the oil in a stainless-steel saucepan. Add the bay leaf, cloves, cinnamon stick, and cardamom. Stir and sizzle for 30 seconds. Add the onion, ginger, garlic, chile, cumin, and coriander, and toss until coated in oil. Cover and sweat over low heat until completely soft but not colored—about 10 minutes.

Remove the hard core from the tomatoes. If using fresh tomatoes, put them in a deep bowl and cover with boiling water for 10 seconds. Then remove and peel off the skins. Slice the tomatoes and add to the onion. Season with salt, black pepper, and sugar to taste. Add the cilantro and cook for another 10–20 minutes, or until the tomato softens.

Meanwhile, blanch the cauliflower florets in lightly salted water for 2–3 minutes. Drain, refresh under cold water, and drain again. Blanch and refresh the beans in the same way, but for 1 minute only.

When the tomatoes are soft, add the cauliflower and beans. Taste and correct the seasoning, if necessary. Top with flat-leaf parsley and serve.

Pears Poached in a Saffron Syrup

Most exotic of all the fruit compotes, pears cooked this way turn a wonderful deep golden color and are delicately infused with the flavors of saffron and cardamom, two of the world's most precious spices. We use Conference and Doyenne du Comice pears. This compote is rich and intensely sweet and best served well chilled. (Be careful not to use too much saffron or the pears will be too strong.) The juice is delicious so serve lots with the pears. If there is some left over, set with gelatin to make delicious pear and saffron jellies. Use 3 teaspoons of powdered gelatin to 2 cups of juice.

Serves 4

1 cup granulated sugar
2 cups water
6 whole cardamom pods, lightly crushed
¼ teaspoon good-quality saffron threads
3 tablespoons freshly squeezed lemon juice
4 firm pears

Put the sugar, water, cardamom pods, saffron, and lemon juice into a shallow, wide pan: we use a stainless-steel sauté pan. Stir to dissolve the sugar and bring to a simmer.

Meanwhile, peel the pears, cut them in half, and remove the cores. As you prepare each pear, drop it straight into the simmering syrup, cut-side up.

Cover the pan with a circle of baking parchment and put the lid on the pan as well. Simmer away gently until the pears are tender, for about 20–30 minutes, spooning the syrup over them every now and then.

Once the pears are cooked, carefully lift them out of the pan and arrange them in a single layer, cut-side down, in a serving dish. Pour the syrup over the pears. Alternatively, you can reduce the syrup first so that it thickens slightly. (For a more concentrated flavor, the syrup may be reduced a little after the pears have been removed to a serving dish. Be careful not to cook for too long, or the syrup will caramelize.) Serve chilled.

Note: This compote keeps for several weeks, covered, in the fridge.

Variations

Poached Pears
Omit the saffron, cardamom pods, and 3 tablespoons of lemon juice and simply add the thinly pared rind and juice of 1 lemon instead.

Poached Pears with Sweet Geranium Leaves
Omit the saffron and cardamom pods and add 3–4 large sweet-scented geranium leaves instead.

Poached Pears with Lemon Verbena Leaves
Omit the saffron and cardamom pods and add 4–6 lemon verbena leaves instead.

Poached Pears with Grated Ginger
Omit the saffron and cardamom pods and add a 1in piece of peeled and thinly sliced fresh ginger instead.

Keeping Chickens

I don't ever remember a time when we didn't have hens. When I was a child my mother always kept a flock of Rhode Island Reds crossed with Leghorn. The hens had a large patch of grass at the far end of the vegetable garden, fenced in with chicken wire. The food scraps from the house were mixed with soaked "presto" (rolled corn) and some chicken feed and fed to the hens every day. As children, we took turns feeding the hens, and freshly laid eggs were part of our life. When the weather turned cold and wet the hens laid less but we had an abundance of eggs from around Easter throughout the summer. From Easter onward, Mummy preserved

Above: A free-roaming Ballymaloe chicken, strutting her stuff in front of the Cookery School.
Right: We have 6–7 different traditional breeds of hen at Ballymaloe, all of which are suited to free-range production. Hens are naturally forestial, so they enjoy being able to shelter from the sun and perch on the branches of the trees. (Sussex white hens are pictured.)

some of this glut in buckets of Isinglass, also known as Waterglass, a substance derived from the swim bladders of fish and a form of collagen. It was sold in a can and mixed with water in a bucket and used as a preservative for eggs. The eggs were carefully layered in this solution in the bucket and covered. They were kept in a cool place and used mainly for baking in winter, when the hens virtually stopped laying and their fresh eggs were too scarce to be used for baking. They kept well for a few months and were very precious, even though they had an odd taste.

When Tim and I got married in 1970, I immediately thought of getting a few hens for Ballymaloe. Frank Walsh, who had worked on the farm for over 60 years, cleared out a little toolshed in the farmyard for my half a dozen birds. They were free-range but went indoors at night to roost.

When we started the School in 1983 we increased the flock in order to have enough eggs to use in the classes. Later, when our yellow Transit van conked out, we converted it into a larger henhouse, much to the amusement of the students. Now we have about 300 organic hens divided into three flocks, a mixture of traditional breeds: Maran, Rhode Island Red, Light Sussex, Leghorn, and Ancona. I prefer the traditional breeds for the flavor and quality of the eggs, plus they are more suited to free-range production.

Aside from the Speckledy and Hebden Blacks, we've got quite a collection of rare breeds, which I'd love to add to even further—we have Silkies, Cochins, Buff Orpingtons, Marans, Pekin, Hamburgs, Araucanas, Campines, and Welsummers. Some lay brown speckledy eggs; others, like the Anconas, lay beautiful, almost blue, eggs. In fact, if I had to choose my last meal it would be a delicious boiled free-range egg with little "soldiers" of Timmy's soda bread—a forgotten flavor for most people these days. I was convinced that absolutely everyone knew about boiled eggs, but recently, to our astonishment, we met not one but two people who had never eaten a boiled egg before, so we delighted in introducing them to the most fundamental gourmet experience by collecting a few eggs from

the nest underneath the rosemary bush outside our kitchen door, boiling them gently so the yolk was still soft and the white just set. We showed them how to lift off the top and enjoy the boiled egg with sea salt, freshly ground pepper, and "soldiers" of hot toast sticks smothered with homemade butter.

On the 12-week certificate courses the students take turns feeding the hens as part of their duties. The scraps from the morning's cooking that don't qualify for the stockpot, e.g., some vegetable peelings, scorched offerings, overcooked bread, and other culinary mistakes, are relegated to the hens' bucket. It's an integral part of the students' education on how food is produced. They understand the wonderfully holistic system, where the leftover food scraps get fed to the hens, who reward us with beautiful fresh eggs a few days later. No waste, and we don't have to pay the city to dispose of the garbage in a landfill.

The system we operate is dual purpose. In each hen run, we have a Dumpster beside the gate. The hens now associate it with food so when we pour the bucket of food scraps in, the hens hop up and gobble up the tasty morsels. We scatter a layer of straw over the top in the evening. Usually the Dumpster is full by the end of the week. It's a perfect combination of straw, vegetable matter, and chicken manure, which activates the compost. This is taken down on the front loader to the compost area and deposited onto a compost bay. The students understand the cycle and know that the compost will be returned to the ground to enrich and enhance the fertility of the soil when it is spread out on the land about nine months later.

The eggs from the grass-fed free-range hens are an essential part of our cooking and baking. Because the hens are allowed to forage and peck around in different areas with access to a variety of grasses, weeds, and worms, the birds are healthy and the eggs absolutely delicious.

The students learn how to keep hens and many can't wait to get a little flock of their own. Having tasted and cooked with these beautiful eggs, they realize the phenomenal difference that eggs of this quality make to the finished product. Some students love the hens and are intrigued by their antics, while others are actually scared of them. One girl was so terrified when she saw the hens running toward her, she dropped the buckets and ran. Now we explain that the hens are not remotely interested in the person, just the food!

We had a student a few years ago who really enjoyed feeding the hens and regularly offered to feed them for his classmates. He was always amused when the hens ran toward him and joked that they were the only appreciative females he ever met!

Left: Michael Dwane, who has been working with us part-time on the farm for many years.
Above: This Barnevelder hen hatched a duck egg, which Eileen O'Donovan's mother had given me as a present. The hen was delighted but a bit puzzled by her achievement, especially when the little duckling found the pond and swam merrily away as the hen pranced up and down on the bank squawking in alarm!

*Above (top): One of our "fancy fowl"—the heirloom varieties
we have a Ballymaloe—perched on the garden seat for a siesta.
Above (middle): A Maran made a nest and hatched a clutch
of chicks on the top of the wall close to the courtyard barn.
Above (bottom): A chicken chorus line, on top of the wall.
Right: My daughter Lydia's painted illustration on the chick house,
where we transfer the baby chicks after hatching them in the incubator.
They then graduate to the Palais des Poulets next door when they reach
about five months old.*

Visitors to the School love to see the fancy fowl pecking around by the Palais des Poulets—this is a very grand name for a simple stone farm building with whitewashed walls and a chandelier hanging rather incongruously from the ceiling.

We regularly got requests for advice on how to keep a few hens, so in May 2005 we offered our first How to Keep a Few Chickens in the Garden course. Such was the interest that almost 80 people signed up. We have continued to offer these courses as a part of our Forgotten Skills series, and it is heartening to see that there has been a phenomenal increase in the number of people keeping hens, both in urban and rural areas, in recent years. I was recently in New York, and guess what the coolest new hobbies were?—keeping chickens in your backyard and bees on your roof. Can you imagine? Public demand is such that the by-laws have changed in many areas to enable people to keep their own fowl. At one dinner party in Brooklyn, guests spent over half an hour comparing notes on how to keep chickens!

At the farmers' market in Union Square they were selling eggs from several different rare breeds of hen, the beautiful blue-green eggs of the Araucanas were selling at several dollars a dozen more than the others, and at Dean & DeLuca in Manhattan beautiful duck eggs sell individually for two or three dollars each.

Eggs were starring on restaurant menus, too; at The Green Table in Chelsea Market I had a beautiful plate of deviled eggs on a bed of red watercress, with crusty bread from Amy's Bakery next door. Scotch eggs were everywhere, with even quail's eggs wrapped in a succulent mix of heritage pork sausage meat. At Buvette, a chic little French café on Grove St. in the West Village, I had a bowl of slow-cooked kale topped with poached eggs and some grilled bread with crumbly pecorino for breakfast, and 'ino on Bedford Street served Truffled egg on toast, both of which were worth flying over for.

Like many people who keep their own hens, I'm frightfully fussy about eating eggs away from home, but these days in New York there are actually places where you can trust the quality of the eggs—they may even come from someone's backyard or a roof garden in the neighborhood.

In 2006, we bought an incubator. We also keep some breeding pairs of traditional and rarer poultry in chicken arks (mobile miniature henhouses) in the orchard, so we have fertilized eggs for hatching. The problem is, the fancier the breed, the less inclined they are to lay—sort of "too posh to push!" They strut around being decorative rather than functional, but I love them nonetheless. Every term when we put eggs into the incubator and we demonstrate this to both the Cookery School students and the children from the local school (9–12 years old) who are part of the East Cork Slow Food Educational Project. Twenty-one days later the chicks start to hatch from their shells—you can't imagine the excitement from "children" of all ages. It's yet another lesson in how food is produced. After several hours, the chicks fluff up and get perky enough to be moved out under the infrared lamp in the Palais des Poulets. They remain warm and cozy under an infrared lamp in the chicken shed for at least another month until they are hardy enough to go outdoors. After a few weeks they grow pin feathers and eventually proper plumage. We have to wait to see which birds grow little tails: those will grow into fine roosters and the others will mature into hens. We fatten up the roosters for the pot and the hens keep us supplied with beautiful eggs. In many countries, there is a tradition of dyeing and painting eggs to be given as presents at Easter, a tradition that we very much foster in our family and, in fact, our clever hens actually lay colored eggs with children's names on them on Easter Sunday!

Research has shown that organic, free-range eggs are considerably lower in cholesterol than eggs from intensive production systems. Hens lay a maximum of one a day, on average five days a week,

depending on season or weather. Five or six hens will provide plenty of eggs for an average household. You don't need much space to keep a couple of hens, unlike cattle, sheep, or pigs, which need much more room and are a totally different proposition. They also generate a supply of nitrogen and phosphate-rich manure that will turn into a rich compost for your garden. They are excellent for pest and weed control; we let the hens into the vegetable garden in the winter to gobble up slugs and insects. From a cook's point of view, the quality of an egg hugely affects the flavor and texture of food. The best mayonnaise, béarnaise, and hollandaise sauce is made from fresh free-range eggs.

If students or visitors want to get a little flock of their own, I always advise first checking the planning regulations in their area. Usually regulations do not expressly forbid keeping livestock in your yard, so long as the animals are for family use rather than business purposes. Chickens are sometimes sold at livestock markets, farmers' markets, or after summer agricultural fairs. Buy from a reputable supplier and ask for a certificate to prove that the chickens are disease-free.

Eggs Bhurji

Geoffrey Dobbs owns several of the most beautiful hotels in Sri Lanka. I love the food he serves and have made a number of return trips. I have cooked several dinners there and always take some cooking classes from the Sri Lankan chefs in the kitchens. Even breakfast is a feast, with freshly cut, perfectly ripe fruit, curd and jaggery, Ceylon tea, chile eggs, stringhoppers (a Sri Lankan noodle specialty), or Eggs Bhurji—a memorable breakfast dish and easy to reproduce in less exotic climes.

Serves 2

2 tablespoons butter
1 teaspoon mustard seeds
a few small fresh curry leaves
2 scallions, finely sliced
½ teaspoon grated fresh ginger
½ hot green chile, seeded and thinly sliced
pinch of ground turmeric
½ teaspoon ground cumin
1 tomato, skinned and diced
4 organic eggs, beaten

To serve
toast or fried bread

Melt the butter in a frying pan over medium heat. Add the mustard seeds, stir once, then add the curry leaves and scallions. Stir and cook over low to medium heat until the onions are soft. Add the ginger, chile, turmeric, cumin, and diced tomato and fry gently for a couple of minutes, stirring regularly.

Add the beaten eggs and continue to stir over low heat until the eggs are softly scrambled. Serve on warm plates, accompanied by hot toast or fried bread.

Kuku Kadoo—Persian Zucchini Omelet

This is the Persian version of a Spanish tortilla, Italian frittata, or an Arabic eggah (also known as ajjah). There are myriad versions and some use baking powder instead of baking soda. Traditionally, this is cooked in a frying pan and flipped over, but it also works very well in the oven. Kuku Kadoo is one of my favorites.

Serves 6–8

2 tablespoons extra virgin olive oil, plus extra for greasing
1lb onions, finely chopped
3 garlic cloves, peeled and crushed
¼ teaspoon grated fresh ginger
6 small zucchini, halved lengthwise and cut into thin slices
sea salt and freshly ground black pepper
8 organic eggs
1 teaspoon ground turmeric
3 tablespoons all-purpose flour
½ teaspoon baking soda

To serve
flat-leaf parsley sprigs and sumac

Preheat the oven to 350°F and grease a 10in gratin dish with a little oil.

Heat the oil in a frying pan over medium heat. Add the onion, garlic, and ginger, cover with a lid, and sweat for 6–8 minutes, until soft but not colored. Add the zucchini, season with salt and pepper, and cook for 6–8 minutes, stirring.

Whisk the eggs in a large mixing bowl with the turmeric, flour, and baking soda. Add the cooked zucchini mixture to the eggs and stir well. Pour into the greased gratin dish and bake for 25–30 minutes, until just set. Serve sprinkled with parsley sprigs and sumac.

Asian Soy and Five-Spice Chicken Breasts with Cucumber, Radish, and Mint Salad

The free-range chickens on Dan Aherne's organic farm in East Cork are reared for a minimum of 80 days, sometimes longer, so the breasts can be so large we just use four and divide each into two pieces.

Preheat the oven to 350°F. Mix the flour and five-spice powder in a shallow bowl with a good pinch of sea salt and some freshly ground black pepper.

Heat a wok or frying pan over high heat. Add the oil and heat until it is just starting to smoke. Meanwhile, toss the chicken breasts one at a time into the seasoned flour. Deep-fry the chicken breasts in the hot oil, a couple at a time, until the skin is crispy—about 3–5 minutes. Drain on paper towels and set aside, reserving the oil in the pan.

Arrange the lemon slices on a baking sheet and lay the crispy chicken breasts on top. Roast in the hot oven until fully cooked, about 10–12 minutes, depending on size.

To make the salad, cut the cucumber in half lengthwise, then in half again. Cut into ½in dice and transfer to a bowl. Trim the radishes and cut into similar-sized pieces and mix with the cucumber. Season with salt and freshly ground black pepper. Drizzle with the extra virgin olive oil and freshly squeezed lemon juice. Toss gently, add the herbs, and mix. Taste again and correct the seasoning, if necessary.

To finish the chicken, pour away all but 2 tablespoons of the oil in the wok or pan. Return the pan to the heat and add the finely grated ginger, honey, soy sauce, lemon juice, and brown sugar. Bring to a boil and simmer for 3–4 minutes until the sauce starts to thicken. Add the cooked chicken pieces back to the pan and coat them with the sauce.

To serve, transfer the chicken and sauce to a serving dish. Accompany with noodles (or fettuccine) and the Cucumber, Radish, and Mint Salad.

Serves 8

¼ cup all-purpose flour
1½ teaspoons Chinese five-spice powder
sea salt and freshly ground black pepper
½ cup sunflower oil, for deep-frying
8 organic chicken breasts (skin on)
1 lemon, cut into 8 slices
1¼in piece of fresh ginger, peeled and grated
5 tablespoons honey
5 tablespoons soy sauce
freshly squeezed juice of 2 lemons
2 tablespoons brown sugar

For the Cucumber, Radish, and Mint Salad
1 fresh cucumber
18–24 radishes, trimmed and quartered
sea salt and freshly ground black pepper
3 tablespoons extra virgin olive oil
1 tablespoon freshly squeezed lemon juice
a handful of fresh mint leaves
a handful of fresh flat-leaf parsley

Salad of Smoked Chicken with Parsnip Chips and Myrtle Berries

We've got two *Myrtus ugni* planted in large terra-cotta pots on the balcony outside the kitchens. The bittersweet wine-colored berries are delicious in winter salads, particularly with game, guinea fowl, or smoked chicken, as in this recipe.

First, make the parsnip chips. Heat the oil to 300°F in a deep-fryer.

Scrub and peel the parsnip. Either slice into wafter-thin rounds or peel off long slivers lengthwise with a swivel-top peeler. Let dry on paper towels.

Drop a few of the parsnip rounds or slivers at a time into the hot oil; they color and crisp up very quickly. Drain on paper towels and sprinkle lightly with salt. Keep warm in a low oven (225°F).

To make the French dressing, put all the ingredients into a blender and run at medium speed for about 1 minute. Set aside.

Put the salad leaves into a bowl. Sprinkle with a little French dressing and toss until the leaves are nicely coated. Taste and divide the salad between four large plates.

Slice the chicken breast thinly and arrange upward around the salad. Put a clump of warm parsnip chips on top. Sprinkle some myrtle berries (if using) around the salad. Garnish with chervil or flat-leaf parsley and serve immediately.

Serves 4

a selection of mixed salad leaves such as Oak Leaf, Little Gem, or lamb's lettuce, arugula, finely sliced Savoy cabbage, claytonia (winter purslane), Pennywort, and Purslane
2 smoked chicken breasts
olive oil
¾ cup myrtle berries (optional)
sea salt and freshly ground black pepper

For the Parsnip Chips
sunflower or peanut oil
1 large parsnip
sea salt

For the French Dressing (Makes 1 cup)
¼ cup wine vinegar
¾ cup extra virgin olive oil
1 level teaspoon Dijon or English mustard
1 large garlic clove
1 scallion
a sprig of flat-leaf parsley
a sprig of watercress
1 level teaspoon salt
few grinds of black pepper

To serve
chervil or flat-leaf parsley

Blathnaid's Chocolate Cake

We have about 10 chocolate cakes in our repertoire, from Cynthia's Chocolate Cake made with cocoa and buttermilk, to the decadently rich Ballymaloe Chocolate Cake made with the very best chocolate money can buy, lots of ground almonds, and a silky chocolate frosting. But if I had to choose just one, it might have to be this recipe given to me by my sister Blathnaid Bergin. It is deliciously chocolatey, yet light and rich at the same time. You can serve it very simply with the chocolate ganache poured over the top or spruce it up for a birthday cake.

Preheat the oven to 350°F. Grease two 8in cake pans with melted butter, dust with flour, and line the bottom of each one with a circle of wax paper.

To make the cake, put the milk and chopped chocolate into a saucepan and warm gently over low heat until the chocolate melts. Set aside to cool.

Sift the flour, salt, baking soda, and baking power into a bowl. In a separate bowl, cream the butter and sugar until light and fluffy. Beat the eggs with the vanilla extract in another bowl and beat them into the creamed mixture a little at a time, adding 1 tablespoon of the flour with each addition. Fold in the cooled chocolate mixture, followed by the remaining flour. Divide between the two prepared pans and bake for 30–35 minutes, or until the cakes have begun to shrink in slightly from the sides of the pan. Set aside to cool in their pans for a few minutes, and then turn them out carefully and transfer to a wire rack to cool completely.

Meanwhile, make the filling. Melt the chocolate in a heatproof bowl over a saucepan of hot water. Set aside to cool slightly. In a large mixing bowl, cream the butter for at least 10 minutes at high speed, until pale and fluffy. Add the egg yolks and confectioner's sugar and contine to beat vigorously for another 5 minutes. Once the butter mixture is thoroughly mixed, remove 2 tablespoons and stir it into the cooled, melted chocolate. Then slowly pour the melted chocolate down the side of the mixing bowl into the butter mixture and fold it in quickly and gently until fully combined and smooth.

Once the cakes are cold, you can start making the chocolate ganache. Put the chocolate in a large bowl. Heat the cream to boiling point, pour it over the chocolate, and stir until it melts; set aside to cool. Beat the cooled chocolate cream until it barely forms soft peaks, making sure not to overbeat it, or it will become too stiff to spread

Serves 10–12

10 tablespoons butter, plus extra for greasing
1¾ cups all-purpose flour, plus extra for dusting
1 cup milk
3oz dark chocolate (about 52 percent cocoa solids), chopped
pinch of salt
½ teaspoon baking soda
2 level teaspoons baking power
2 cups light brown sugar
3 organic eggs
1 teaspoon pure vanilla extract

For the chocolate filling
7oz dark chocolate (about 52 percent cocoa solids), chopped
17 tablespoons butter, softened
4 organic egg yolks
1¼ cups confectioner's sugar, sifted

For the chocolate ganache
5oz dark chocolate (about 52 percent cocoa solids), chopped
1¼ cups heavy cream

To decorate
chocolate curls
unsweetened cocoa powder and confectioner's sugar, to dust

and may turn into chocolate butter. (Use as soon as possible, or it will become too stiff to spread.)

To assemble the cake, split the cakes in half horizontally with a sharp serrated knife. Spread the chocolate filling onto each layer and sandwich the four layers together. Frost the cake with the chocolate ganache and decorate as you wish—we like to use chocolate curls, dredging them in unsweetened cocoa and confectioner's sugar.

Butchery

There was great excitement in October 2005 when Hugh Fearnley-Whittingstall and his butcher at River Cottage, Ray Mears, came to teach a Cutting Up a Pig in a Day course at the School. Our local butcher, Frank Murphy, slaughtered a couple of our Saddleback pigs for them to butcher. Using these pigs, which had been hung for several days, Ray began by butchering the carcass and then continued on to explain the different cuts and how they can be used. Hugh and Ray demonstrated how to brine a leg to make a ham, then how to dry-cure bacon and salt pork belly. They used the head and feet to make head cheese and the liver and some pork belly were ground to make Ray's Rich Liver Pâté. They made delicious juicy sausages, chorizo, and salami. The tenderloin was stuffed and roasted and the kidneys were deviled; not a scrap was wasted. Both the teachers and students were agog with excitement. Hugh is an inspirational teacher, and he and Ray made a fantastic duo.

In 2005, my youngest daughter, Emily, brought her German boyfriend, Philip Dennhardt, home from New York with her. (He and Emily married down by the pond in the garden in 2011.) Philip is a master butcher from a long line of craft butchers who have passed their skills from generation to generation. He immediately started to teach some of the Forgotten Skills courses at the School, including Butchering; How to Cure a Pig in a Day and Use Every Morsel; How to Build a Smoker and Smoke Your Own Food; Butchery, Charcuterie, and Sausage Making; Hands-on Pork Butchery, as well as tutoring custom courses for those who wanted hands-on butchery classes.

The first of these was in October 2006, when we ran a Pig in a Day course and a Basic Home Butchery Course. We now offer these courses every year, and they are extremely popular. Participants learn how to butcher a side of pork like a professional and transform it into a full range of fresh and cured hams, succulent sausages, and perfect charcuterie. They are instructed in how to produce air-dried ham, brine-cured ham, head cheese, bacon, sausages, chorizos, salamis, and country pâtés and terrines. Every morsel of the pig is put to good use.

Students who have a particular interest in doing their own in-house butchery have the option to learn more when Philip butchers our beef and occasional carcasses of lamb. We buy all our poultry whole and teach the students how to joint a chicken, duck, guinea fowl, quail, or rabbit in a matter of minutes and then show them how to put every single scrap to delicious use and make a fine pot of stock or broth from the carcass and giblets.

Almost every term, Haulie Walsh, our Farm Manager, who has been with us since he was in his teens, takes one of our prime cattle to the local butcher to be slaughtered, so we also have our own dry-aged, well-hung beef for burgers and meat for prime-rib roasts, stews, and casseroles. We show the students how to cut their own steaks and short ribs and explain how to buy and judge good meat. We urge them to build up a relationship with their local butcher, to inquire about the breed and feed, and to seek out dry-aged meat, rather than vacuum-packed meat joints. They also learn about hanging times. We encourage them to ask their butcher about the different cuts that are available and how best to cook them; you can learn something new every time you shop.

Left: Hugh Fearnley-Whittingstall and his River Cottage butcher, Ray Mears, when they came to Ballymaloe in October 2005. In addition to butchering the carcasses of two of our Saddleback pigs, they got students involved in making sausages. Above: Our black Berkshire cross sow with her motley crew of piglets snuffling around in the paddock.

The rise in interest in home-butchery has been phenomenal over the past decade. Both male and female students want to learn how to butcher, cure meat, and make charcuterie. There's great excitement when we get one of our pigs back from our local butcher. Even though it's an extracurricular activity on the 12-week course, there's always a line of students who want to learn about the various meat cuts and discover how to butcher the carcass. We get a wide range of nationalities, but all seem to be fascinated. This trend is reflected in the proliferation of butchery classes everywhere from The Ginger Pig in London to The Meat Hook in Brooklyn—all are overbooked.

There's also a resurgence of interest in nose to tail eating for a variety of reasons, not least economic. Chefs such as Fergus Henderson of St. John in London have blazed a trail and put marrow bones, pigs' ears, and scrag end back on their menus and reminded us how delicious the lesser-known cuts can be. The skill of cooking the cheaper cuts was all but lost until a combination of food trends and necessity forced us to reevaluate. Now there's a realization that anyone can slap a steak into a pan, but it takes greater skill and patience to coax a more muscular cut to melting tenderness and the added bonus is the sensational flavor. We now incorporate an increased number of slow-cooked dishes and offal into our menus at the School and the reaction is overwhelmingly positive.

There are other changes afoot, as dieticians regularly remind us that too much red meat can be detrimental to our hearts. Recent food scares like the horsemeat scandal have highlighted the dangers of cheap meat and consequently more people seem to be deciding to eat less, but better quality free-range and organic meat.

The notion of eating less meat, but sourcing heritage breeds from small, less intensive production systems is gathering momentum. The general public has become more aware and concerned about animal welfare issues and sustainability. In the US and farther afield, the idea of meat-free Monday has started to gain credence for health, environmental, and ethical reasons. It received a boost in 2009 when Sir Paul McCartney and his daughters Stella and Mary launched their Meat Free Monday campaign. In April 2010, Mario Batali launched Meat Free Monday menus in all 14 of his restaurants, and many other high profile chefs, including Wolfgang Puck, have followed suit.

The Food and Agriculture Organization of the United Nations (FAO) estimates that livestock production is responsible for up to 18 percent of global greenhouse gas emissions. Some estimates put the figure even higher. Global meat production also uses massive amounts of water. Here in Ireland, however, our animals are predominantly grass-fed, and we are certainly not short of water thus far, but who knows what lies ahead with global warming. Another good reason for Meat Free Monday is the growing body of research that indicates that meat- and dairy-heavy diets can play a role in obesity, which increases people's risk of developing many chronic diseases, including cancer, heart disease, and stroke.

Slow Food also promotes the idea that responsible meat consumption means eating less meat and only eating meat from animals that have been raised with a high quality of life. The movements tries to teach people to pay a fair price for meat, one that reflects the true cost of production and that respects animal welfare. Slow Food's consumer guide, "Too Much at Steak," outlines good practice that can be applied to everyday life, when shopping and eating at home or in restaurants.

Above: Student Emily Ashworth making sausages with Philip Dennhardt on the 12-week course.
Right: Preparing a leg of lamb for roasting—I have removed the chine bone and am about to trim the knuckle. I really enjoy butchering; at Ballymaloe we buy all our joints of meat unprepared so that we can teach students this skill.

Dawn Chorus

Dennis O'Sullivan has worked with us as a painter, plasterer, slater, and glazier for over 40 years and has been involved in the process of converting many of the farm buildings into the cottages where the students reside when they are at the School. Dennis's absorbing hobby is birdwatching. It is fantastic to have an almost resident ornithologist on site. He's extraordinarily knowledgeable and observant and can always tell us where there's a nesting pair of this or that species on the farm or in the local area.

In 2006, Dennis offered to do a bird survey of the farm and he has been doing it brilliantly ever since. It's been a very interesting exercise and Dennis has been fascinated to discover the biodiversity of species on our 100 acres. There are 46 different bird species at present, much higher than the average, but consistent with Soil Association surveys that show increased biodiversity on organic farms.

The farm is rich in trees and hedgerows and we have always resisted the temptation to chop hedges, which is the common practice in modern farming. My father-in-law, Ivan Allen, had a lifelong interest in birds and was made a fellow of The Royal Society for the Protection of Birds (RSPB) in the late 1980s. Even though he was a progressive conventional farmer for most of his life, he always created and protected the bird habitats on the farm, sometimes delaying or mowing around nests in the grass so as not to disturb the nesting birds.

I'm not sure why it took me so long to think to ask Dennis to take the students on a Dawn Chorus walk. We introduced it in 2008 and it's been a regular facet of the summer courses ever since; more recently, Dennis has introduced Dusk Chorus walks as well. The students love them, as do we, and they greatly enhance our enjoyment of the environment in which we are fortunate enough to live.

Slow-cooked Beef Shank

❧❧❦❧❧

This slow-cooked beef shank is fantastic winter food. Gillian Hegarty, who teaches at the School and worked at the River Café, loves to cook this dish, one of Rose and Ruthie's favorites. It takes 12 hours of gentle simmering to reduce the beef shank to a rich, melting tenderness, but it is so worth it. The beef is wonderful served with polenta, but we also love it with potato and rosemary gratin and a good green salad.

Serves 6–8

1 beef shank on the bone, weighing about 6lb 8oz
750ml bottle of Chianti Classico (or more)
50 garlic cloves, peeled
8 thyme sprigs
3 tablespoons freshly ground black pepper
sea salt

To serve
½ loaf of sourdough bread, sliced and toasted
freshly grated Parmesan (optional)
extra virgin olive oil, for drizzling

Preheat the oven to 325°F. If necessary, ask your butcher to cut the beef shank from knuckle to knuckle into shorter lengths, about 7in long.

Put the beef shank into a large casserole or Dutch oven with a good tight-fitting lid. Cover with the wine. Add the garlic, thyme, pepper, and a little salt and slowly bring to a boil. Cover with a wax-paper lid and the lid of the Dutch oven. Cook gently in the preheated oven for 12 hours. Check every 3–4 hours, and add more wine if the beef is uncovered. You may need to use more than one bottle of wine.

To serve, put the toasted sourdough bread in a bowl and the meat and juices on top. Sprinkle with Parmesan, if using, and a generous drizzle of extra virgin olive oil. This dish can also be served with soft polenta.

Grilled Bavette or Hanger Steak with Shallots

❧❧❦❧❧

A bit chewy, but juicy and packed with flavor, this cut is a lot cheaper than fillet or sirloin steak. It probably won't remain inexpensive for long, however, as more and more chefs discover this secret butcher's cut, which the French call bavette.

Serves 4–6

¼ cup extra virgin olive oil
2 garlic cloves, peeled and crushed
2 teaspoons freshly ground black pepper
1½–2lb bavette or hanger steak
Maldon sea salt
2 tablespoons butter
6–10 shallots, finely sliced
1–2 tablespoons red wine vinegar

To serve
freshly chopped flat-leaf parsley

First, marinate the steaks. Mix the olive oil, garlic, and cracked pepper together in a shallow dish, add the steaks, and turn a couple of times. Cover with plastic wrap and set aside to marinate in the fridge for at least 4 hours. Remove the steaks from the marinade and pat dry with paper towels.

Preheat a grill pan over high heat. Season the beef generously with sea salt and freshly ground black pepper. Sear well on all sides, reduce the heat, and cook until rare (125°F) or medium (130°F). Remove the steaks from the pan and set aside to rest, covered with an upturned plate, while you deglaze the pan.

Melt the butter in the pan, add the shallots, and sweat gently for 3–4 minutes, until soft and slightly colored. Increase the heat, add the vinegar, and bring to a boil. Reduce the heat and stir well with a wooden spoon to scrape all the nice caramelized pieces from the bottom of the pan.

To serve, cut the steaks into thin slices across the grain and sprinkle with the shallots and some freshly chopped parsley. The steaks are delicious accompanied with a béarnaise sauce and lots of fries or sautéed potatoes.

Ham Hocks with Navy Bean and Tomato Stew

Ham hocks are delicious with so many things—bean stew, cabbage and champ, lentils, shredded into a broth with diced vegetables, or in a split pea soup. We also love to add chunks of quartered cabbages to the cooking water about 30 minutes before the end of cooking. Ham hocks are excellent value for money; one will easily feed two people or more when added to a chunky bean or lentil soup.

Soak the beans overnight in plenty of cold water.

Put the ham hocks into a deep saucepan, add the vegetables and seasonings. Cover with cold water, bring to a boil, and simmer for 2–2½ hours, or until the meat is virtually falling off the bones.

While the ham hocks are cooking, strain the beans, put in a saucepan, and cover with fresh cold water. Add the bouquet garni, carrot, and onion, cover and simmer until the beans are soft but not mushy—anything from 30–60 minutes. Just before the end of the cooking time, add a pinch of salt. Remove the bouquet garni and vegetables and discard.

Meanwhile, sweat the chopped onion gently in olive oil in a wide saucepan until soft but not colored, about 7–8 minutes. Add the garlic and cook for another 1–2 minutes, then add the chopped tomatoes and their juice and cook for 6–8 minutes. Add the cooked beans and rosemary and cook for another 5 minutes.

Remove the meat from the ham hocks, including the skin, and add to the bean stew. Simmer for 3–4 minutes, adding some of the bean liquid, if necessary, and season well with salt, freshly ground black pepper, and sugar. The mixture should be juicy but not swimming in liquid.

Sprinkle with lots of flat-leaf parsley and garnish with a sprig of rosemary to serve.

To make Ham Hock and Bean Soup, add 4 cups of chicken stock and some bean water to the stew for a deliciously robust soup.

Serves 4

2 fresh or smoked ham hocks
1 onion
4 garlic cloves
1 carrot, thickly sliced
2 celery stalks, chopped
1 bay leaf
1 teaspoon black peppercorns

For the Navy Bean and Tomato Stew
7oz dried navy beans
bouquet garni
1 whole carrot
1 whole onion
3 tablespoons olive oil
1 cup chopped onion
4 large garlic cloves, crushed
1 x 14oz can chopped tomatoes
1–2 tablespoons freshly chopped rosemary
sea salt, freshly ground black pepper, and sugar

To serve
lots of flat-leaf parsley
a sprig of rosemary

Self-sufficiency

During the Celtic Tiger period between 1995–2008, Ireland witnessed rapid economic growth, and along with it came a building boom. The country became quite wealthy, and a lot of people had much more disposable income than they had been used to. Many lost a grip on reality, and there was a frenzy of consumerism. Why bother to sow or grow or cook? If something could be bought, it was bought. But the music suddenly died in September 2008, when there was a serious banking crisis, and Ireland, along with many other European countries, went into a recession. Many people lost their jobs and were unable to pay mortgages on property they had bought during the "good times," when property was overvalued. A period of serious austerity followed, and people were forced to come down to earth and face a somewhat unpalatable reality. The adjustment wasn't easy, but soon many began to see the value of a degree of self-sufficiency.

As a result, the interest in relearning almost forgotten skills has gathered momentum in recent years. Many of our series of Forgotten Skills courses at the School were started in response to requests from people who had never learned to make do and now needed to make their money stretch much further. These courses teach techniques such as preserving, pickling, and smoking, as well as how to keep your own chickens to show people how to make the most of their food and also how to produce their own. A course on How to Make Homemade Butter, Yogurt, and Several Cheeses was first run in May 2006 to encourage people to make some dairy products at home or to add value to their produce on the farm. From day one it got an enthusiastic response; participants are given the option to arrive early to help bring in the cows and watch them being milked, and they love it.

The first lesson in the class shows how to separate the cream from the milk in the electric separator. The cream is churned into rich yellow butter and the milk is transformed into a variety of dairy products, from thick yogurt and labneh to paneer, cottage cheese, and myriad other cheeses. The whey is used to make beautiful, tender ricotta (which means recooked). The average Holstein

Friesian milk produces 4–4.5 percent butterfat (or milkfat), but our Jersey milk produces up to 6–7 percent butterfat, depending on the time of year. The thick yellow cream is sublime, with anything from oatmeal to coffee granita. This simple course takes the mystery out of these basic skills and gives people the confidence they need to experiment at home.

In 2008, we converted the henhouse below the School into a milking parlor and dairy. Eileen O'Donovan and Tim started to make the Jersey milk into delicious, smooth yogurt and, buoyed by this success, began to experiment with making a semihard cheese in 2009. The 12-week students were fascinated and soon became involved in making their own cheese. Now cheese is made several times a week, and any students who wish to can make their own cheese, care for it during the term, and take it home when they leave. Students who make cheese later in the term often come back to collect their cheese, which normally takes 12 weeks to mature.

The apple orchards in Kinoith were first planted by my father-in-law, Ivan Allen, in about 1935–1936, and there were beehives scattered throughout the orchards to enhance pollination. He grew about 15 varieties of apple in total, with a mixture of tart and sweet. Grenadier apples were ripe for using in September for compotes and apple pies, Bramley's Seedling matured later and could be stored through the winter in cold stores in the farmyard, several of which have now been converted into student cottages. The 13 or more apple varieties, including Beauty of Bath, Lady Sudeley, James Grieve, Worcester Pearmain, and Cox's Orange Pippin, were chosen for flavor and keeping quality. The apples were sold from the apple-packing shed (now the Cookery School) and to wholesalers and a supermarket in Cork for a brief period in the late 1970s. Each year the price decreased, and when we learned that thousands of acres of apples were being planted in Chile, we realized that the writing was on the wall for a small apple production unit such as ours.

We made the decision to dig up most of the apple orchards, but we kept the orchard in the front of our house, which contains a mixture of Worcester Pearmain, Grenadier, Bramley's Seeding, and a few Cox's Orange Pippin. This, plus the new heirloom varieties that

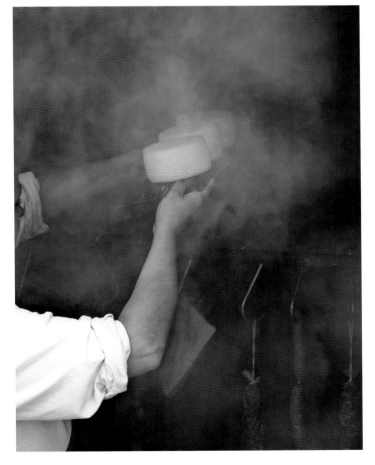

Left: The students' cheeses with their names and details of the process on each label. Each cheese will taste slightly different, depending on the way each person has handled it and interpreted the cheesemaking process. Right: Cheese going into the smoker. Emer Fitzgerald, a long-term teacher at the School, has a particular passion for the forgotten skills of foraging, pickling, and smoking. Students love to experiment with smoking all different types of food, not just the traditional fish.

we have planted in recent years behind the Shell House, provides us with apples for the School and Ballymaloe House. We carefully store the Bramley's Seedling for winter use and in good years manage to have baking apples until late February or early March.

Left: We are fortunate to be situated in the middle of a farm, so we can grow most of our own produce. Some crops are seasonal, but with onions, for example, we try to grow enough to provide for the whole year, since onions can be dried and preserved for use over the winter.
Above: My daughter Emily picking potatoes.
Right: We preserve food throughout the seasons in a variety of ways, starting with marmalade during the citrus fruit season, when the Seville and Malaga oranges reach the stores just after Christmas. In addition to teaching preserving on the 12-week course, we also run shorter pickling, preserving, and fermentation courses, and have recently been inspired by Sandor Ellix Katz, the fermentation revivalist, after he visited Ballymaloe for the inaugural Literary Festival of Food and Wine in 2013.

Beekeeping

Up until the late 1970s, our orchardist, Sean Mullane, also managed to look after the beehives located throughout the orchards. We extracted the honey in the late summer, and apple blossom honey was the most sought-after honey. It was extracted cold, and the raw honey recrystallized in the jars. It was truly delicious—a taste of Ballymaloe containing the antibodies of the area.

For many years we had no bees, but we now have several hives back in the orchard. Initially, they were looked after by our son Toby, but he became allergic to bee stings and so was forced to stop in 2008. A local beekeeper, Gary O'Keeffe, now cares for the bees, and we purchase the honey from him in return for taking care of the apiary. The students are fascinated, and some want to learn how to keep bees and manage a beehive. We teach them about the crisis in bees around the world, as more colonies are wiped out by disease. Given the importance of bees in the ecosystem and the food chain, plus the multiple services they provide to humans, their survival is essential. The European Food Safety Authority (EFSA) has the mandate to improve EU food safety and to ensure a high level of consumer protection, so has an important role to play in protecting the survival of bees. The EFSA has completed a review of neonicotinoids (some of the most widely used insecticides in the world) as part of ongoing activities related to bees, and further research is being pursued. Other studies have shown that exposure to neonicotinoids at sublethal doses can have significant effects on bee health and bee colonies; even doses that are not fatal may have damaging effects. So it was very welcome news when it was announced in April 2013 that the EU has imposed a two-year ban on the use of three neonicotinoid pesticides.

We try to keep students up-to-date on the latest research on the effect of neonicotinoids and other factors on bee colonies. Varroa, a parasitic mite that attacks honey bees, and foulbrood, which also attacks bee colonies, have both had serious effects on the bee population.

Many students have gone on to keep bees at home on the roofs or balconies of their buildings, as well as on farms and in yards. In 2000, I gave my four children the present of a beehive for Christmas—it was no problem getting a beehive, but it's really tough to get a nook of bees!

Above: A bee collecting pollen from a Nicotiana plant in the gardens at Ballymaloe.
Right: Delicious honey, rich in antibodies.
Far right: Our beekeeper, Gary O'Keeffe, checking the beehives.
We were all thrilled and relieved in the summer of 2013 to discover that we had not lost any of our bees in a year when most beekeepers were happy if 50 percent of their bees had survived the winter. This created considerable interest from beekeepers, and some think our bees' survival could be linked to the biodiversity on the farm.

Bee Bedlam

In the summer of 2009, we had a young guy mowing the lawns who fancied himself a Formula One driver; despite multiple warnings, he drove the riding mower like a racecar and, of course, collided with a couple of beehives. The irate bees poured out, and he made a quick getaway on the mower, but several visitors were forced to make a run for it, and the grounds had to be closed for the afternoon!

Pickled Vegetables

We are crazy about pickled vegetables and find all kinds of ways to serve them. I first came across lightly pickled vegetables at Momofuku in New York.

Makes about 1 quart

prepared fruit or vegetables of your choice (see right)

For the brine
2 cups hot water
1 cup rice vinegar
9 tablespoons sugar
4½ teaspoons dairy salt

Put all the ingredients for the brine into a bowl. Stir until the sugar and salt have dissolved. Pack the vegetables or fruit tightly into a 1½ quart sterilized canning jar, pressing them down well. Cover with the brine and fasten the lid.

Transfer the jar to the fridge to cure. Most pickled vegetables will keep for about 1 month. They can be eaten immediately, although they are best kept for at least 2–3 days before opening.

Pickled Carrots

2lb baby carrots, well scrubbed, peeled, and trimmed

If very fresh, leave a little of the green stems attached, but wash well. Pack tightly into jars and cover with the brine. Refrigerate and mature for 2–3 days before eating.

Pickled Fennel

2lb fennel, cut into quarters and then sliced thinly lengthwise
1 teaspoon coriander seeds

Pack tightly into jars and cover with the brine. Refrigerate and mature for 2–3 days before eating.

Pickled Beets

2lb small young beets, peeled and thinly sliced into disks or half-moons

Pack tightly into jars and cover with the brine. Refrigerate and mature for 2–3 days before eating.

Pickled Cherries

2lb cherries

Halve and pit the cherries, keeping the pits. Crush the pits in a mortar and pestle, pour into a muslin bag, and tie the bag.

Place the bag of pits in a saucepan along with the ingredients for the brine (omitting the salt). Bring to a boil. Pack the cherries into a jar and pour in the hot brine. Cool and refrigerate. Mature for 2–3 days before eating with goat cheese or duck.

Pickling and other types of preserving have changed from something that we do out of necessity into a real trend. Many restaurants are now lined with jars of pickles and jams made in-house from scratch by the chefs.

Ballymaloe Homemade Yogurt

~~≈≋≈~~

Yogurt can be made from fresh milk, but it must be brought to 194°F to pasteurize first, then allowed to cool to a lukewarm 108°F before use. Boiling destroys unwanted bacteria in the milk, which can interfere with the good bacterial action of *bacillus*.

2 cups fresh whole milk
2–3 teaspoons natural "live" yogurt

Heat the milk to 194°F and allow to cool to 108°F. Stir in the live yogurt. Pour into a deep bowl, cover, and set aside in a warm, draft-free place until set. This usually takes about 14 hours. The cooler the temperature, the longer the yogurt will take to set, but too high a temperature will kill the *bacillus* and the yogurt will not form.

Yogurt can be set in a warm pantry or utility room, in a vacuum flask with a wide neck or an insulated ice bucket. Alternatively, an earthenware pot with a lid, wrapped up in a thick towel or blanket and put near a radiator, will also do the job. The simple goal is to provide steady, even warmth to allow the *bacillus* to grow.

Remember to keep back 2 tablespoons of yogurt as the starter for the next batch. After two or three batches, you may need to use a fresh starter. Special yogurt starters can be purchased online.

Yogurt with Honey and Dates

unsweetened natural yogurt, very cold
fresh Medjool dates
thick cream
local honey
fresh almonds or lightly roasted almonds
fresh mint leaves, to garnish

Half-fill a bowl or glass with yogurt. Pit and coursely chop the dates. Put a few on the top of each helping of yogurt. Spoon a good dollop of thick cream over the top and then trickle 1 teaspoon of honey over the top. Scatter a few almonds and some shredded mint leaves on top and serve.

Penny's Kraut-Chi (Sauerkraut)

~~≈≋≈~~

Sandor Ellix Katz, a fermentation revivalist from the US, has a global cult following and came to Ireland for the Ballymaloe Literary Festival of Food and Wine in 2013. We are all fans, including my daughter-in-law Penny, who has been experimenting with all manner of fermented foods. This is her recipe, which keeps for three months or more and is delicious served with cold meats, cheese, salads, or toasted sourdough sandwiches.

Makes 1½ quarts

10oz cabbage (red or green), thinly sliced
10oz carrots, scrubbed then grated
8oz onions, thinly sliced
3 large garlic cloves, peeled and coarsely chopped
14oz beets, scrubbed then grated
½ level tablespoon salt
½–1 teaspoon red pepper flakes

Scrub and wash your vegetables well. Don't peel the carrots or the beets—the skin contains the highest density of microbes to get fermentation off to a good start.

Put all the ingredients, except the red pepper flakes, into a large bowl and mix thoroughly. Squeeze between your hands as much as possible to get the juices coming out of the vegetables. Add the red pepper flakes.

After a few minutes' mixing, pack the vegetables very tightly into a sterilized 1½ quart canning jar. Weigh down the top of the vegetables with something heavy (e.g., a sterilized jar filled with water). The vegetables should be submerged under a layer of their own juices. Fermentation happens anaerobically to produce the beneficial bacteria that you want.

Keep the jar out of the fridge for about 5 days, until it reaches the desired level of sourness—it may take a little longer if you like a quite sour taste. Many people then transfer the pickled vegetables to the fridge, but they will keep stored outside of the fridge indefinitely as long as they are covered in a layer of the juices. Penny eats this dish with everything—it can be an acquired taste at first, but, as Penny has discovered, it is one that you can become completely hooked on. She enjoys it with her own homemade buckwheat bread and occasionally with a sweet chutney for a particularly appealing mix of sweet and sour flavors.

Sustainable Fishing

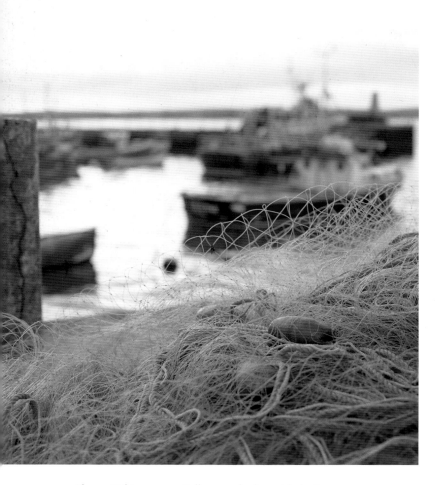

Above: Fishing nets at Ballycotton harbor with the famous Ballycotton lifeboats in the background.

Ballymaloe Cookery School is just minutes from Shanagarry Strand and the little fishing village of Ballycotton. In January or February it is sometimes difficult to predict when the herring will come in, but if we are really lucky we get a bucket or two of sprats. When the sprats are in, the herring chase them right to the shore and it's easy to scoop them up, but you must be there. We cook the sprats whole right away, dipped in well-seasoned flour and deep-fried (they are delicious with almost any kind of mayonnaise-based sauce) and we always eat the whole fish, which takes some courage for the uninitiated, but they soon become addicted. Sprats are also delicious served simply with aioli or tomatoes and mustard seeds. Whitebait come in late summer and are cooked in a similar way, served with a few arugula leaves and chile crème fraîche or made into whitebait fritters, with a wedge of lemon on the side.

As the years pass, despite our proximity to the sea, it becomes increasingly difficult to source really fresh day-boat fish. As the stocks become scarcer, due to a combination of overfishing and the discard policy, many of the fishermen have to go farther afield for their catch and some boats are at sea for up to five days. Landed fish may therefore vary from 0–5 days old, and the carbon footprint of the process has increased appreciably by using vessels that stay offshore for so long. The fish is iced to preserve it in prime condition, but still, wherever possible, our preference, both for the Cookery School and the restaurant at Ballymaloe House, is for day-boat fish caught by small, day-tripper boats that land their catch when it has only been out of the water for a few hours. Most chefs acknowledge that fish landed this way is of the greatest quality, with the best flavor, and it is much sought-after, although sadly, these days, it's hard to come by.

I became aware of the sustainable seafood issue in the early noughties at a Slow Food Conference in Turin (Slow Food has been running a Slow Fish conference since 2003). I was shocked by the statistics. For example, the International Council for Exploration of the Seas (ICES) estimated in 2005 that 95 percent of assessed EU fish stocks were overfished. While that figure has fallen to 40 percent in 2013, the EU Commission estimates that 20 percent of wild fish

Above (left): Even though Ballycotton harbor is small, with a few day boats and a couple of larger vessels, a huge variety of fish and seafood is landed there throughout the year.

Above (right): Collecting lobster directly from the boats at Ballycotton. We only serve lobster when we can get them directly from Ballycotton because we don't like to keep them in tanks. In 2008, I was awarded the Chef of the Year Award at the Conservation Leadership Awards at the Monterey Bay Aquarium, California. I collected my award and met Julie Packard, Executive Director and Vice Chair of the Aquarium's Board of Trustees, who is committed to advancing ocean conservation. I returned home even more determined to spread the word about the impact of our food choices on the environment.

consumed worldwide has been caught outside official supervision. In the US, the reviews are mixed: on the one hand, the National Oceanic and Atmospheric Administration (NOAA) found that the US seafood catch was at a 17-year high in 2012, thanks to policies to rebuild domestic fisheries. On the other, some US fisheries have been declared disaster zones—particularly the cod fisheries in New England and oyster and crab fisheries in the Mississippi. Such statistics ensured I immediately resolved to try to heighten awareness of the issue.

"Sustainable" is a widely used term, but it is not a straightforward concept. In the context of food production it means that we can interact with the environment and the creatures with which we share it to harvest food and provide for the needs of today, without damaging the ability of that environment to provide for the needs of

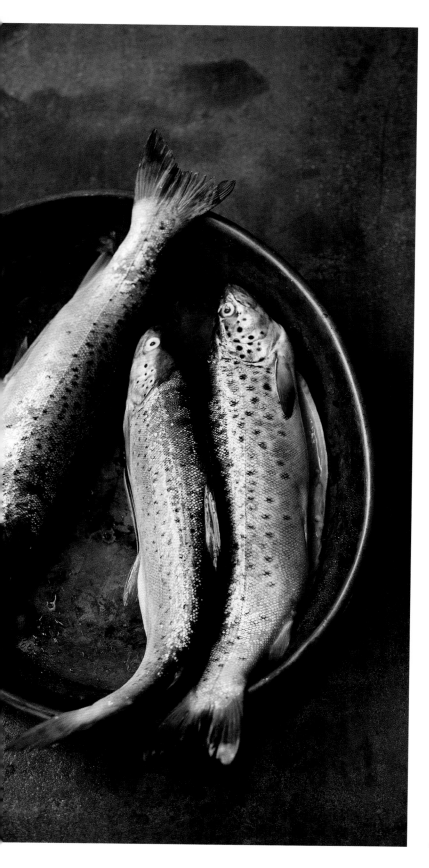

tomorrow and future generations. Sustainable fishing of wild-caught sea fish includes measures to ensure that enough fish are allowed to breed to maintain the population at viable levels, but it also includes the wider environmental footprint of this form of food production, e.g., fossil-fuel usage of boats and their impact on the ocean floor ecosystem. It is therefore unwise or even foolhardy to regard a particular species as truly sustainable. For just one species of fish there exists differences in its "sustainability," depending on which stock it comes from, the catch area and catch methods. Conversely, for highly migratory fish stocks, e.g., blue-fin tuna, they may be managed sustainably in one region, yet overexploited in another. There exist entire bureaucratic and regulatory strictures limiting what fishermen can do in the interests of sustainability, but these have to date failed in balancing society's competing desires for cheap, constantly available seafood, vibrant fishing industries, habitat protection, and sustainable fish stocks. We teach the students that the best we as consumers can do is to make informed choices and understand where our seafood comes from, how it was caught, transported, and landed—in short, where our money goes. Those who fish responsibly are usually proud to impart their passion and deserve our support.

We therefore put a Sustainable Seafood course on the Cookery School program in 2006 (we had been offering a Seafood Course since the early years of the School), emphasizing the importance of not buying or serving endangered species such as shark, or fish from stocks that are under threat such as Irish Sea cod. We educate students about alternative species that can be substituted for some threatened species, for example, rather than using cod or hake to get flaky, white fish-meat, pollock or coley (saithe) may be good alternatives. We give both the students on the Sustainable Seafood course and the 12-week students a pocket fish guide to take with them so that they have an accessible reference to check which species are endangered and what substitutes they can use.

Most people who don't live within sight of the sea will probably buy their fish in a supermarket, but we tell students who are fortunate to have a good fishmonger close by to build a relationship with him in the same way as with a local butcher, and to ask lots of questions to increase their fish knowledge—the different species, when they are in season, and how to cook them.

Schooling fish, such as mackerel or herring, tend to be particularly good at recovering from commercial exploitation, so we encourage students to use these species. The Northern Ireland Pelagic Sustainability Group (NIPSG) Irish Sea herring fishery entered into Marine Stewardship Council (MSC) assessment in

2013. The MSC is a commercial company that examines individual fisheries and accredits the acceptable exploitation of that fishery by boats that are members of the group. It is a concept that only applies to "clean" fisheries where a fisherman can have a reasonable target and only catch a particular fish type. The blue MSC logo appears on fish that have been caught at one of its certified fisheries and is a quick shorthand for buying sustainable fish. American fisheries take part in the MSC assessment program and, increasinly, US supermarkets carry MSC-labeled fish. However, because of its assessment methods, MSC certification is not applicable to a mixed bottom-trawl or beam-trawl fishery where various bottom-dwelling species are caught in proportion to the mixture on the seafloor. In other words, the absence of MSC-labeling is not necessarily the absence of a responsible approach.

Hugh Fearnley-Whittingstall has done considerable work to influence changes to the EU fisheries policy with regard to discards, which includes the wasteful practice of throwing overboard fish that fishermen have caught without a quota. However, discards only arise if fishermen use a fishing method that catches those fish. And it only happens repeatedly if fishermen return to an area and continually use that fishing method, catching fish for which they do not have a quota. Discards also arise when fishermen catch undersize fish or when they try to boost the value of their fishing trip and available quota by throwing out smaller, but legal, fish to retain onboard higher-value larger fish and maximize their return on a limited quota. Thankfully, there have been policy initiatives to address this area, which will broadly consist of measures to minimize discards, such as quota allocation proportionate to fish presence, technical gear modifications to target specific fish, plus an obligation to land all catches regardless of marketability and value.

It is important to conserve fish so it is available as a food choice, particularly since it has many health benefits. Packed with vitamins and minerals, and a major source of omega-3 fatty acids, fish can help protect against a range of diseases. We need to ensure that the rich and complex ecosystem of our seas is maintained so that future generations can enjoy the advantages of fish

Left: Beautiful fresh trout.
Right (top): There is a skill in picking up lobsters so you don't get nipped.
Right (middle): The late Tommy Sliney, who used to sell fish from his donkey and cart on the pier in Ballycotton, where he would fillet your purchase for you.
Right (bottom): Tommy Sliney bringing in a box of fish. I dedicated my Simply Delicious Fish book to him—he gave away more fish than he ever sold!

Deep-fried Squid with Aioli and Tomato and Chile Jam

One of my favorite squid recipes is from Gillian Hegarty, a past student and now head chef at Ballymaloe House. Squid can be a bit intimidating for some people to cook, but you should cook it either for a few seconds, so it turns from translucent to white, or for a long time, otherwise it can become tough and rubbery.

First, make the Tomato and Chile Jam. Preheat the oven to 400°F. Arrange the tomatoes in a roasting pan in a single layer and roast in the hot oven for about 30 minutes.

Meanwhile, put the sugar in a heavy-bottomed saucepan and dissolve over low heat. Once the sugar has dissolved, increase the heat and continue to cook until the sugar caramelizes to a pale golden brown. Pour in the roasted tomatoes, along with the cooking juices, and add the remaining ingredients for the jam. Bring to a boil and reduce by half. Liquidize until really fine and smooth. Set aside.

To make the Aioli, put all the ingredients, except the olive oil, in a food processor and blend until smooth. Keeping the motor running, add the olive oil in a slow, steady trickle through the feeder tube until emulsified. Set aside.

Prepare the squid flour by mixing together the rice flour, potato flour, and milk powder in a shallow dish. Season with the salt and white pepper.

Cut each squid in half and open out. Score the flesh deeply at an angle, and then cut each piece into 1½in squares. Pour the milk into a shallow bowl.

Preheat the oil in a deep-fat fryer to 350°F. Dip the squid in the milk and shake off any excess. Coat in the flour mixture and deep-fry in the hot oil until golden brown (don't overcrowd the deep-fryer). Season with a sprinkle of cayenne pepper and extra salt if needed. Serve with the Aioli and the Tomato and Chile Jam.

Any leftover jam can be stored in an airtight jar in the fridge. Serve with goat cheese and cold meats and use in sandwiches.

Serves 8

2 large squid
2 cups milk
sunflower oil, for deep-frying
cayenne pepper, for dusting

For the squid flour
1½ cups rice flour
1½ cups potato flour
1 tablespoon rice milk powder
1 tablespoon salt
½ tablespoon ground white pepper

For the Aioli
4 organic egg yolks
1 teaspoon Dijon mustard
½ tablespoon ground turmeric
4 garlic cloves, peeled
freshly squeezed juice of 1 lemon
2 cups extra virgin olive oil
sea salt and freshly ground black pepper

For the Tomato and Chile Jam
18oz very ripe tomatoes, halved
1½ cups turbinado sugar
4 red chiles, smashed with a rolling pin
4 garlic cloves, peeled and coarsely crushed
2in piece of fresh ginger, peeled and coarsely chopped
1 tablespoon fish sauce (nam pla)
½ cup red wine vinegar

Crab and Asparagus with Thai Mayonnaise on Sourdough

There is no shortage of common crabs to be had from the fishermen in Ballycotton these days, a big change from when I first came to Ballymaloe 40 years ago. Myrtle and Ivan were still trying to coax the fishermen to bring in crab so we could serve it on the menu. We had to promise to take the entire catch, be it four or 40, so it was feast or famine. Myrtle would never accept crab claws, for fear of encouraging the practice of harvesting the claws and throwing the crabs back into the sea, preferring instead to buy whole crabs so she could use both the flaky white meat and the creamy brown meat from the body in her repertoire of Ballymaloe recipes. This is one of the rare recipes where we use just white meat.

Bring some water to a boil in an oval casserole or saucepan that will fit the asparagus spears. Season with 1 teaspoon salt per 2 cups water. Prepare the asparagus spears by snapping off the tough end where it breaks naturally. Lay the asparagus in the boiling water and cook for 2–4 minutes, depending on the thickness. The asparagus should still be crisp and al dente for this recipe. Remove the asparagus with a slotted spoon and plunge immediately into cold water. Refresh under cold running water and drain thoroughly.

To make the Thai Mayonnaise, stir the garlic, chile, lime zest, fish sauce, and chopped cilantro into the mayonnaise. Taste and correct the seasoning, if necessary. Mix in the crabmeat and set aside.

To serve, toast or broil the bread. Drizzle with a little extra virgin olive oil and scatter a few arugula leaves over each slice. Pile the crab mixture on top. Toss the cold asparagus spears in a little extra virgin olive oil and split each spear in half lengthwise. Arrange the asparagus over the crabmeat and serve immediately.

Serves 4

6 asparagus spears
sea salt
8oz white crabmeat
4 slices of sourdough bread (see page 172), thinly sliced
    no more than ½in thick
extra virgin olive oil, for drizzling
a handful of arugula leaves

For the Thai Mayonnaise
1 garlic clove, peeled and crushed
½ red chile, seeded and finely diced
freshly grated zest of ½ lime
3 tablespoons fish sauce (nam pla)
2 teaspoons freshly chopped cilantro
¼ cup homemade mayonnaise (see page 72)
sea salt and freshly ground black pepper (optional)

Salmon with Tomato, Ginger, and Fresh Cilantro

Claudia Roden first introduced me to Salmon with Ginger and Cilantro. It sounds like an extraordinary combination, but try it; it's delicious hot or cold. For the past couple of years we have had a few beautiful wild salmon from the Blackwater River, less than an hour's drive from Shanagarry, and have appreciated every precious mouthful.

Put the olive oil in a wide, stainless-steel sauté pan, add the garlic and tomatoes and cook over medium heat until the tomatoes soften and break down, about 10–15 minutes. Add the grated ginger and cook for another 5 minutes. Season with salt, pepper, and sugar. Remove from the heat and set aside.

Cook the salmon gently in a little butter in a wide frying pan for about 3 minutes on each side. (Alternatively, put the salmon into the sauce, cover, and cook gently in the sauce.)

Remove the salmon fillets from the pan and arrange on hot serving plates. Just before serving, add the cilantro and spoon the sauce over the salmon. Serve immediately.

Serves 6

1 teaspoon olive oil
2–4 garlic cloves, peeled and finely chopped
8 very ripe tomatoes, peeled and chopped
1 tablespoon freshly grated ginger
sea salt, freshly ground black pepper, and sugar
6 x 4oz fresh wild salmon fillets
butter, for frying
2 tablespoons freshly chopped cilantro leaves, plus extra to garnish

Salmon was one of the first victims of overfishing and so fishing was restricted for a number of years to allow the stocks to build up again. Anglers feel that the proliferation of salmon farms around the coast has also affected salmon stocks and argue that escapees from such farms have bred with the wild salmon to the latter's detriment.

Roast Fish with Dill Butter and Zucchini

The fish can be cooked whole or cut into portions.
Allow 4oz for an appetizer, 6oz for a main course.
This is a fantastically easy way to cook fish—haddock,
hake, or wild salmon can all be used.

Preheat the oven to 475°F. Gut the fish and descale it, if necessary.

Line a roasting pan with foil or wax paper, put the fish on top,
and brush all over with the melted butter and oil. Season well with
salt and freshly ground pepper.

Bake the fish for about 5–8 minutes, depending on the
thickness of the fish. The fish is cooked when the flesh changes
from transparent to opaque.

Meanwhile, prepare the zucchini. Trim both ends of the zucchini,
then cut them into ¼in slices. Melt the butter or olive oil in a frying
pan, toss in the zucchini, and coat well. Cook until barely tender,
about 4–5 minutes. Add the chopped marjoram, season with salt and
freshly ground black pepper, and pour into a hot serving dish. It is
vital that the zucchini are undercooked because they will continue
to cook after they have been removed from the heat.

To make the Dill Butter, melt the butter in a small pan and stir
in the freshly chopped dill.

To serve, carefully transfer the fish onto a serving dish. Spoon
a little of the dill butter over the hot fish and serve the remainder
separately. Garnish with the chervil sprigs and accompany with
the hot zucchini.

Serves 4–6

1 whole fresh fish fillet, such as haddock or wild salmon
2 tablespoons butter, melted
2 tablespoons extra virgin oil
sea salt and freshly ground black pepper

For the Zucchini
1lb zucchini, no larger than 5in in length
2 tablespoons butter or 2 tablespoons extra virgin olive oil
1 tablespoon freshly chopped marjoram

For the Dill Butter
8 tablespoons butter
2–4 tablespoons freshly chopped dill

To serve
sprigs of chervil

Thomasina Miers

❝ I had never been to Ireland before I left for Ballymaloe. I was 25 years old and deeply depressed by life and my own inability to find a career that I could stick with; I was in serious need of inspiration. If there is anything that Ballymaloe does unfailingly, it is inspire. From the moment I drove off the ferry from Holyhead and set foot on Irish soil I had an inkling that I was finally on the right track.

I was right. From the beautiful cottages with their roaring log fires, to the chickens (and their wonderful eggs) that ate the scraps of delicious food from our cooking; the greenhouses that provided the mustard, arugula, mizuna, and baby bull that made those delicious salads we had every day for lunch; the wild sea on our doorstep that produced the mackerel and mussels and Carrageen moss that we learned to prepare. These were some of the tangible things that I remember with nostalgia, reinforced by the knowledge that for the Allens this is their normal, everyday way of life.

Less tangible but just as vivid for me were the lessons we learned. Lessons in bread making and the magic of sourdough from Timmy, lessons in it-didn't-matter-what from Rory O'Connell, so skillful and elegant was his cooking and way with words. Then there was the whole story of food from Darina—where it came from, how it was grown, what impact its growing and our eating had on the planet, how terroir affected flavor, how love and passion for food inspired a whole gallery of producers to make cheeses, cured meats, smoked fish, and other delicacies up and down the country. Nuggets of information from the mighty Myrtle Allen that I gleaned while earning my keep as a girl Friday at Ballymaloe House only deepened my thirst for knowledge.

It doesn't harm the School that it is tucked away in one of the prettiest parts of the world, or that this corner of Ireland is full of Ballymaloe alumni cooking fresh local ingredients with tested skills and enormous energy. It doesn't hurt that the local pubs were brimming with gnarled and vibrant characters who could have stepped out of the radio and who treated you like a long-lost cousin within days of meeting. In my memory there seemed to be a jam happening every other night with wild boys in wild bands who

Left: Thomasina Miers at the Ballymaloe Literary Festival of Food and Wine in 2013.

Right (top): Thomasina Miers with the instantly recognizable Pamela Black, a senior teacher at the School. Thomasina has returned to the School several times to teach guest chef courses on Mexican food, which has become her passion and the focus of her chain of Wahaca restaurants.

Right (bottom): Thomasina Miers demonstrating with Stevie Parle, her fellow classmate at Ballymaloe on the 12-week course in January 2002, and Rachel Allen—some of the new young voices in food.

played intoxicatingly beautiful Irish ballads in houses found down winding country lanes.

Darina has spawned generations of cooks who have scattered across the globe to weave their own food stories in their own particular way, but all with her maxims ringing in their ears. If I close my eyes today, all these years later, I can see her clearly in the classroom rubbing her hands together, eyes shining brightly with the fun of the recipe.

You go to Ballymaloe not solely to learn to become a chef, but to learn an approach to food that is inextricably bound up in the pleasure gained from preparing and eating food, a pleasure that is ingeniously intensified when shared with either family or friends. You learn along the way skills such as boiling an egg, making the perfect meringue, sweating vegetables, clarifying stock, or deglazing a pan, but you never forget that the most important aspect is the simple joy of making good food. **"**

Oaxacan Chicken Soup

Mexico and Mexican food most definitely have a special place in my heart, a passion that I share with Thomasina Miers. I particularly love Oaxaca, a colorful colonial town in the Sierra Nevada Valley, where this soup comes from. Adding extra bits to a bowl of soup always adds to the enjoyment for me.

Serves 6

6–7 cups flavorful chicken stock, well skimmed
sea salt and freshly ground black pepper
8oz shredded chicken (cooked or raw)

To serve
2–3 ripe Hass avocados, cut into ¼in dice
6 medium tomatoes, cut into ¼in dice
2 medium red onions, cut into ¼in dice
3 green serrano or jalapeño chiles, thinly sliced
4–6 tablespoons freshly chopped cilantro leaves
3 limes, cut into wedges

Put the chicken stock into a wide saucepan and bring to a boil. Taste and season—it should have a full rich flavor, otherwise the soup with be bland and insipid.

Add the shredded chicken—I sometimes use scraps from the chicken carcass from the stockpot, however, you can use either raw or cooked chicken. Cooked chicken just needs to be reheated in the broth. Raw white meat will take a few minutes to cook and dark meat a little longer. Poach it gently, so it doesn't toughen. Taste again and correct the seasoning, if necessary.

To serve, ladle the soup into bowls. Provide each guest with a side plate containing some diced avocado, tomato, red onions, thinly sliced green chiles, chopped cilantro, and lime segments to add to the soup as they choose.

Chilaquiles Verdes o Rojos

Mexican culture, like many other cultures, has many ways of using up leftovers and a tradition that it is sinful and unlucky to waste even a scrap of tortilla. Chilaquiles are one of the many ways to use up tortillas deliciously.

Many of the chickens in Mexico are corn fed so the skin is a rich golden color. One chicken produces a mound of shredded meat when it is pulled apart along the natural grain.

Preheat the over to 450°F.

First, poach the chicken breast. Put it in a small saucepan, cover with the chicken stock, and simmer gently until cooked, about 15–18 minutes, depending on size. Shred the flesh and set aside, reserving the poaching liquid.

Meanwhile, cut each tortilla into eight pieces. If they are moist and floppy, dry them out in a moderate oven for a few minutes; they are best stale and leathery for this dish.

Preheat the oil in a deep-fat fryer and cook the tortilla pieces in batches, until crisp and lightly golden. Drain on paper towels.

To make the salsa, peel off the husks from the tomatillos and discard. Put them into a saucepan with the chiles and cover with cold water. Bring to a boil and cook until soft, about 10 minutes. Drain through a strainer, discarding the cooking liquid, and transfer the cooked tomatoes and chiles to a food processor. Add the onion, garlic, cilantro, salt, and water and pulse for several minutes. Taste and correct the seasoning, if necessary.

To assemble the dish, arrange half of the tortillas over the bottom of a deep-sided 8 x 5in ovenproof dish. Scatter the shredded chicken over the top and season with salt and freshly ground black pepper. Top with the remaining tortillas. Thin out the tomatillo sauce with a little of the chicken broth, if necessary, and pour over the tortillas. Sprinkle a little grated cheese over the top and bake for 5–10 minutes until hot and bubbling.

Serve immediately with the sour cream and cheese and scatter the sliced onions (if using) and fresh cilantro over the top.

Serves 4

1 large chicken breast
1 cup chicken stock
6–8 corn tortillas (stale is fine)
sunflower oil, for deep-frying
sea salt and freshly ground black pepper
4 tablespoons crumbled Queso Fresco (or grated mozzarella and Cheddar cheese mixed together)

For the Tomatillo Salsa
6 tomatillos (green tomatoes covered with a papery husk), weighing about 18oz
4 serrano chiles
1 heaping tablespoon chopped onion
1 small garlic clove, peeled
a handful of fresh cilantro (leaves and soft stems)
½ teaspoon salt
2 tablespoons water

To serve
2–4 tablespoons sour cream
4 tablespoons crumbled Queso Fresco (or grated mozzarella and Cheddar cheese mixed together)
1 onion, thinly sliced (optional)
fresh cilantro leaves

Hoja Santa Quesadilla

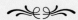

Hoja santa is an aromatic South American herb with a very particular flavor. Its name means "sacred leaf" in Spanish. The treelike plants grow well in warm parts of the US, and the fresh herbs are available at Mexican grocery stores and online. Do use the herb if you can find it, because its magical flavor adds to so many dishes. If hoja santa is not available, any number of other fresh herbs would be good here—wild garlic, even scallions and some chopped chile, a little diced chorizo, or some tapenade.

Serves 1

2–3 white corn tortillas
1 hoja santa leaf (*Piper auritum*), about 8in across
Oaxaca string cheese (or a mixture of grated mozzarella cheese and mature Cheddar cheese)
pinch of salt

To serve
Tomatillo Salsa (see left)

Lay a tortilla on a cutting board. Tear off a few pieces of fresh hoja santa leaf and scatter over the tortilla. Sprinkle with the cheese and season with a pinch of salt.

Heat a grill pan or heavy frying pan over medium heat. Cook the tortilla for a couple of minutes. As soon as the cheese starts to melt, fold over and cook the other side until slightly crisp on both sides. Serve with the Tomatillo Salsa.

The Soft Fruit Garden

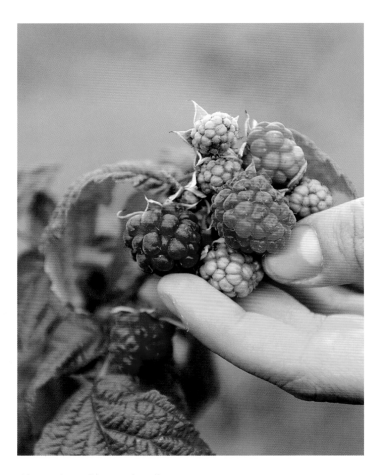

Above: An early crop of raspberries.
Right: A selection of soft fruits from our berry and currant garden.

For many years we were able to get beautiful summer berries and currants for the Cookery School, such as raspberries, tayberries, loganberries, and black, white, and red currants from Sunnyside Farm near Fermoy. But John Howard eventually gave up growing berries in 2009, defeated by inclement weather and new labor laws, which made it difficult to get fruit pickers at opportune times. Sourcing consistent supplies of organic fruit in any significant quantity had become problematic, so in 2010 we decided to plant a currant and berry garden next to the Celtic Maze to have our own supply of organic fruit.

This approximately half-acre fruit garden is planted in straight rows interspersed with grass paths. Clumps of lavender, chives, and other edible flowers are planted at the end of each row to attract bees, butterflies, and beneficial insects into the gardens to help with pollination. We grow a variety of soft fruits including strawberries, raspberries, black currants, red currants, white currants, tayberries, and gooseberries. Black currants are one of the first fruits to come into leaf in spring. Green gooseberries are ready in May and, even though they are still hard and green, this is when they are best for pies, compotes, and fools and are particularly delicious with elderflower, which is in full bloom at that time. Next come strawberries in June, followed by raspberries and all the currants in July, then loganberries, tayberries, and boysenberries in August. Autumn raspberries ripen in September and October—they are a more mellow and flavorsome crop than the summer raspberries. The fruit is picked daily by hand and is used to make jams, cakes, desserts, popsicles, and ice cream by our students and by Julija Makejeva, who cooks for the Ballymaloe stall at Midleton Farmers' Market.

In 2012 we added a blueberry patch for the joy of being able to pick our own, having first added lots of acid components to our naturally limey soil, as blueberries need acid soil to flourish. The birds really love blueberries, so we've built a protective cage over the plants to stop the birds from eating them. My husband Tim also bought two scary inflatable "men" from an English farm website,

Above: Loganberries growing in the currant and berry garden. You need to resist picking them until they are dark red, or they taste bitter and unappealing. We never seem to have enough of them since their bittersweet flavor makes super pies, jams, ice creams, and fools. If we do have a surplus, they also freeze well. They are well worth growing because, unlike raspberries, they can be difficult to buy.

who leap up at irregular intervals and scare both garden visitors and the birds—very effective.

As well as supplying the School with delicious produce to cook with, the fruit garden is also used as a teaching garden. The students, many for the first time, see how fruit grows and learn how to pick it directly off the bushes. They are excited to learn that they can also use some of the young leaves for cordials and granita; black currant leaf sorbet is particularly delicious. We tell them raspberry leaf tea is supposed to induce labor, information they can store up for another time!

The berry and currant garden forms part of the larger farm and gardens to provide an ever-changing outdoor classroom where students can observe the changing seasons and learn how to judge when the vegetables, fruit, and herbs are perfect for picking. The fact that fruit and vegetables are not all identical in size and perfectly shaped comes as quite a shock to many people who buy only from the supermarket shelves. We teach them about the phenomenal amount of waste resulting from customers' demands for perfect produce—farmers reckon they have done well if 40–50 percent of a crop reaches the supermarket shelves; the remainder is wasted or ploughed back into the ground. A shocking realization at any time, but particularly in Ireland today, where just one of the charities in Cork, Penny Dinners, is feeding 900–1,000 people a week. (Hearing this, some of the students are moved to volunteer to help this charity on weekends.)

When the students pick and taste the fresh fruit and vegetables directly from the plants and bushes, the flavor can be a revelation, so they are less interested in buying imported produce in the winter when it is out of season and much more expensive. We also discuss air miles and the challenge of reducing our carbon footprint, something we can do by buying fruit from local suppliers in season rather than strawberries in the middle of winter, when they will have to have been flown in from halfway across the world.

We also teach the students how to use up a surplus of fruit and vegetables and to have fun pickling and preserving.

In addition the School offers a variety of gardening courses on Designing a Herbaceous Border, Creating a Fruit Garden, and Winter Pruning. These are taught by Susan Turner, our consultant head gardener, who was previously head gardener at Yalding Organic Gardens in the UK.

Above: Students making pasta from scratch at the Ballymaloe Cookery School.

Mike Butt Award

In 2010 I was honored by the Restaurants Association of Ireland (RAI) for my contribution to the Irish Restaurant Industry and the Food Movement. When I accepted this award in Dublin, I spoke of my concerns about the loss of basic skills among chefs, at a time when an increasing number of restaurants were just opting for "catalog cooking." Some are choosing this option for economic reasons and others because it is the path of least resistance from the food hygiene and food safety perspective.

If the food arrives pre-packaged in plastic, it has the seal of approval of the FSA (Food Safety Authority). All chefs need to do is pop the food portion in a microwave or water bath, and slit open the top of the package. Fish is filleted, poultry is cut up, racks of lamb are French trimmed, sauces are already made, perfect tartlets come waiting to be filled, and chocolate curls ready to be popped onto ice creams or mousses.

It is all terrifically convenient and very tempting, and indeed it can be very impressive, but the price of this compromise (to convenience) is a sameness in menus all over the country. What is even more serious is that many chefs are becoming increasingly deskilled, since in many kitchens they no longer need to be able to make a loaf of bread, whip up a bowl of mayonnaise, or produce buttery feather-light puff pastry, not to mention a jar of jam.

I encouraged the inclusion of a class in the curriculum in the catering colleges, or Institutes of Technology as they are now called, to encourage sourcing and to introduce artisan food producers to the students. I got a resounding round of applause from the audience, many of whom were restaurant owners and head chefs who were having to cope with the very difficulties I had outlined. I also encouraged the colleges to consider planting vegetable, herb, and fruit gardens in their extensive grounds, so students could learn how to grow and harvest.

Pan-grilled Summer Mackerel with Green Gooseberry Sauce

We eat mackerel only when they come into Ballycotton Bay from early summer and become more plentiful toward the end of August. There have recently been concerns over the sustainability of mackerel, but it is worth checking in your area as the stocks vary from place to place. This is a master recipe for pan-grilling fish. The simplest and possibly the most delicious way to cook really fresh mackerel.

First make the Green Gooseberry Sauce. Top and tail the gooseberries (or cut up the rhubarb into 1in pieces), put them into a stainless-steel saucepan, and barely cover with the simple syrup. Bring to a boil and simmer until the fruit bursts. Taste. Stir in a small pat of butter if you like, but it is very good without it.

Preheat a grill pan. Dip each fish fillet into seasoned flour and shake off any excess. Spread a little softened butter over the flesh side of each fillet, as though you were buttering a slice of bread rather lightly. When the pan is quite hot, but not smoking, put the fish fillets, butter-side down, in the pan; they should sizzle as soon as they touch the pan. Reduce the heat slightly. Cook the fillets for 4–5 minutes on the first side, then turn over and cook on the skin side until crisp and golden. Serve on a hot plate, accompanied by the warm gooseberry sauce and lemon wedges.

Serves 1–2

2–4 fillets of very fresh mackerel (allow 6oz fish per person as a main course, or 3oz as an appetizer)
flour, seasoned with salt and pepper
small pat of butter, softened

For the Green Gooseberry Sauce
10oz fresh green gooseberries (or rhubarb)
approx. ¾ cup simple syrup (see page 284), to cover
pat of butter (optional)

To serve
lemon wedges

Black Currant Popsicles

We use all the summer fruits to make popsicles—raspberries, strawberries, and black currants—with combinations like blackberry and sweet geranium, red currant and strawberry, peach and raspberry, or raspberry and basil. In the winter we make a variety of citrus popsicles, including blood orange and tangerine. They are loved not just by children but people of all ages, and I particularly enjoy serving them at the end of a dinner party.

Makes 6

1lb black currants
1–1¼ cups simple syrup (see below)

Put the black currants in a medium saucepan, pour in the syrup, and bring to a boil. Cook for 3–5 minutes until the black currants burst, and then purée. Strain through a nylon sieve and set aside to cool.

Taste and add a little more syrup if necessary. It needs to taste sweeter than you would like because the freezing dulls the sweetness. Pour into popsicle molds, cover, insert a stick, and freeze until needed. These are best eaten within a few days.

Simple Syrup

Makes 2½ cups

2¼ cups granulated sugar
2½ cups water

Dissolve the sugar in the water over low heat. Bring to a boil, and boil hard for 2 minutes. Set aside to cool. Any leftover syrup can be stored in a sealed container in the fridge for approx. 1 month.

Camilla's Strawberry and Rose Petal Jam

When my friend Camilla Plum, Danish cook, farmer, and food writer, comes to stay, she wanders through the farm, gardens, and greenhouses, picking and collecting fresh ingredients and cooking nonstop. Last summer, she filled her apron with rose petals from the scented old roses—she tossed them into a saucepan with some fresh strawberries and made this exquisite jam. We also made rose syrup and crystallized the petals to decorate desserts and cakes.

Makes 2–3 x 13oz jars

2¼ cups granulated sugar
2¼lb fresh strawberries
4 cups rose petals from fragrant roses
juice of 1 lemon

Preheat the oven to 275°F. Pour the sugar into an ovenproof dish lined with parchment paper and warm it in the oven for 20 minutes.

Meanwhile, put the strawberries in a wide, heavy-bottomed stainless-steel saucepan and cook over a high heat until the juices run and the fruit breaks down. Add the rose petals and the warmed sugar and stir until the sugar has dissolved. Bring to a boil, and continue to cook for 5–8 minutes until a set is reached. To test for a set, spoon a teaspoon of the hot jam onto a cold plate and set aside for a few minutes in a cool place. If setting point has been reached, the jam should wrinkle when pressed with a finger. (If the jam isn't set, return the pan to the heat and boil for a few minutes longer.) Stir in the freshly squeezed lemon juice, remove from the heat, and pour into sterilized jars with nonreactive lids. Fasten the lids. Store in a cool, dark place and in the fridge once opened.

Rachel Allen

" Of course I'd seen Darina on television before, but never in real life. I was a teenager when she first appeared on our screens in Ireland with her bright red glasses, long linen skirts, and her no-fuss approach to food. At that stage I was toying with the idea of becoming a fashion designer, a shoe designer, or maybe even an actress. So when my sister and parents encouraged me to leave Dublin to go down to Ballymaloe to learn how to cook at the age of 18, I really didn't know what to expect.

Darina came racing into the demonstration kitchen on the first morning of the 12-week certificate course (I was soon to learn that she never goes anywhere slowly!) and began to speak to us about food. She was talking about provenance, sustainability, seasonality, and something called organic growing. This was January 1990 and food was in a very different place back then. The big trend was "vertical food"; one thing sitting on top of another and then another and then topped with a turned carrot or something similar. So why on earth was this woman talking passionately about the soil, keeping chickens, and growing vegetables without chemicals or pesticides? I thought I had come here to learn how to cook.

It took a few hours of fervent and tireless talk during which Darina also spoke about her mother-in-law, Myrtle Allen, and the radically integrated approach here at Ballymaloe before it finally clicked. To get great food, we need great produce—and to get great produce, we need great soil.

Over the next 12 weeks, I was to learn a tremendous amount from Darina and her brother, the equally extraordinary Rory O'Connell. Each has a distinctive style of teaching, yet both share the same passion for great food, drive to eliminate food waste, and an unwavering commitment to their extremely high standards. It is an ethos that runs throughout the School and is practiced by the many, many people who work here, each with a crucial part to play in making Ballymaloe what it is.

I was so encouraged by the approach to food here that I decided to stay around for a while and got a job working in the restaurant kitchen at Ballymaloe House (though Darina tells me now that she

Left: Rachel and me, enjoying a cup of tea in a moment's rest outside the Cookery School.
Above (top): Rachel and me at the School in the mid-1990s.
Above (bottom): Claire Cullinane, Rachel O'Neill (later to be Rachel Allen), and Breda Murphy. I wish I knew what had attracted their attention.

Left: Rachel and me posing together for a piece in Observer Food Monthly on "What's it like to run a restaurant with your family?"

Below (top): Myrtle Allen, Rachel, and me in the Blue Dining Room of the Cookery School with my grandson Joshua.

Below (bottom): Rachel chatting to Triana and Sue Cullinane as they prepare for a long-table dinner, with Rory O'Connell in the background.

Right: Rachel and me demonstrating together at the Ballymaloe Cookery School. Rachel teaches regularly at the School and we occasionally demonstrate together. The afternoon demonstrations throughout the year, such as this one, are open to the public, but demand is usually high so it's always wise to book ahead.

knew only too well that it was the lure of her eldest son that kept me here!)

At Ballymaloe House the ethos was no different to that of the School. The menu there changes every day and is dictated by what's growing at the time and what fish is available that day. Myrtle, or Mrs. Allen as everyone calls her, is another unbelievably impressive woman and, like her daughter-in-law, is indefatigable.

After cooking and learning so much at Ballymaloe House, I eventually went back to the Cookery School to teach. I was drawn to the electric atmosphere of so many learning minds. I continue to be inspired each day by the School, especially when a student masters a new technique or discovers a love of some new dish.

When I'm writing a cookbook, I always think of my teaching at the School. It is at the core of all my work, and I feel an immense privilege to be a part of the School. I get the same thrill whenever I see a new group of students arriving. Often from as many as 15 different countries, they begin their journey at Ballymaloe. They learn at once about the fundamental relationship between growing good food and cooking good food. They become a part of the harvest and the dairy. Then of course there are the kitchens, where countless people have received the tools and knowledge to go on either to great professional achievement or simply better quality home-cooked meals. Whatever they do and wherever they go, Ballymaloe can always be credited with instilling in its students a lifelong passion and enthusiasm for growing, cooking, and sharing great food. **"**

Long-table Dinners

Since 2010, we have organized a feast in the greenhouses to celebrate the work of the gardeners and farmers. As soon as the early potatoes are harvested we plant a lawn in one of the greenhouse bays. By July we have a lush green carpet. We lay a long table with starched white-linen tablecloths in the midst of the scarlet runner beans, tomatoes, and edible flowers. All the meat and vegetables come from the farm and gardens and the fish and shellfish from nearby Ballycotton. When the tickets go on sale, they sell out within a matter of days and many people come back year after year. Some travel from the US, UK, and Holland.

We welcome the guests in mid-afternoon with a glass of Prosecco and some freshly grilled sourdough bread from Arbutus artisanal bakery, simply drizzled with Capezzana extra virgin olive oil and a few flakes of sea salt, as well as heirloom tomatoes and a little basil, or scattered wild chanterelles foraged by Melissa Odendahl, or topped with a chunky purée of broad beans. After a little talk, we divide into two or three groups to walk through the farm, gardens, and orchards, stopping on the way to visit the milking parlor, where our small herd of Jersey cows is milked every morning, and the dairy, where we separate the milk from the cream to make butter, cheese, and yogurt. Then through the fruit garden, past the Palais des Poulets, through the little wooded area into the kitchen garden where the willow scarecrows keep guard over the vegetables. It's then across the courtyard and into Lydia's Garden, pausing to look at the summerhouse floor made from broken china

by the Quaker Strangman sisters. It incorporates the shamrock, rose, and thistle, the emblem of these islands, and the date it was made—1912. Those who would like to have a bird's eye view of the herb garden climb up onto the treehouse, while others walk through the arches in the beech hedge into the formal herb garden with its boxwood hedges and limestone sundial. Then it's on down into the pleasure garden, to the pond, past the walnuts, nut trees, and ancient magnolia.

The ducks and geese glide past the classical folly and chase each other around the fountain. Farther on we pass the happy, lazy pigs snoozing in the field—Saddlebacks and Gloucester Old Spots blissfully unaware that their slow-roasted sibling is on the menu in the greenhouse close by. From there we walk under the bridal arch created for our daughter Emily's and her husband Philip's wedding, and on through the herbaceous borders to the Shell House, an octagonal folly with a seashell-crusted interior created by Blott Kerr Wilson in 1995 to celebrate our 25th wedding anniversary. The currant and berry garden is over to the left, close to the Celtic maze where the latest Petal Folly, designed by Jeremy Williams, peeps up over the hornbeam, yew and beech hedges. The interior was richly embellished with exotic birds and flowers by Michael Dillon in 2012. Then on through the wildflower meadow, through the field vegetables, such as asparagus, sea kale, and Jerusalem artichokes, and into the greenhouse. There, my son-in-law, Rupert Hugh-Jones, and his friends are playing a mix of traditional, classical, and hip-hop music.

In mid-July there is an abundance of produce interspersed with flowers, so it is a breathtaking scene. My brother Rory, his ace team of teachers, and our housekeepers beaver away in the field kitchen they have set up in the bay of the greenhouses next to the long table. The 100 guests take their places at the table. In 2013 many were drawn down to the end of the greenhouse where, just outside the door, Adam O'Connor and my grandson Joshua were working on a huge graffiti piece of pesky birds, snails, and insects about to attack the organic produce. The feast begins with one delicious dish after another. I cannot imagine how they create such delicious food. In 2013, Baroness Julia Neuberger, a rabbi friend, said grace and we all gave thanks for the bounty of the earth and celebrated the work of those who produce our beautiful, nourishing food.

My daughter Lydia creates a hand-drawn, watercolor menu for each guest, and these are now becoming collector's items. (She also creates these menus for the Farewell dinners that the 12-week students have at the end of every course, as well as for other special celebrations we have at the School.)

The proceeds of the long-table dinners go to support the East Cork Slow Food Educational Project, which links with nine local schools to teach the children how to grow, cook, and keep hens.

In 2011 the Outstanding in the Field team came to Ballymaloe with their founder, Jim Denevan, whose brainchild it was to have long-table dinners on farms and vineyards, in apple orchards, and community gardens, and on mountaintops and beaches right across the US and Canada. The event came about after my daughter Emily met Leif Hedendal in a pub in California. He told her how he and his friends had been organizing these dinners, which had been a phenomenal success, and their next stop was Europe. They were scouting for a venue in Ireland, the UK, France, Spain, or Denmark. Did she know of anywhere? Emily explained that a dinner in a field in Ireland was a risky business, but how about a greenhouse? And so a plan was hatched.

We had already had several long-table dinners in the greenhouses to celebrate the work of the farmers and gardeners so had had some practice. The School farm and garden gang snipped and clipped for several weeks to have the whole place looking its best for the event. The weather forecast was for rain and gale-force winds. We all held our breath and pleaded with our friends who had a direct line to the Holy Ghost to intercede on our behalf. We'd be happy with just one drizzle-free hour to walk through the farm. And so it was.

People traveled from the US, Mexico, Holland, and the UK to join the Irish guests. We invited some of the Irish artisanal producers whose food we were serving, so it was a wonderfully convivial event, enjoying and celebrating their delicious produce.

Left: The guests sit down to a long-table dinner in the greenhouse.
Right (top): The beautifully laid long table, covered with crisp white linen, before the guests arrive.
Right (middle): Rory O'Connell with petit fours for the guests to finish off their dinner.
Right (bottom): The band providing musical entertainment in the greenhouse.

Sumac Lamb Chops with Tomato and Cucumber Salad

Sumac is a Middle Eastern berry that is crushed and sold as a red spice powder. The flavor is quite distinctive, delivering a uniquely sour taste. You can find sumac in specialist food shops and some big supermarkets.

Put a large grill pan or frying pan over high heat and allow it to get quite hot. As the pan heats up, drizzle 1 teaspoon of olive oil over each lamb chop and rub in well on both sides. Season each chop with ½ teaspoon of sumac and plenty of salt and pepper, rubbing in the spice and seasoning with your fingers.

Put the chops in the hot pan and fry for 2–4 minutes on each side, depending on the thickness of the chops and how pink you like them.

As the lamb chops cook, mix together the ingredients for the salad in a bowl and season with salt and pepper. Divide the lamb chops and salad between plates and sprinkle each one with a pinch of sumac to serve.

Serves 4

8 lamb chops, each weighing approx. 6–8oz
8 teaspoons olive oil
4 teaspoons sumac, plus extra to serve
sea salt and freshly ground black pepper

For the Tomato and Cucumber salad
2 tomatoes, cut into ½in dice
2¼ cups chopped cucumber, cut into ½in dice
¾ cup plain yogurt

Roasted Vegetable Coconut Curry

The creamy coconut milk and myriad spices grant these vegetables both elegance and luxury. Roasting the vegetables in the paste really brings out their sweetness. Making your own curry paste takes minutes, and the complex depth of flavor means it's always worth doing. Chana masala is made up of equal quantities of ground coriander seeds, cumin seeds, and turmeric.

Preheat the oven to 325°F. First make the curry paste. Put a small frying pan over medium heat, and add the coriander seeds, cumin seeds, and chana masala. Cook, tossing frequently, for approx. 1 minute or until they start to pop. Pour into a spice grinder or mortar and pestle, and crush to a fine powder.

Put the ginger, garlic, chiles, onions, and vegetable oil in a food processor and process for 2–3 minutes or until smooth. Pour this mixture into a large saucepan and stir in the freshly ground spices, along with the turmeric, sugar, and salt. Set over medium to low heat and cook, stirring occasionally, for approx. 5 minutes or until the mixture has reduced slightly.

Remove the curry paste from the heat and pour half of the mixture into a large bowl. Keep the remaining paste in the pan and stir in the coconut milk and stock, mixing well until combined.

Add the yogurt to the spice paste in the bowl and stir well, then add the root vegetables and onions. Stir well until the vegetables are thoroughly coated, and then divide the contents of the bowl between two roasting pans. Cook in the preheated oven until the vegetables are lightly browned, approx. 1 hour.

Remove the vegetables from the oven and pour them into the saucepan with the coconut milk mixture. Warm over medium heat for a few minutes, and then stir in the spinach. Cook for a few minutes until the spinach has wilted.

To serve, spoon the curried vegetables into serving bowls and sprinkle with the fresh cilantro and a scattering of toasted cashew nuts. Drizzle a spoonful of yogurt or crème fraîche over each portion.

Serves 8–10

For the curry paste
1 tablespoon coriander seeds
2 teaspoons cumin seeds
2 teaspoons chana masala
½ cup peeled and roughly chopped ginger
12 garlic cloves, peeled
4 red chiles, seeded and roughly chopped
2 medium onions, peeled and quartered
¼ cup vegetable oil
1 tablespoon ground turmeric
2 teaspoons sugar
2 teaspoons sea salt

2 x 14oz cans of coconut milk
2½ cups vegetable stock
1¾ cups plain yogurt
4 large carrots, peeled and cut into ¾in cubes
6 parsnips, peeled, cores removed, and flesh cut into ¾in cubes
1½lb sweet potatoes, peeled and cut into ¾in cubes
4 onions, peeled and cut into eighths
5oz spinach (any large stems removed), chopped

To serve
large bunch of cilantro, freshly chopped
3 cups cashew nuts, toasted and chopped
1 cup plain yogurt or crème fraîche

White Chocolate Mendiants with Dried Cranberries, Cherries, and Pistachios

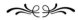

Mendiants are a traditional French treat. They are unbelievably fast and easy to make, yet they look so elegant served at the end of a meal. The French would use different nuts and dried fruits to represent the four mendicant, or monastic, orders of the Dominicans (raisins), Augustians (hazel nuts), Franciscans (dried figs), and Carmelites (almonds). These can be made a few days in advance; make sure to store them somewhere cool, but preferably not the fridge as they will sweat.

Makes 28

4oz white chocolate (we use Valrhona)
1 heaping tablespoon dried cranberries and cherries
1 heaping tablespoon shelled pistachios, coarsely chopped
2oz dark chocolate
edible gold leaf (optional)

Line two baking sheets with parchment paper.

Put the white chocolate into a Pyrex bowl and set over a saucepan of hot water, making sure that the bottom of the bowl doesn't touch the water. Bring the water to a boil, then immediately remove from the heat and set aside until the chocolate has melted.

Put teaspoons of the melted white chocolate, spaced a little apart, onto the parchment paper. Shake gently to level, then quickly dot them with a few dried cranberries and cherries and some coarsely chopped pistachios. Allow to set.

Meanwhile, melt and cool the dark chocolate. Peel the medallions of white chocolate off the paper and brush the bases with the dark chocolate. Arrange the mendiants upside down on the parchment paper and leave to set. These look wonderfully festive scattered with edible gold leaf or served on a gold doily on a chilled plate.

The New Nordic Movement

A table at Noma restaurant in Copenhagen is one of the hottest, most sought-after meals in the world. In 2012 Noma was named best restaurant in the world by *Restaurant* magazine in the influential World's Best 50 list for the third consecutive year. Curious chefs and food lovers from around the globe fly into Copenhagen to eat at this simple establishment, which has defined the gastronomy of a whole nation and generated a flow of food tourism that benefits not only Noma but a growing number of restaurants in Copenhagen and the hinterland. So why is Noma causing such a sensation? Well, chef René Redzepi and his team cook and serve Nordic ingredients proudly. The food is fresh and seasonal, and much is foraged from the wild. It is incredibly delicious. But Noma is not just about the food; the whole experience challenged many of our concepts of how it should taste and be served.

In just a few short years, the center of the gastronomic world has moved from Spain to the Nordic countries. Spain's Ferran Adrià, a genius whose food I have enjoyed many times, is unique. He and his acolytes concentrate on transforming textures and flavors, often to stunning effect, but even though I listened hard, one never heard the words "fresh" or "seasonal" and there was no discussion about breeds, feed, or tradition. The new culinary movement, spear-headed by René Redzepi and Magnus Nilsson, is flowing not from Spain, France, Italy, or the Mediterranean, but from Copenhagen and Stockholm and as far north as Lapland. It began in 2004 when prominent chefs from the region, including Redzepi and Claus Meyer, signed a Kitchen Manifesto emphasizing the need for purity, simplicity, and freshness in their cooking, and for the increased use of seasonal foods. Restaurants were encouraged to develop traditional dishes using ingredients benefiting from their local region's specific climate, water, and soil. Just as many chefs began investing in water baths, siphons, gels, and expensive gadgets, it became clear that the huge wave of technical cooking was on its way out. Instead, what is catching young chefs' imaginations is the New Nordic or authentic cuisine. This new movement, honoring nature and the seasons, resonates much more with me.

To quote Julia Moskin in *The New York Times*, this style of cooking is "earthy and refined, ancient and modern, both playful and deeply serious. Instead of the new (techniques, stabilizers, ingredients), it emphasizes the old (drying, smoking, pickling, curing), with a larger goal of returning balance to the earth itself." Challenging in the extreme Nordic climate where chefs say goodbye to fresh ingredients at the beginning of October and don't see them again until they welcome their re-emergence in April. Food is presented on plates in the midst of rocks and shells, moss, twigs and bark, lichen, hay, and pine, in a recreation of its natural environment.

On arrival at Noma, a converted herring warehouse, you walk down three or four steps—the kitchen is directly ahead—and are greeted by several of the chefs and shown to your table. The room is simple yet incredibly sophisticated. And then the feast begins. Lots of little snacks arrive in quick succession, then the pace slows down and the dishes become slightly larger. Virtually all are vegetarian. In an exquisite meal of almost 20 courses, we had meat just twice: tiny medallions of bone marrow in one dish and paper-thin slices of duck breast in another. I hadn't even noticed the absence of meat until someone mentioned it in passing. It was a beautiful celebration of vegetables and wild foods. At Noma the chefs not only plate the food in the kitchen but also help to serve it to the guests—such a simple yet brilliant concept. The chefs, normally hidden behind closed doors, get to experience the guests' reaction to their food. Noma has simply one of the best dining experiences I've ever had.

There were three Irish chefs in the Noma kitchen, one of whom is a past student of the Ballymaloe Cookery School. Louise Bannon, who did the 12-week course in 2002, baked the bread and produced many of the tempting desserts on our visit. The bread was mouthwatering, served warm in a little felt nest with the most incredibly delicious butter I have ever tasted. It's made by a Swedish couple who have just five goats. They stop the butter just when the cream is starting to split, drain and wash it, then serve the curdled butter fat at that stage—completely delicious.

Noma alone is worth the trip to Copenhagen, but one can have many memorable breakfasts, brunches, lunches, afternoon teas, and dinners there, although there never seems to be enough time to enjoy them all. At Nimb Herman in Tivoli we had a fantastically good lunch. The first "course" was two pieces of oysterleaf (also known as oysterplant) served on a little mound of empty oyster shells. This intriguing little plant, *Mertensia maritima*, tastes distantly of oysters, a little teaser at the beginning of the meal. The next three courses were oyster-related. A cushion of oyster-flavored foam was served on a flat pebble, with instructions to allow it to slide off the pebble into your mouth. It dissolved into a little pool of briny deliciousness. This was followed by a couple of oysters with smoked olive oil, and then a pine-flavored granita served on a plate of seaweed and rocks with little sprigs of pine tucked in here and there. Next up, oyster, veal, and sour cream, served in a marrow bone—sublime—and on it went. We enjoyed a plate of Danish farmhouse cheeses: Red Christian from Jutland, Trope Need Krondil, a hay cheese, and a blue cheese from Fyn, served with a little loaf of warm walnut bread with rose-hip marmalade and chutney. Several desserts and three cheeky petit fours signaled the end of the meal. I forgot to count the courses, each was tiny and perfectly pitched, a celebration of Nordic seasonal ingredients with a mischevious, fun element running throughout.

Denmark is not the only Scandinavian country producing food fitting the tenets of the New Nordic movment. I've been lucky enough to visit Jukka Oresto, a past student, in his homeland to taste traditional Finnish foods, visit the markets, and bake bread in a wood-burning stove on a farm in Karppala, north of Tampere. Eila Haapaniemi, her daughter Eija, and her daughter-in-law Sari, lovingly taught me how to make some of the traditional Finnish breads passed down from generation to generation. We ate Pullo, a sweet bread flavored with anise and topped with crunchy sugar, straight from the oven with glasses of cold milk. I tasted elk for the first time and was greatly surprised to discover that it was not at all strong, but juicy and succulent. The meal incorporated many Finnish specialties—herring dishes, Finnish pancakes, and a particularly distinctive Finnish potato dish called rosolli.

The market in any country provides a peephole into the food and lifestyle of the people. Helsinki's neat and tidy covered markets gave a fascinating insight into the traditional food of the Finns. A tantalizing array of smoked fish, several types of gravlax, Finnish cheese, wonderful breads (rye, barley and wheat), a variety of crispbreads, plus a special dark bread to serve with reindeer, pleated

Karelian pasties, and sugar Possu with different fillings were all on offer. It is these traditional foods that the Nordic movement is keen on using, promoting and preserving.

We've also brought Scandinavian food trends to the School, with multiple visits from guest chef Camilla Plum. She came from Fuglebjerggaard in Denmark to stay in 2012 and showed me how to make beautiful herb salts and preserve tomatoes using Maldon sea salt or Sel de Guérande—she's a totally natural cook. Camilla sprinkled chopped verbena salt over and into a chicken, which we roasted several hours later and ate accompanied by roast potatoes with lemon and bay leaves. It is one of the best things I have ever eaten and her simple salt transformed the chicken. I now teach the students how to make these delicious salts.

The whole ethos of the New Nordic movement excites me in a way that molecular gastronomy didn't. I love the honoring of tradition and find myself searching in the deepest recesses of my memory to try to recollect forgotten skills, such as how Pa made vegetable pits in our kitchen garden in Cullohill years ago to store root vegetables and apples for use over the winter.

Above: Camilla Plum, Danish organic cook, farmer, and cookbook author, during the Ballymaloe Literary Festival of Food and Wine in 2013.

Thanksgiving

Since the second year of the School, we have had American students on virtually every course. For them, Thanksgiving is the big celebration of the year. If they are at the School when Thanksgiving falls, they often decide to cook a huge dinner for all their class. The centerpiece is a fine free-range turkey from Nora Aherne who has been supplying poultry to the School since the beginning. However, many have never cooked a Thanksgiving dinner before and rely on childhood memories rather than experience to guide them.

So, in November 2012 we decided to add a Thanksgiving Course to our brochure. It proved to be a resounding success. We invited all of our American students to tell us about their favorite Thanksgiving meal. Several wanted to share a recipe; some sounded a little strange to us, but Sweet Potato and Marshmallows is definitely a favorite. A version from Jared Batson, one of our American students, got a terrific reaction. Several others talked about Green Beans and Mushrooms. I enquired about how it was made. There was much giggling and then they told me: "Take a couple of cans of green beans, top with a can of mushroom soup, sprinkle with sliced crispy onion, and put into the oven." Definitely a step too far for me, so we decided to try a more homemade version with the last of the season's beans, blanched and refreshed, mushroom a la crème, crispy onion, and flaked almonds. It was sooo good, everyone fought over the last morsel. Pumpkin Pie is another Thanksgiving favorite. The American version is made with canned Libby's pumpkin purée, but Eoin Cluskey, a student from Dublin, made this pie with finely chopped fresh pumpkin flesh, by far the best anyone had ever eaten. We made three stuffings with the turkey: chestnut and sausage, oyster stuffing, and our own special buttery, herby bread stuffing, which seemed to be the favorite.

Kale Crisps

Suddenly kale is the coolest ingredient—it's all over the place, on restaurant menus, at farmers' markets, even on supermarket shelves, and kale crisps are the snack of the moment. I'm not complaining since I love kale—it's super nutritious and we grow four different varieties here at the School—Red Russian, Ragged Jack, asparagus, and curly kale. I find the latter works best for this recipe.

A couple of years ago we invested in a dehydrator—it's not a must-have bit of kitchen equipment, but if you do decide to buy one you can have fun experimenting. It's brilliant for drying fresh herbs, tomatoes, and wild mushrooms—in a good mushroom season it will pay for itself in no time. Kale crisps will only take approx. 3–4 hours in a dehydrator at 135°F.

Makes lots

9oz curly kale
2 tablespoons extra virgin olive oil
sea salt and sugar

Preheat the oven to 300°F. Strip the leaves off the kale, tear into bite-sized pieces, and put in a bowl. Sprinkle with extra virgin olive oil, a little salt, and a pinch of sugar, and toss well. Spread out in a single layer on two baking sheets.

Bake in the preheated oven for approx. 20 minutes until crisp. Transfer to a wire rack to cool and crisp more. Enjoy.

Yannick and Louise's Banana Shallots with Anchovy Crème Fraîche

Yannick Van Aeken and Louise Bannon both spent five years in the kitchen at Noma in Copenhagen. In November 2012 they gave a pop-up dinner in the Garden Café at Ballymaloe using ingredients that they gathered from the hedgerows, seashore, and the farm. This recipe is one they cooked when they returned to do another pop-up at the Ballymaloe Literary Festival of Food and Wine in May 2013.

Makes approx. 40 crisps

4 banana shallots
sunflower oil or duck fat, to cover

For the Anchovy Crème Fraîche
4oz anchovy fillets
1 cup crème fraîche

Preheat the oven to 250°F and line two baking sheets with parchment paper.

Cut the banana shallots in half lengthwise. Put them in a saucepan or sauté pan, cover them with the sunflower oil or duck fat, and simmer over low heat until they are beginning to soften, approx. 20 minutes. Set aside to cool. Drain the shallots, reserving the oil. (The shallot-infused oil can be used for salad dressings or roast potatoes. It has a light shallot-confit flavor. Store in a glass jar in the fridge.)

Remove the skins from the cooled shallots and carefully separate the layers one by one. Arrange them on the prepared baking sheets in a single layer and cover them with another layer of parchment paper. Lay another baking sheet on top of each to flatten the shallots completely.

Cook for 1 hour or until the shallots are dark brown and caramelized. Remove and drain on paper towels.

To make the anchovy cream, process the anchovies with the crème fraîche and spoon into a little dish.

Serve the shallot crisps in a little bowl, accompanied by the anchovy crème fraîche.

Oysterleaf and Sea Urchins

We had a wonderful lunch in 2012 at Nimb Herman in Tivoli Gardens in Copenhagen. The first "course" was just two leaves presented on a flat stone. The waiter was mightily impressed when I recognized them as oysterleaf, which we have been growing here in the greenhouses from a plant given to me by Giana Ferguson of Gubbeen. Oysterleaf tastes distinctly of oysters even if you are blindfolded.

If you can get flat, smooth beach stones to serve the sea urchins and oysterleaf on it makes a lovely presentation. If not, just use small plates. Seawater adds an extra dimension to this dish but if you do not have access to fresh seawater then just leave it out.

Serves 4

4 sea urchins
8 pieces of oysterleaf (*Mertensia maritima*)
4 tablespoons seawater

Open the sea urchins carefully and remove the corals. Check to make sure they are free of the urchin spines or shell.

For each serving, put two oysterleaves and the corals from a sea urchin on each plate. Drizzle with a little seawater and serve immediately.

Shrimp in the Shell with Bacon Mayonnaise

This is another recipe that Louise Bannon and Yannick Van Aeken cooked at their pop-up restaurant in the Garden Café at the Cookery School. We get wonderful fresh shrimp directly from the boats in Ballycotton for a good part of the year and Yannick and Louise showed us how to deep-fry them whole in the shell. They were unbelievably delicious and we have been cooking them this way ever since.

Start with the mayonnaise. Preheat the oven to 325°F.

Scatter the diced bacon in a roasting pan and cook for 20 minutes. Remove from the oven and set aside to cool. Pour the vegetable oil into a sterilized 1 quart jar and add the bacon. Leave to infuse in the oil overnight.

The following morning, drain the oil through a sieve, discarding the bacon. In a bowl, whisk the egg yolks, white wine vinegar, mustard, and sea salt together. Holding the bacon-infused oil in one hand and the whisk in the other, gradually add the oil in a steady stream, whisking all the time until the mayonnaise is thick and smooth. (If the mayonnaise starts to split, just add a little hot water to re-emulsify.) Taste and correct the seasoning if necessary.

Preheat the sunflower oil in a deep fryer. Toss the whole shrimp, a few at a time, in the seasoned flour. Shake off the excess and fry in batches in the hot oil for 1–2 minutes or until crisp. Drain on paper towels.

Serve the shrimp with a bowl of the Bacon Mayonnaise. Eat the lot, shells and all—they will be crunchy and delicious—the best flavor comes from the heads, so it's a must to eat everything.

Serves 16 as a canapé or 8 as a starter

For the Bacon Mayonnaise
7oz smoked bacon, diced
1 quart (4 cups) vegetable oil
12 organic egg yolks
3 tablespoons white wine vinegar
3 tablespoons Dijon mustard
big pinch of sea salt

sunflower oil, for deep-frying
2¼lb whole fresh raw shrimp in the shell
flour seasoned with salt and pepper

The Students

Over the past 30 years we've had students from Ireland, Great Britain, Sweden, Norway, Finland, Denmark, Holland, Austria, Germany, Alaska, USA, Mexico, Chile, Italy, France, Belgium, Sicily, Japan, India, Malaysia, Sri Lanka, Singapore, Hong Kong and mainland China, Dubai, Latvia, Cyprus, Poland, Switzerland, Russia, Korea, Lithuania, Australia, New Zealand, South Africa, Kenya, Peru, Zimbabwe and Zambia. Fourteen nationalities in one group was our most diverse so far, and we've had a wide range of ages from officially 18 (but there have been several highly-motivated 16-year-olds) to 69. One lovely American celebrated his 70th birthday while he was with us and achieved his lifelong ambition of being able to cook.

So our little village of Shanagarry becomes very cosmopolitan with students from all over the world mingling with the local community in the pubs and restaurants. Local shopkeepers also tell me that the school greatly enhances the economy and atmosphere of the village. You can also imagine how tempting it is to have so many beautiful young people in the area for months at a time. We've had lots of romances and several weddings, so we've been instrumental in bringing "new blood" into the area! Needless to say even a whisper of a party or a celebration at the Cookery School causes a flurry of excitement and I've been known to chase away "likely lads" with six packs from the School on several occasions in the middle of the night, until they get the message that "the old bat" will appear out in her nightgown. They have now reluctantly realized that the Cookery School, with all its tempting morsels, is out of bounds for all non-students.

Even though we do stress it in the brochure, the intensity of the 12-week course invariably comes as a surprise to the students. For those who have already gone to college, the fact that they must turn up for every class sometimes comes as a shock—it's not an optional extra and a "hangover" is not a legitimate excuse, as many groggy students have discovered when they wake up to find me peering down at them, giving them the option of going to the doctor (50 euros) or putting on their whites!

Left: At Ballymaloe Cookery School we use the gardens and farm as an outdoor classroom and the School as indoor classroom. I show the students our Egremont Russet heritage variety of apples, which has a lovely, full crop every year and grows outside the Blue Dining Room. Above: A busy hands-on session in Kitchen Two during a 12-week course in the early days of the School.

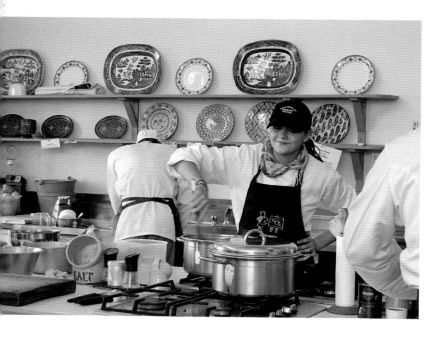

Sounds like gastro-bootcamp, but we really want everyone who comes to not only get value for money, but much, much more.

Past students tell us that the Ballymaloe Cookery School is not just about learning to cook, but it's also an introduction to a particular way of life. In the cottages, students quickly learn many life skills, including how to wash the dishes and use an iron and a vacuum cleaner; a first, and a shock, for many who have never before shared a house with anyone except their family.

I suppose it shouldn't come as a surprise in these days of central heating that so many young people don't know how to light an open fire or a stove. Even though the cottages are toasty warm, they love the comfort of an open fire, so we show them how to set a fire with newspaper, kindling, dried citrus peels, and dry wood. A wheelbarrow always sits in the courtyard to encourage students to collect fallen twigs and miscellaneous bits of wood when they go for a walk in the garden or the woods. One student told me that the fire always feels warmer when she collects the wood herself!

Students enroll on the 12-week course for any number of reasons. Many are determined to be professional cooks or chefs and are here to gain the skills to earn their living from cooking. Others take a career break to fulfil a dream of learning to cook so they can cook and entertain their family and friends with confidence and panache. For some it's a chance to reskill or change career, but the majority want to be able to earn a living from their cooking skills. They can travel all over the world and get a job. Being able to cook is one of the easiest ways to win friends and influence people and

there are a myriad of opportunities for those who can cook to use their new skills—in restaurant kitchens, catering businesses, and farmers' markets; by food styling or food writing; cooking on boats, in ski chalets, on television, or as personal chefs. If students are unsure of the opportunities, the deal is this: if they make me a pot of tea after class any day and produce a homemade cookie, I will explore the possibilities with them. Because I'm a member of the IACP, Slow Food, Euro-Toques, Guild of Food Writers in UK, and Irish Food Writers' Guild, I am fortunate enough to have contacts all over the world, which I can share with them. Fortunately, many restaurants and food businesses love to have the Ballymaloe Cookery School students in their kitchens because of their passion for real food and their interest in sustainable food issues, and of course the skills they have learned from our "everything from scratch" approach.

Students use their skills in a diverse range of ways. Ireland's Whitbread Round the World crew were the best fed crew in the 23-boat fleet according to a piece in *The Irish Times* in 1989, as Richard Gibson, from Baltimore, Maryland, who did the 12-week certificate course in 1987, was the chef on board. He had a hugely challenging task; on a racing yacht the galley is tiny, with a limited number of pots and pans and storage space and a weight limit for provisions (only root vegetables qualify because they keep well). The food must be delicious and, even more importantly, nourishing to give the crew strength and keep them in good humor. During the course of the Whitbread race he provided approximately 13,770 meals to his crewmates with a batterie de cuisine of three pots, a chef's knife, and a mixing bowl, using a four-ring stovetop and one oven. Sadly their hopes were dashed after the yacht's boom broke halfway through the last leg, but Richard gave the despondent crew a treat he'd been saving for an occasion when they might need their spirits lifted—he produced some freshly baked cookies!

It's a few years ago now since a chap called Paddy Daly, a shoe-polish salesman from Dublin, arrived to do a one-week Introductory Course at the Cookery School. When he arrived in the parking in his camper van, it took him all the courage he could muster to actually walk into the School. Paddy, a man in his sixties, was going through a harrowing time, nursing his much-loved wife

Above: Students on the 12-week course wear chef's whites while students on the shorter courses wear their "civvies."
Right: Students relaxing in the courtyard after a busy day's cooking at the School.

through a long illness. He was bereft and had lost his will to live. She had been a wonderful cook—Paddy missed her delicious food so much and was becoming more and more despondent when he was unable to cook tasty, delicious food to cheer her up as her health deteriorated. In a concerted effort to provide new hope and enthusiasm in his life, his family had clubbed together to give him a present of a cooking course. Paddy himself wasn't at all eager, but he was dispatched to Cork and felt he had to make the effort in response to their generous gesture.

He eventually plucked up the courage to venture into the School and, somehow, the experience changed his life. It renewed his zest for living, and the skills he learned enabled him to brighten his wife's last months and have given both him and his family and friends endless pleasure ever since. He has made several return visits over the years. Paddy telephones us periodically, and I was particularly touched by hearing how, on noticing that many other people are alone in his neighborhood, he and some friends started something on the SOS—"share our skills principle"—that is quietly making a difference to many people's lives. He invites and welcomes the person into his house and teaches them how to make a loaf of bread, a pot of stew, and a soup, and then they sit down and eat it together and chat. The "student" can then make it at

home and pass on the skill to someone else. No money changes hands. Paddy says the reward is in the sharing and the delight of the recipient. What a beautiful idea—those of us who have learned how to cook can make such a difference to people's lives by passing on our skills to those less fortunate.

Since 2005, two French horticultural colleges have been sending their students as interns. Both say that there is nowhere else in Europe where they can get such a range of experience, or the combination of farm, gardens, greenhouse, animals, poultry, dairy, cheesemaking, and delicious food. The latter is certainly a big attraction, and we understand that there's huge competition to be chosen for a "stage" at the Ballymaloe Cookery School Organic Farm and Gardens. We too love to have them with us and their presence enriches our lives. They come with a brilliant work ethic, eager to learn and properly equipped with all-weather clothes and footwear. Before they leave, as a little thank-you, many cook us a family dinner—we've had not only French, but also Ukrainian, Lithuanian, Russian, and Croatian farewell meals.

Early in 2001, an executive from the Farm Apprenticeship Board telephoned to ask whether we could offer work experience on our farm to a young Ukrainian girl. She had been working on a dairy farm in the Midlands since her arrival in Ireland in November, milking 80 cows, and was ready for a change of scene. We arranged to meet, and we chatted about the Ukraine and her family. Her grandmother had a farm, but Elena herself had studied economics at the Zhytomyr National Agroecological University and was highly educated and eager to travel and improve her languages. The Farm Apprenticeship Scheme gives her and many others like her this opportunity. When they come to Ireland, they get a warm welcome and are treated with respect and given comfortable accommodation and delicious food. Elena loved working here on the farm and in the gardens and enjoyed the food. Nonetheless, like so many travelers, she missed the food of her native country. For many of us, foods are inextricably linked with happy memories of childhood.

I'm always fascinated to learn about other food cultures. Elena described the food of her region of Ukraine and then offered to cook some of her favorite dishes for us. She telephoned her mother and grandmother who really entered into the spirit, and not only gave her lots of advice but sent a huge can of caviar for our aperitif; it was delicious. We were spreading it sparingly on some thinly sliced white bread, but Elena said, "Nonsense, we spread it like butter at home." We invited some friends and Elena cooked a delicious meal for us.

Occasionally a past student comes back to the school to do a cooking demonstration for the students. In March 2013 Maria Cho from Korea, who did the 12-week course with us in September 2009, returned to teach us all the basics of Korean food through some of her favorite dishes. The students loved her food and were inspired by her stories about how, after a series of emails and letters had failed to get a response, she secured work experience in many of her favorite restaurants (such as Locanda Locatelli, Moro and Marcus Wareing in London, the sustainable food project at the American Academy in Rome—which was her favorite—and Boulette's Larder and Chez Panisse in the US), simply by turning up at the kitchen door and more or less refusing to go until they gave her a chance.

Far left: Sign welcoming students to the School.
Left: The Garden Café at the School, where the students eat the food they have cooked during a morning session for lunch alongside the teachers.
Above (left): The huge overhead mirror and TV monitors ensure that the students can see right into the saucepans during demonstrations.
Above (middle): For students on the summer 12-week course the courtyard provides a lovely place to relax.
Above (right): 12-week students get the chance for some leisure activites during time off from cooking, such as exploring the surrounding local area by bike.

Arun Kapil's Garam Masala Cookies

Arun Kapil is an Anglo-Indian past student from the 12-week course in September 2004. He was previously a DJ but when he came to the Ballymaloe Cookery School he discovered his real passion was food. He realized there was an opportunity to import fresh spices, which he now does from his relatives' spice gardens in India. He sometimes includes recipes alongside the packets of spice mix that he sells.

Preheat the oven to 425°F.

First make the cookie dough. Put the butter and sugar in the bowl of a food processor. Turn the food processor on a high speed and cream the butter and sugar together for a few minutes until pale. (You may need to cream the butter by itself for a while before adding the sugar if it's straight out of the fridge.)

In a separate bowl, mix all the dry ingredients together: the flour, oats, baking powder, and garam masala.

Reduce the speed of the food processor to slow and add the dry ingredients, a handful at a time to avoid clouds of flour engulfing you and your kitchen. Once the mixture has come together, turn off the food processor, take out the dough, and put it on a lightly floured, clean surface.

Using your favorite rolling pin, roll out the dough to a thickness of approx. ¾in—don't forget to keep rubbing flour onto your rolling pin to prevent the dough from sticking to it. Cut out the cookies using the cutter of your choice—the lid of an empty jar will do fine.

Put the cookie shapes onto a baking sheet (there is no need to flour it, oil it, or use any sort of parchment paper). Pop the baking sheet onto the middle shelf of the oven. Bake the cookies for 10–15 minutes or until golden brown, then remove them from the oven and transfer to a wire rack to cool.

Wait until they've cooled down completely before serving.

Serve these excellent cookies with a pot of chai for an alternative, fragrant afternoon chill-out, with rhubarb fool, or crumbled up and used as an alternative base for a creamy cheesecake.

Makes 30–40 cookies, depending on the size of your cutter

8 tablespoons (1 stick) salted butter
⅓ cup superfine sugar
½ cup all-purpose flour, plus extra for dusting
1 cup oats
pinch of baking powder
3 teaspoons garam masala

Many students have shared recipes with us over the past 30 years and some become part of our repertoire, even making an appearance in some of my books!

Alison Heafey's Autumn Nut and Caramel Tart

This recipe comes from former student Alison Heafey, who got it from her friend Cindy Mushet, author of *The Art and Soul of Baking*. I always encourage students to share recipes as well as asking for recipes in restaurants; it's a great way to expand your culinary skills.

Preheat the oven to 350°F.

First make the pastry. Put the flour, sugar, and salt in a food processor fitted with the metal blade. Pulse five times to blend the ingredients. Add the butter and pulse 6–8 times until it is the size of large peas. In a small bowl, whisk together the egg yolks, vanilla extract and 1 teaspoon of water. Add to the food processor, then process until the dough begins to form small clumps. To test the dough, squeeze a handful of clumps—when you open your hand they should hold together. If they fall apart, sprinkle the remaining water over the dough and pulse several times. If necessary, add up to one more teaspoon of water to bring the dough together.

Remove the dough from the bowl and knead it gently 2–3 times, to bring the dough together. Shape it into a round disk approx. 6in across. Set aside in the fridge to chill for 30 minutes.

Break the cold dough into 1–2in pieces and scatter them evenly over the bottom of a 9in tart pan. Use the heel of your hand to press the dough flat, connecting the pieces in a smooth layer. Press from the center of the pan outward, building up some extra dough around the base at the edge of the tart. Using your thumbs, press this excess up the sides of the pan, making sure it is the same thickness as the dough on the bottom. Roll your thumb over the top edge of the pan to remove any excess dough (save this for patching any cracks that might form during baking). Chill for at least 30 minutes.

Bake blind for 20–22 minutes or until the edges and center are set. (If the shell is cracking and sticking to the parchment paper lining, replace it and continue to bake for another 5–6 minutes.) Remove the parchment paper and beans and set aside to cool.

Once cooled, return the pastry shell to the oven and bake for another 10–12 minutes or until the crust is a pale tan color. Transfer to a rack and cool completely before adding the filling.

Meanwhile, make the frangipane filling. Put the almonds and sugar in the bowl of a food processor and process until finely ground. Add the butter and blend. Add the eggs, flour, and almond extract and mix thoroughly. Pour the filling into the tart shell and bake for 30–35 minutes, or until firm in the center and lightly browned. Set aside to cool completely.

To make the topping, put the water, sugar and corn syrup in a saucepan large enough to eventually hold all the nuts as well. Heat slowly until the sugar has dissolved and the liquid is clear. Then increase the heat to high and boil rapidly until the sugar darkens to a rich golden-brown color.

Remove the pan from the heat and immediately add the butter and cream (be careful, as the mixture will rise in the pan and splutter). Stir briefly with a wooden spoon to blend, then add the toasted nuts. Stir gently to coat the nuts in the caramel sauce, then immediately spoon the nuts over the cooled frangipane tart, reserving the caramel in the pan. Use two spoons, not your fingers, because the mixture will be very hot. Finish, if you like, by spooning some of the caramel sauce over the nuts. Set aside to cool.

Remove from the pan just before serving. Serve at room temperature.

Serves 10–12

For the vanilla pastry
1½ cups all-purpose flour
¼ cup sugar
¼ teaspoon sea salt
8 tablespoons (1 stick) cold unsalted butter, cut into ½in pieces
2 large organic egg yolks
2 teaspoons pure vanilla extract
1–2 teaspoons water

For the frangipane filling
1 cup whole natural almonds, lightly toasted
½ cup superfine sugar
4 tablespoons unsalted butter, softened
2 large organic eggs
2 tablespoons all-purpose flour
½ teaspoon almond extract

For the nut and caramel topping
½ cup water
1½ cups sugar
2 tablespoons corn syrup
8 tablespoons (1 stick) unsalted butter, softened
½ cup heavy cream, at room temperature
½ cup whole unsalted almonds, lightly toasted
⅔ cup pecan halves, lightly toasted
½ cup walnut halves, lightly toasted

Kaitlyn's Lemon Curd Meringue Cake

We love the way some of our students add their own creative touch to a basic recipe. Kaitlyn Brenner from Massachusetts, a student on the 12-week course in January 2012, served this at her exam.

Preheat the oven to 300°F and line a baking sheet with parchment paper.

Start with the meringue kisses. Put the egg whites and sugar in the bowl of a mixer and whisk at high speed until the mixture forms stiff, dry peaks. Spoon into a piping bag fitted with a star nozzle and pipe approx. 30 rosettes onto the parchment paper, making each one approx. 1½in in diameter. Bake immediately in the oven for 45–50 minutes or until crisp. Remove from the oven and set aside to cool.

Meanwhile, make the lemon curd. Beat together the whole eggs and egg yolks together in a bowl. Melt the butter in a saucepan over very low heat. Add the sugar, lemon zest, and juice, followed by the beaten eggs. Stir carefully over low heat with a straight-ended wooden spatula until the mixture coats the back of it. Remove the lemon curd from the heat and set aside to cool.

Once the meringues are cooked, raise the oven temperature to 375°F. Grease two 7in cake pans with a little melted butter, put a round of parchment paper in the bottom of each pan, and dust lightly with flour.

To make the cake, cream the butter with the sugar and lemon zest until pale and fluffy. Beat in the eggs, one at a time, adding a tablespoon of flour with each addition. Beat very well, and then fold in the remaining flour. Divide the mixture evenly between the prepared pans and bake in the oven for 20–25 minutes or until the cakes are well risen, golden, and feel spongy to the touch.

Remove the cakes from the oven and set aside to cool in the pans for a few minutes before turning them out onto a wire rack to cool completely.

Meanwhile, make the icing. Mix 8 tablespoons of the cooled lemon curd into the mascarpone and beat in the sifted confectioners' sugar.

To serve, split the cakes in half horizontally with a sharp serrated knife. Sandwich the four layers together with the lemon curd and lemon mascarpone icing, reserving some of the icing for the top and sides of the cake. Put the cake on a stand and use a warm offset spatula to spread the top and sides of the cake with the reserved icing. While the icing is still wet, stick the meringue kisses all over the cake and decorate with fresh or frosted lemon balm leaves, if using.

Serves 8–10

For the meringue kisses
2 organic egg whites (reserve the yolks for the lemon curd)
½ cup superfine sugar

For the lemon curd
4 organic eggs, plus 2 organic egg yolks
8 tablespoons (1 stick) butter
1 cup superfine sugar
grated zest and juice of 4 lemons

12 tablespoons butter, plus extra for greasing
¾ cup superfine sugar
1⅓ cups self-rising flour, plus extra for dusting
grated zest of 2 lemons
3 organic eggs

For the lemon mascarpone icing
8 tablespoons lemon curd (see above)
1 cup mascarpone
4 tablespoons confectioners' sugar, sifted

To decorate
fresh or frosted lemon balm leaves (optional)

Madhulika's Grandmother's Pork Masala

Madhulika Sundaram came from Chennai in South India to do the 12-week certificate course in April 2013. She showed us how to cook several of her family recipes, including this delicious Pork Masala. You can reduce the amount of chiles in this recipe if you like a milder flavor.

Serves 6

½ cup sunflower oil
2 rounded tablespoons brown mustard seeds
1 rounded tablespoon cumin seeds
3 cups finely chopped onion
2¼lb pork shoulder, cut into 1in dice
1 cup peeled and finely diced fresh ginger
¾ cup peeled and finely chopped garlic
1 level teaspoon ground turmeric
6–10 red chiles, sliced into rings
1½–2 cups water
sea salt
1 teaspoon brown sugar

Put the oil in a saucepan over high heat, and when it begins to bubble, add the mustard seeds and cumin. As soon as the mustard seeds pop, add the onions and cook until light brown. Reduce the heat to medium and add the diced pork, ginger, garlic, turmeric, and chiles to the pan. Stir well, cover, and leave to cook over medium heat for 15 minutes.

Add 1½ cups of water, season lightly with salt, and stir. Cover the pan and allow to cook gently for 40 minutes over medium heat, stirring at regular intervals, adding more water if it is starting to stick. The water should be almost fully reduced after 40 minutes. Add half the sugar, stir well, and add more if desired.

Serve in a warm bowl with rice and a fruit raita.

Cilantro Kimchi

This simple kimchi works well with other Korean dishes, such as Bulgogi (see right).

7oz cilantro leaves
1 tablespoon soy sauce (preferably Korean)
1 tablespoon cider vinegar
$\frac{1}{3}$ tablespoon organic superfine sugar
½ tablespoon chile powder
1 teaspoon toasted sesame seed oil
1 teaspoon toasted sesame seeds

Wash or rinse the cilantro leaves gently under cold water.

Mix the soy sauce and vinegar with the sugar and chile powder in a small bowl. Just before serving, add the sesame oil and seeds and toss with the cilantro. Serve with Bulgogi (see right) or steamed white rice.

Bulgogi

When former student Maria Cho from Korea returned to give a cooking demonstration at the School, the students went crazy for her food. Bulgogi is quite a mission to make, but so good it's certainly worth the effort. Matganjang is a seasoned soy sauce and a very useful marinade that can be prepared ahead of time and used for many dishes. It will keep in the fridge for up to a month.

First make the matganjang. Put the soy sauce, sugar, and water in a large saucepan and bring to a boil. Once boiling, add the mirin and sake or vermouth. Bring to a boil again, add the apple and lemon, then remove from the heat. Cover with a lid. Allow to cool completely, then return to the heat and bring to a boil.

Getting the meat for this dish can be tricky, but worth it. You need to ask your butcher for a beef tenderloin and to freeze it for you, thus making it easier for him to slice it thinly for you.

To defrost the meat, put it in a sieve and leave it at room temperature, so the blood can drain out. Once defrosted, cut the meat into ½in strips.

While the meat is defrosting, prepare the vegetables.

Drain the mushrooms and trim the stems off the mushrooms and discard. Slice the caps into ¼in slivers. Chop the onions and scallions.

Mix together the matganjang, crushed garlic, ginger paste, pear (if using) and a little pepper and pour over the vegetables and beef. Mix well with your hands. Leave to marinate for 20 minutes.

Cook the mixture in a wok or frying pan to heat through—approx. 5–6 minutes—and serve immediately with rice, garnished with sesame oil and seeds.

Serves 4–6

For the matganjang
2½ cups organic soy sauce
2½ cups organic sugar
½ cup water
½ cup mirin
½ cup sake or vermouth
½ apple, thinly sliced
½ lemon, thinly sliced

18oz beef, sliced (lean beef tenderloin roast, eye of round, or sirloin)
4oz dried shiitake mushrooms, soaked in boiling water for 30 minutes
⅔ cup finely chopped onions, cut into ⅛in dice
½ cup chopped scallions, chopped into 1¼in lengths
½ cup matganjang
2 tablespoons crushed garlic
1 tablespoon ginger paste
1 pear, peeled and grated (optional)
freshly ground black pepper

To serve
½ tablespoon sesame oil
1 tablespoon toasted sesame seeds

Index

Note: page numbers in **bold** refer to information contained in captions.

Adrià, Ferran 296
aioli 218–19, 266
Allen, Myrtle 8, 10, 20, 22, 28, 30, 33–4, 42–3, **48**, 52, 68, **70**, 75, 80, 83, 100, 116–17, **117**, 118, 126, 131, **149**, **188**, 189, 223, 267, 272, 287, 288, **288**
almond 78
    green 77
    praline 114–15
    tart 30–1
Alston, Rod 176
anchovy 112–13
    crème fraîche 302
apple 38, 71, 77, **77–8**, **176**, 253–5, 256, **305**
    granola 144
apricot 78
    poached, and sweet geranium compote 75
arjard 155
art 19
Asian pear 78
asparagus
    and crab with Thai mayonnaise on sourdough 267
    with romesco 187
asthma 88, 92
avocado, pecans, and Brussels sprouts 132

bacon 28, 64, 120
    glazed loin of 29
    mayonnaise 303
    Savoy cabbage and cream with pheasant or partridge 66
Balfour, Lady Eve 130
Ballycotton Seafood 33
Ballymaloe Literary Festival of Food and Wine (LitFest) 15–17, **16**, 43, 187, 199, **199**, **255**, **273**, **297**, 302
Bannon, Louise 296, 302–3
barbecues 105
Barber, Dan 131
barnacles 71
basil 50, **125**, **176**, 223
    opal, with fig, bocconcini, and mizuna salad 84
Batali, Mario 246
batter 109

bay 51
beef 13, 34
    bistecca alla Fiorentina 114
    bulgogi 315
    grilled bavette or hanger steak with shallots 248
    rendang 227
    slow-cooked shank of 248
beekeeping 33, 50, 256–7, **256**
beets 260
    pickled 258
    purée, with toasted cumin seeds and buffalo curd on poppadom 186
berries 103, 278–80
see also specific berries
bilberry 103
biodiversity 148, 152, 247
birds 247
bistecca alla Fiorentina 114
bitter greens, wild, buffalo mozzarella and spruce syrup 108
blackberry
    granola 144
    vodka 109
black currant popsicles 284
blood orange, Toonsbridge Mozzarella and watercress salad 41
blue cheese, parsley, lemon, and broad bean pizza 171
blueberry 278
    raspberry and peach autumn crumble tart 86
    scones 146
bocconcini, mizuna and fig salad with opal basil 84
borage 50
bread
    Ballymaloe brown yeast 122
    Ballymaloe white sourdough 172–3, 267
Brenner, Kaitlyn 312
brine 258
broth
    vegetable and red lentil 132
    watercress, sorrel, and wild leek 160
Brown, Henry Clifton 171
Brussels sprouts with avocado and pecans 132
buffalo curd, beet purée, and toasted cumin seeds on poppadom 186
buffalo mozzarella with spruce syrup and bitter greens 108
bulgogi 315
butchery **34–5**, 34–5, 138, 244–6, **245**
butter 93, 94
    corn with butter and sea

salt 185
dill 270
hot buttered oysters 118
spinach sauce 119
buttermilk 94
Byrne, Gay 80, 82, 83

cabbage 67, 260
    Savoy, cream and bacon with pheasant or partridge 66
cake
    Blathnaid's chocolate 242
    Kaitlyn's lemon curd meringue 312
    parsnip and maple syrup 137
caramel
    and chocolate mousse 221
    ice cream with salted peanuts, caramel popcorn and dark chocolate sauce 99
    and nut autumn tart 311
carrageen moss pudding with poached apricot and sweet geranium compote 75
carrot 260
    pickled 258
    pickled, with star anise 55
    and sweet potato and cilantro soup 211
Casey, Bill 71, **151**, 155
cashew nut
    and cilantro pesto 211
    curry 202
"catalog cooking" 33, 281
cauliflower
    garlic and oil, penne with 112
    spiced cauliflower with tomato and parsley 227
celeriac remoulade with rabbit and prune terrine 64
celiac disease 205–7
Celtic maze 12, 158, 278, 290
chana masala 294
charcuterie, a plate of Irish 154
Charles, Prince 152
cheese
    hoja santa quesadilla 277
see also specific cheeses
cheesemakers 70–1, 148–50, 153, 189
cheesemaking 93, 110, 178, 179, 252, 253, **253**
cherry 295
    pickled 258
    scones 146
chicken
    Asian soy and five-spice breasts, with cucumber, radish, and mint salad 240
    Ballymaloe pie 120

chilaquiles verdes o rojos 276
    Oaxacan soup 274
    salad of smoked, with parsnip chips and myrtle berries 241
    spatchcock, with rosemary and chile oil 56
chicken-keeping 230–7, **230**, **233**, **236**
chilaquiles verdes con rojos 276
Childs, Beryl & John 20
chile 199, 223–4, **223**
    rosemary and chile oil 56
    sweet chile sauce 196
    and tomato jam 40, 266
Cho, Maria 309, 315
chocolate
    Blathnaid's cake 242
    and caramel mousse 221
    chocolate chip scones 146
    dark sauce 99
    ganache 242
see also white chocolate
cilantro 51, 199
    kimchi 314
    and cashew nut pesto 211
    ginger and tomato with salmon 269
clergy cooking course 141, **141**
cloudberry 103
coconut curry, roasted vegetable 294
Colcannon with venison sausages 67
comfrey 50
companion planting 126
compotes
    green gooseberry and elderflower 85
    poached apricot and sweet geranium 75
Conroy family 35, 154
cookies, fork 29
cookies, garam masala 310
corn with butter and sea salt 185
course structure 15, 20–5
cow farming 34, 88–94, **88**, 178–9
crab and asparagus with Thai mayonnaise on sourdough 267
cream 93, 94
    pheasant or partridge with Savoy cabbage, cream and bacon 66
crème fraîche, anchovy 302
    asparagus with romesco and crème fraîche 187
crisps
    banana shallot 302
    kale 301
    parsnip 241
crumble
    spiced pear, pecan, and ginger 212
    tart, autumn, peach, blueberry

and raspberry 86
cucumber 155
  radish and mint salad 240
  and tomato salad 292
cumin seeds, toasted 186
cured meats, a plate of Irish 154
curing 139, **151**, **152**
currants 278–80
curry
  cashew nut 202
  paste 294
  pumpkin 201
  roasted vegetable coconut 294
  shrimp 201
custard
  egg 85
  wild garlic 106

dairy-free eating 205, 207, 208,
  211, 212
Daly, Paddy 306–8
dandelion flower fritters 109
date(s), honey and yogurt 260
deer 62
Dehillerin, Paris 27
Dennhardt, Philip **164**, 165, 171,
  244, **246**
Desmond, John 15
dill 51
  butter 270
  mayonnaise 72, 73
Dobbs, Geoffrey 15, 238
dressings 38, 40, 54
  French 241
  olive oil and lemon 208
  wasabi mascarpone 194
duck 33, 62
Duignan, Clare 80

eczema 88, 92
Educational Farm walk 179
egg 156, 236–7, 238
  bhurji 238
  boiled 230–3
  custard 85
elder 78
elderflower and green gooseberry
  trifle 85
equipping the school 27
European Union (EU) 148, 207,
  256, 262–3, 265

Farm Shop 11, 37, 92, 190, 196
Farmer, Colette 80–2
farmers' markets 70–1, 93, **188**,
  189–93, **190–3**, 196, 236
fast days 125
fat 34
fava bean, blue cheese, parsley, and
  lemon pizza 171
Fearnley-Whittingstall, Hugh 61,

82, 131, 244, **245**, 265
fennel
  lamb and green bean salad,
    with tomato and chile jam 40
  pickled 258
  pollen 51–2
  sauce 171
Ferguson family 38, 88, 148, **148**,
  150, **151**, 154, 302
fig 78
  bocconcini and mizuna salad
    with opal basil 84
fig leaf and raspberry granita 84
fish 125
  discards 265
  roast, with dill butter and
    zucchini 270
fishing, sustainable 262–5, **262–3**,
  265
flan de naranja (orange flan) 46
flowers, edible 78, 126
Floyd, Keith 80
food allergies/intolerances 205–13
food production 12–15, 33–7, 70–1,
  125–7, 148–53
food scandals 174, 246
foraging **70**, 100–3, 106–9
Forgotten Skills courses 100–3,
  139, 236, 244, 252
fork cookies 29
frangipane 311
Fraughan Sunday 100
French dressing 241
French tarragon 50
fritters, dandelion flower 109
fruit 77–8, **77–8**, 278–80, **278**, **280**

Galle Literary Festival, Sri Lanka 15
game 61–2, 64–7
ganache, chocolate 242
garam masala cookies 310
Garden Café 12, 37, 164–5, **215**,
  302, 303, **309**
Gardner, Alix 17, 20
Gibson, Richard 306
Gill, Michael 82, 83
ginger
  crystallized ginger scones 146
  poached pears with grated ginger
    228
  salmon with tomato and fresh
    cilantro 269
  spiced pear and pecan crumble
    212
  tea 58
glaze, red currant 30
Gleeson, Stevie O'Brien 165
Glenilen Farm 93
globe artichoke 126, **127**
Gloucestershire Old Spot 138, **139**,
  178

gluten-free food 205–3, 212
goat cheese 33
  Ardsallagh 156, 190
  kale and pumpkin tart 134
  and thyme leaf soufflé 156
golden marjoram 50–1
gooseberry, green
  and elderflower trifle 85
  sauce 283
granita, raspberry and fig leaf 84
Grant, Doris 122
Gray, Rose 95, 164, 248
Great Taste Awards 93
green bean, fennel and lamb salad,
  with tomato and chile
  jam 40
gremolata, roast pepper and olive
  pizza 168
Grigson, Jane **13**, 214
grouse 62
growing your own 12–15, 125–7
Gubbeen cheese 38, 88, 148, **149**,
  150, **151**
Gyngell, Skye 15, 17, **17**, 58, 187

Hall, Lyn 20
ham hock with navy bean and
  tomato stew 251
Hazan, Marcella 10, 110–14, **111**,
  223
Heafey, Alison 311
Hederman, Frank 71, **188**, 190, **190**
Hegarty, Gillian 95, 248, 266
Henderson, Fergus 245
herb tisanes, fresh 58
herbs 48–52, **48**, **50–2**, 95, 223, 277
  dried 51
Hogan, Bill 148–50, **149**
hoja santa quesadilla 277
Holden, Patrick 177, 180, 182–3
Hom, Ken 63
honey mousse with lavender jelly
  163
horseradish cream 155
Hsiung, Deh-Ta 63, **63**, 223
hummus, with Moroccan lamb pita
  wrap 45
hyssop 50

ice cream, caramel, with salted
  peanuts, caramel popcorn, and
  chocolate sauce 99
icing, lemon mascarpone 312
International Association of
  Culinary Professionals (IACP)
  15, 68, 100, 205, 306
Irish food 68–71

Jaffrey, Madhur 15, **16**, 77, 80,
  198–9, **198**, 214, 223–4
jam

strawberry and rose petal 284
tomato and chile 40, 266
Jaumaud, Anne-Marie 189
jelly, lavender, with honey mousse
  163
Jersey cows 12–13, 88, **88**, **92**, 93,
  94, 178
Jerusalem artichoke, roast slices
  196

kale
  crisps 301
  pumpkin and goat cheese tart
    134
Kapil, Arun 199, 224
  garam masala cookies 310
Karmel, Elizabeth 105
Katz, Sandor Ellix 17, **255**, 260
Kenedy, Jacob **17**, 93
kimchi, cilantro 314
Kingston, Alan and Valerie 93
kitchens 20, **21**, 27
Kraut-Chi (sauerkraut), Penny's 260
kuku kadoo—Persian zucchini
  omelet 238

La Ferme Irlandaise 8, 28
lamb 34–5
  green bean and fennel salad,
    with tomato and chile jam 40
  Moroccan pita wrap, with
    hummus 45
  roast shoulder, with aioli and
    salsa verde 218–19
  Rory's Moroccan harira soup
    216
  sumac chops, with tomato and
    cucumber salad 292
Late, Late Show (TV show) 80, 82
lavender **48**
  jelly with honey mousse 163
Leith, Prue 20
lemon
  curd meringue cake 312
  fava bean, blue cheese, and
    parsley pizza 171
  fresh lemonade with mint 46
  mascarpone icing 312
  posset with rose geranium 58
lemon verbena 50
  poached pears with lemon
    verbena leaves 228
lentil(s), red, and vegetable broth
  132
library 104–5
local artisan producers 33–7,
  148–50, 174
see also farmers' markets
loganberry **280**
  tartlets with 30–1
long-table dinners 290–1, **291**

mackerel **33**
  pan-grilled summer, with green gooseberry sauce 283
maple syrup and parsnip cake 137
marinades 45, 56
Marine Stewardship Council (MSC) 264–5
masala, pork 314
mascarpone
  cake filling 137
  lemon mascarpone icing 312
  wasabi 194
mayonnaise
  bacon 303
  dill 73
  homemade 72
  Thai 267
McCan, Colm 17, 24, **179**
McCartney, Paul 246
Meat Free Monday campaign 246
Memory Arboretum 159
mendiants, white chocolate, with dried cranberries, cherries, and pistachios 295
meringue cake, lemon curd 312
Meyer, Claus 15, 296
Middle Eastern food 42–3, **43**, 45–6, 208
Midleton Farmers' Market **188**, 190–3, **190–1, 193**
Miers, Thomasina **16**, 17, 95, 272–3, **273**, 274
milk 88–93, 178–9
milking cows 92–3, 178–9
mint 46, 50, 185
  cucumber and radish salad 240
mizuna, fig and bocconcini salad with opal basil 84
mousse
  chocolate and caramel 221
  honey, with lavender jelly 163
mozzarella
  buffalo, with spruce syrup and wild bitter greens 108
  Toons Bridge, watercress and blood orange salad 41
muffins, gluten-free raspberry 212
mulberry, black 77–8
mushroom 103
"Mushroom Hunt" 100–1
mutton, boiled leg of, with wild garlic sauce 162
myrtle berry, parsnip chips, and a salad of smoked chicken 241

New Nordic movement 296–7
Nilsson, Magnus 296
Nimb Herman 297
Noma 15, 94, 101–3, 108, 296–7, 302
nouvelle cuisine 11, 42, 104

nut and caramel autumn tart 311

oatmeal 71
O'Connell, Rory, Moroccan harira soup 216
olive 78
  green and black, tapenade, with pork belly 144
  gremolata, and roast pepper pizza 168
Oliver, Jamie 82
omelet, Persian zucchini 238
onion
  pickled red 155
orange flan (flan de naranja) 46
organic produce 93, 95, 101, 174–80, **179**, 207, 247, 278
Organic Trust 176–7
ovens, wood-burning 164–5
Owen, Sri 223, 224, 227
oyster, hot buttered 118
oysterleaf 297
  and sea urchins 302

panna cotta, rose blossom, with crystallized rose petals 96
pans 27
Parle, Stevie **16**, 17, 95, **273**
Parmigiano Reggiano 110
parsnip
  chips 241
  and maple syrup cake 137
partridge with Savoy cabbage, cream and bacon 66
pastry
  puff 120
  shortcrust 134–5
  sweet 30
  sweet shortcrust 86
  vanilla shortcrust 311
pea **176**
  garden, with fresh mint 185
  in the pod 185
peach 78
  blueberry and raspberry autumn crumble tart 86
peanut(s), salted 98–9
pear
  poached in a saffron syrup 228
  spiced, pecan, and ginger crumble 212
pearl barley and Smoked Gubbeen cheese salad with toasted almonds, apple and pomegranate seeds 38
pecan(s)
  Brussels sprouts and avocado 132
  ginger and spiced pear crumble 212
penne with cauliflower, garlic, and oil 112

pepper **180**
  roast, olive and gremolata pizza 168
pesticides 256
pesto, cilantro, and cashew nut 211
Petrini, Carlo 148, 150
pheasant **61**, 62
  with Savoy cabbage, cream, and bacon 66
pickled vegetables 258
pie, Ballymaloe chicken 120
pig keeping 138–9, **139**, 154, 178–9, 244
pita wrap, Moroccan lamb, with hummus 45
pizza **164**, 165
  fava bean, blue cheese, parsley, and lemon 170
  with roast peppers, olives, and gremolata 168
Plum, Camilla 284, 297, **297**
plum pudding 83
popcorn, caramel 99
poppadoms, with beet purée, roasted cumin seeds, and buffalo curd 186
popsicles, blackncurrant 284
pork 13, 138–9
  belly, with green and black olive tapenade 144
  masala 314
posset, lemon, with rose geranium 58
potato 67, 71, 125, **255**
praline 114
preserves **255**, 258
  see also jam
"Producer of the Week" concept 35
prune and rabbit terrine 64
Puck, Wolfgang 164, 246
pumpkin
  curry 201
  goat cheese and kale tart 134

quail, spatchcock 56
quality of food 18
quesadilla, hoja santa 277
quinoa, red, tabbouleh, with roasted pine nuts and pomegranate 208

rabbit and prune terrine with celeriac remoulade 64
radish, mint, and cucumber salad 240
raspberry
  and fig leaf granita 84
  gluten-free muffins 212
  granola 144
  peach and blueberry autumn crumble tart 86

tart or tartlets with 30
red currant glaze 30
Redzepi, René 103, 296
remoulade, celeriac 64
rendang, beef 227
Restaurant Association of Ireland (RAI) 281
rice noodles and prawn crackers with shrimp salad 54
River Café 95, 164, 248
Roden, Claudia 15, 42–3, **43**, 80, 214, 216, 223–4, 269
Rogers, Ruth 95, 164, 248
romesco, with asparagus and crème fraîche 187
rose
  blossom panna cotta, with crystallized rose petals 96
  petal, and strawberry jam 284
rosemary 51
RTÉ 80–2
Ryall, J.R. 163
Ryan, Declan 63, 193

Saddleback pig 138, **139**, 154, 178, 244, **245**
saffron syrup, pear poached in 228
sage 50
salad
  cucumber, radish, and mint 240
  fig, bocconcini, and mizuna, with opal basil 84
  heirloom tomato 194
  of lamb, green beans and fennel with tomato and chile jam 40
  shrimp 54
  of smoked chicken with parsnip chips and myrtle berries 241
  Smoked Gubbeen cheese and pearl barley 38
  tomato and cucumber 292
  watercress, blood orange, and Toons Bridge Mozzarella 41
salad burnet 50
salmon **151**
  smoked wild Irish, with horseradish cream, arjard, and pickled red onions 155
  with tomato, ginger, and fresh cilantro 269
Salone del Gusto 151–2, 153
salsa, tomatillo 276
salsa verde and aioli with roast shoulder of lamb 218–19
Sami (reindeer people) 102–3
Sardo, Renato 148
sauerkraut 260
sausages, venison, with Colcannon 67
Scannell, Willie 190, 193, **193**

scones, Mother's sweet white 146
sea urchin and oysterleaf 302
seeds, sowing 14–15
self-sufficiency 252–5
see also growing your own
semifreddo, zabaglione 114–15
shallots, banana, with anchovy
    crème fraîche 302
Shaw, Debbie 208
Shell House 142, **143**, 290
shrimp
    Ballycotton, whole in their
        shells, with watercress and
        dill mayonnaise 73
    curry 201
    salad, with rice noodles and
        prawn crackers 54
    in the shell, with bacon
        mayonnaise 303
Simmonds, Toby 148, **188**, 190
simple syrup 284
Simply Delicious (TV series) 13,
    80–2, **81**, 83, 146, 189
Simply Delicious Versatile Vegetables
    (TV series) 125, 176
Slow Food 102–3, 148–53, 237,
    246, 262–3, 291, 306
slow roast shoulder of lamb with
    aioli and salsa verde 218–9
smoked foods **151**, 155
Smoked Gubbeen cheese and pearl
    barley salad with
        toasted almonds, apple and
        pomegranate seeds 39
soil 127–30
Soil Association 130, 177, 180,
    182, 247
sorrel, wild leek and watercress
    broth 160
soufflé, Ardsallagh goat cheese and
    thyme leaf 156
soup
    carrot and sweet potato with
        cilantro and cashew nut pesto
        211
    French peasant 28
    Oaxacan chicken 274
    Rory's Moroccan harira 216
see also broth
sourdough 172–3
    with crab, asparagus, and Thai
        mayonnaise 267
    spatchcock chicken with rosemary
        and chile oil 56
    spiced cauliflower with tomato and
        parsley 227
spices 223–4, **223–4**
sponge, trifle 85
spruce syrup 108
squid, deep-fried, with aioli and
    tomato and chile jam 266

starters, sourdough 172
Staunton, Ross 191
steak
    grilled bavette or hanger steak
        with shallots 248
    grilled T-bone, Florentine style
        114
stew, tomato and navy bean with
    ham hock 251
strawberry
    granola 144
    and rose petal jam 284
students 15, 304–9, **305**, **306**, **309**
sumac lamb chops 292
sustainable fishing 262–5, **262–3**,
    265
sweet cicely 50
sweet geranium 58, 75, 85, 109,
    228, 284
    and poached apricot compote
        75
sweet potato and carrot soup 211
syrups
    saffron 228
    spruce 108

tabbouleh, red quinoa, with roasted
    pine nuts, and pomegranate 208
Tanis, David 17
tapenade, green and black olive
    144
tartlets with raspberries or
    loganberries 30
tarts
    almond 30
    autumn nut and caramel 311
    peach, blueberry, and raspberry
        autumn crumble 86
    pumpkin, goat cheese, and
        kale 134
television 13, 80–3, **81**, 125, 146,
    176, 189
Terra Madre 151, 152, 153
terrine, rabbit and prune, with
    celeriac remoulade 64
Thanksgiving 299
Thompson, Antony Worrall **13**
tisanes, fresh herb 58
tomatillo salsa 276
tomato **174**
    and chile jam 40, 266
    and cucumber salad 292
    and spiced cauliflower with
        parsley 227
    ginger and fresh cilantro with
        salmon 269
    and navy bean stew with
        ham hock 251
    heirloom, salad, with wasabi
        mascarpone 194
    Isaac's roasted tomato pizza

sauce 168
    with tripe 74
tortillas 277
Travers, Kitty 78, 84
trifle, green gooseberry, and
    elderflower 85
tripe with tomatoes 74
trout, baked, with spinach butter
    sauce 119

Van Aeken, Yannick 302, 303
vegan food 130, 131
vegetable(s) 125–31, **125**, **127**
    pickled 258
    and red lentil broth 132
    roasted, coconut curry 294
vegetarian food 130–1, 296
venison sausages with Colcannon
    67
violet 78
vodka, blackberry 109

Walsh, Scott 55
wasabi mascarpone 194
watercress
    blood orange and Toons Bridge
        Mozzarella salad 41
    dill mayonnaise and whole
        Ballycotton shrimp in their
        shells 73
    sorrel and wild leek broth 160
Waters, Alice 6, 15, 68, 164
wheat allergy 205–7
white chocolate mendiants with
    dried cranberries, cherries, and
    pistachios 295
wild garlic
    custards 106
    sauce 162
wild leek, watercress, and sorrel
    broth 160
Willan, Anne 15, 68
wine courses 17, 24

yeast 122
yogurt 93, 178, 253
    Ballymaloe homemade 260
    with dates and honey 260
Yosses, Bill 17

zabaglione semifreddo 114
zucchini **125**, **178**
    dill butter and roast fish 270
    Persian omelet 238

Picture Credits

*All photographs by Laura Edwards
except for the following:*

Tim Allen: 10 (*bottom*), 11,
12, 17, 18, 19, 20, 21, 22, 23,
24, 25, 27 (*top*), 28, 34, 35, 37,
42, 43 (*top*), 49, 50, 52, 63,
78, 81, 82, 92, 93, 101, 102,
104, 111, 116, 127 (*left*), 138,
139 (*top*), 143, 150, 151, 152,
153, 158, 164, 165, 177 (*left*),
180 (*bottom*), 188 (*except bottom
right*), 190, 191 (*top*), 192, 193,
194, 198, 199 (*except bottom*),
214, 215, 224, 233, 236 (*except
bottom*), 237, 244, 245, 252,
254 (*top left and right*), 255 (*top
left and bottom right*), 257 (*top
to bottom right*), 263 (*left*), 265,
273, 274, 287, 288 (*middle
and bottom*), 290, 291; **Peter
Cassidy**: 7, 32, 33, 60, 62, 69,
70, 72, 79, 88, 100, 109, 117
(*bottom*), 125, 128, 167, 177
(*right*), 200, 222, 254 (*bottom
left*), 255 (*top right*), 278, 299,
309 (*left and middle*); **Kevin
Dunne**: 13, 61, 305; **Cullen
Allen**: 16, 230; **Ray Main**: 26,
220, 247; **Joleen Cronin**: 43
(*bottom*), 199 (*bottom*), 297;
John Minihan: 149; **Melanie
Eclare**: 180 (*top*), 252, 263
(*right*); **Emily Ashworth**: 188
(*bottom right*), 191 (*bottom*), 236
(*bottom*), 246, 281, 308 (*right*),
309 (*right*); **Francine Lawrence**:
223; **Ray Roberts/Impact Photo
Library**: 225; **Cristian Barnett**:
257; **Diane Cusack**: 272; **Pål
Hansen**: 288 (*top*); **Susan
McKeown**: 306.

Newspaper articles: The Boston
Globe (*p.14*); The Irish Times
(*p. 83*); Guardian (*p.141*).

Acknowledgments

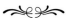

Where to start?! Thirty-plus years of thank yous would fill every page of this book. I must start with the late Mór Murnahan, kindly senior lecturer at the catering college in Cathal Brugha Street, Dublin, who stuffed a piece of paper into my hand in 1968 with a name and address on it and said "write to her." The name on the piece of paper was Myrtle Allen, who is now my mother-in-law. She and my late father-in-law Ivan Allen have been a lifelong inspiration and support—a heartfelt thank you to you both.

Special mention also for my brother Rory O'Connell, who started the School with me in 1983 and who has continued to support me and teach here at the School as well as organizing all the events and celebrations with the Cookery School team.

To all the wonderful people, past and present, who have worked with us here in every area of the enterprise over the years. We owe each and every one of you a huge debt of gratitude for the way you welcome, care for, and so generously and enthusiastically pass on your knowledge to everyone who comes to the School. This book is also your celebration and achievement.

To Emer Fitzgerald, who patiently and meticulously tested recipes over and over for this book.

Then there's Haulie Walsh, Eileen O'Donovan, Susan Turner, and their team: the gardeners and organic farmers, all our suppliers, artisanal producers, fishermen and fishmongers, butchers, bakers, poultry producers, fish smokers, cheesemakers......Where would we be without you? We are enormously grateful to you all.

Some other longstanding members of staff have been with us for in some cases over 30 years: Adrienne Forbes; Doreen Costine; Evelyn Ryan; Florrie Cullinane; Joe Cronin; Mary Dewane; Maura Daly; Pam Black; Sharon Hogan and Sue Cullinane. Will Kenneally, Dennis O'Sullivan, Jimmy Lee and all the builders and decorators of the "no problem team" were involved every step of the way.

A particular tribute to Aunt Florence, who welcomes and entertains everyone who visits the Cookery School.

A huge thanks also to the many students who shared their recipes with us and now with all of you.

We are also indebted to Colm McCan, consultant sommelier at Ballymaloe House, who takes the mystery out of wine and also enthuses the students with a passion for organic, biodynamic, and natural wines. Over the years, he has enticed some of the most iconic winemakers in the world to the Ballymaloe Cookery School and The Grainstore as well as inspirational speakers such as Jancis Robinson and Nick Lander.

Kyle Cathie has published seven of my cookbooks, a huge thank you for your encouragement, support and patience. Special thanks also to my editor Vicky Orchard, for her guidance and astute editing. And to Catherine Ward, for copy editing the recipes; to Louise Leffler, for the beautiful design, Linda Tubby and Polly Webb-Wilson, the ace team who cooked, propped, and styled my foods for the photographs.

To Laura Edwards for her beautiful photos of the food and Kinoith. And to Emily Ashworth for generously sharing her photographs of her time at the School.

To the photographers who kindly gave us permission to use their images: Peter Cassidy, Ray Main, Melanie Eclare, Kevin Dunne, Cullen Allen, Joleen Cronin, Diane Cusack, John Minihan, Pål Hansen, Susan McKeown, Cristian Barnett, Francine Lawrence, and Ray Roberts.

A special acknowledgment also to Susan McKeown, for trawling through and collating old photos for weeks on end.

Rosalie Dunne, my PA of 24 years, came out of retirement to help with research. Her exceptional recall has been invaluable in piecing together the many wonderful memories of the last 30 years. I simply couldn't have put this book together without her input—a heartfelt thank you.

To Tim, for his constant support and for creating such a beautiful environment around the Cookery School. Last, but not least, our children: Isaac, Toby, Lydia, and Emily, and their partners Rachel, Penny, Rupert, and Philip, all of whom contribute in a myriad significant ways. Finally our nine grandchildren: Joshua, Lucca, Scarlet, Willow, India, Amelia, Jasper, Ottilie, and Zaiah, who will hopefully carry on the legacy that Ivan and Myrtle entrusted to us.

Guest Chefs

To the myriad guest chefs who have come to the Ballymaloe Cookery School since 1984 to share their knowledge with us. The list of names reads like a Who's Who of the food world.

Deh-Ta Hsiung; John Desmond; Claudia Roden; Madhur Jaffrey; Ada Parasiliti; Lady Suzanne Mahon; Alicia Ríos; Sri Owen; Jane Grigson; Antony Worrall Thompson; Rose Gray & Ruth Rogers; Frances Bissell; Margaret Ryan; Anne Willan; Marcella Hazan; Sophie Grigson; Roger & Olivia Goodwillie; Alastair Little; Paul & Jeanne Rankin; Ursula Ferrigno; John Ash (Fetzer Vineyard); Seamus O'Connell; Rory O'Connell; Naranjan McCormack; Nina Simonds; Kevin Orbell-McSean; Rachel Allen; Rick Bayless; Julia Wight; Marie-José Sevilla; Sam Clark; George Gossip; Denis Cotter; Doris Lehnigk; Eric Treuille; Wasinee Soratee Beech; Paul Flynn; Maggie Beer; Merrilees Parker; Suzie McCully; Hugh Fearnley-Whittingstall; Peter Gordon; Skye Gyngell; Claire Ptak; Richard Corrigan; Thomasina Miers; Gerard Coleman; Yotam Ottolenghi & Sami Tamimi; Jean-Pierre Moullé; Philip Dennhardt; Debbie Shaw; Eddie O'Neill; Barny Haughton; Shermin Mustafa; Sunil Ghai; Gillian Hegarty; Pamela Black; Mary Jo McMillin; Jeremy Lee; Mickael Viljanen; Kitty Travers (La Grotta Ices); J.R. Ryall; Jacob Kenedy; Chad Robertson & Richard Hart (Tartine Bakery); Maria Cho; David Thompson; Stevie Parle; Camilla Plum; Bill Yosses; David Tanis; Yannick Van Aeken & Louise Bannon.